INVENTORY OF A LIFE MISLAID

An Unreliable Memoir

MARINA WARNER

WITH VIGNETTES BY SOPHIE HERXHEIMER

WILLIAM
COLLINS

William Collins
An imprint of HarperCollins*Publishers*
1 London Bridge Street
London SE1 9GF

WilliamCollinsBooks.com

HarperCollins*Publishers*
1st Floor, Watermarque Building, Ringsend Road
Dublin 4, Ireland

First published in Great Britain in 2021 by William Collins

1

A catalogue record for this book
is available from the British Library

HB ISBN 978-0-00-834758-1
TPB ISBN 978-0-00-834759-8

Typeset in Garamond 3 LT Std by
Palimpsest Book Production Ltd, Falkirk, Stirlingshire
Printed and bound in Great Britain by CPI Group (UK) Ltd, Croydon CR0 4YY

INVENTORY
OF A LIFE
MISLAID

Also by Marina Warner

To Maggie S, dear friend over the years
To Hartley and Jack, in hope for the time to come

'Here I am' you shall say when you are summoned at any time, to do all the work that is to be done in the necropolis, in order to make the fields grow, irrigate the channels, ferry the sands of the east to the west and west to east. Now indeed when you face these tasks, you shall say, 'Here I am'.

Shabti spell, *The Book of the Dead*

La lingua va dove il dente duole
(The tongue goes where the tooth aches)

Contents

Part III 1947–1949: In Cairo

Part IV 1950–1951: Balm in Gilead

Part V 1952: Revolution

Prologue

You are somewhere you know very well and a door appears; when you open it you find yourself in a backstage area you've never entered before. You're following those you have lost: they're lingering in obscure recesses, shadowy as the interior of a confessional box when you were a child and you knelt down on the foam-cushioned prie-dieu and leant in towards the battered colander screen and the priest concealed on the other side lifted the half curtain and appeared, a blurred outline through pinpricks of light, and in awe you whispered very low:

'Forgive me, Father, for I have sinned. I have had unkind thoughts. I have lied. I have said bad things. I stole some of Annie's sweets from her drawer.'

The verdict when it came was a relief, spoken in an undertone so that the waiting queue could not overhear:

'My child, for your penance, say three Hail Marys.'

Your sins would grow in seriousness, later, and also in embarrassment.

When you find that place backstage there will be an exit — it might take the form of a trapdoor leading down to a disused coal-hole or an area under glass bricks laid in the York stone pavement. At other times, access lies through a picket gate with a broken catch; you bend to adjust it to let yourself through; or a lift might beckon, the shaft rising against the exterior wall, as on tall SoHo buildings from the time they were sweatshops, before conversion into lofts. Pass on, and you will meet the lost there, too, murmuring.

Some time ago I thought I'd set this unreliable memoir in a City of the Dead – no, not a dream underworld like Hades, but in *the* City of the Dead in Cairo, where dusty piles of once grand ornate and crumbling tombs stretch beside the elevated motorway that runs alongside the old Mameluk aqueduct; its peaked stone arches are now ruinous, cadenced rhythmically like pages of a book turning as the car I was travelling in grumbled along in the notorious choked traffic of Cairo. Such a cemetery offers cold storage for stories: find a copper ring in the stone flag under a layer of grimy sand and lift it, and then the chambers and corridors snake through the darkness this way and that, with a half-frozen prince moaning or a hexed sister pinned down by the magic of her brother's shirt that she put on to disguise herself when she ran away with him.

If your loved one has been ill for a time, it comes as a relief to go over to the other side, and to enter this place which you learn, from the angel who comes up to you to take your name, is the holding area of memory, where all details will be registered, the story hoard rummaged, and the account of a life entered in the archive. Then you realise that this chamber stretches infinitely on all sides; you now see you are in a glazed capsule, as if you were a ship and the room a bottle, and all around, multiplied as far as you can see, as if in mirrors set at slight angles to one another, more presences are thronging. You realise the glazed vessel is humming: those who have come through before you are passing on information to one another. It's a memory palace – the figures evoked in these testimonies cast a shadow on the floorboards or leave a hollow in a bed they've just quitted; a door will close quietly, footsteps begin to move away, as voices rise and fall from rooms on the other side of the glass. The stories need a stenographer because that was what such a recording angel was called in the period when this inventory was made. Now, she might be using a small handheld device or an app on a phone.

~~~

Of all the rivers in eternity the best known is Lethe, flowing with water that wipes away the past and sinks you into a deep blank sleep, but also consigns you to be forgotten. Some of the dead are content with this, because forgetting what they were and what they did is soothing. But there's another river, which was not known to the ancients and has remained much less mapped by the more recently departed, and it is called Eunoe, meaning good memories or good mind, and fewer characters in stories or in real life can reach it.

The story you tell will prompt the angel who hears you to bathe you in one or the other. Neither is a punishment – it is a form of bliss to forget and happiness follows bathing in Eunoe, the waters of good memories. To be given a bath in both, as Dante imagines in the earthly paradise where Matilda sings in a flowery meadow, brings with it the deepest happiness.

But you are unsettled, as when a dark dry moth was once blown into your face through the wound-down window of a car one hot night when you were driving to the country, and its wings got stuck to your lip. You choked and for a moment lost control of the wheel as you gasped and hit out at it to rid yourself of its dustiness as it clung and fluttered there.

This same sensation emanated at first from the voices you heard humming.

The angel who is to take your statement says to you, 'It doesn't have to be like that.' She bends to your ear and adds something, and though you can't decipher her exact words, and her breath makes you shiver, and then you remember how your mother's breath also made you shiver – with pleasure – when she cut your fringe so that it would not fall into your eyes and then blew on your face to scatter the snippets from your cheeks and round your eyes. Her breath was soft and warm. 'Mmmmm,' you said, 'do that again.'

A sliver of light appears in the dimness.

'See,' says the angel, 'you remembered something . . .'

The scintilla has already faded.

'Try and remember,' she says again.

Call for lights. Hold up the lamp and itemise the things that you know because they belonged to them and through them became part of you.

~~

Today would have been my father's 111th birthday; tomorrow my mother's 96th.

PART I

Italy

to

England

1944–1946

Magari

If only. As if! Touch wood. Crossing fingers. Maybe. Inshallah. I wish!

Or, as my father wrote in his letters home, 'DV I shall be back soon.' 'DV things are going well.' *Deo volente*. God willing.

Magari turns up sprinkled here and there in the flow of Italian colloquial speech, especially in the south, among Neapolitans and the region of former Magna Grecia, for it most likely derives from the Greek *makarios*, which means blessed, lucky. In Italian, it's a synonym for *beato*, fortunate, and it punctuates a sentence or a phrase with a small cry of yearning and hope, the equivalent of saying, 'What luck it would be if I had, if I could, if I were . . .' In conversation, it's a pause, an intake of breath, a filler, technically phatic, a close relation of 'like, you know, like' and 'sort of' in English, when a speaker is searching for the next thought and wants to assure the person on the receiving end that they're both in tune with each other, that they're *simpatici*, friendly. It behaves like a customised punctuation mark – ?? or a burst of exclamations or both !!!??? It could now be supplanted on page and screen with an emoticon. And like such interlocutions, the filler is asking the interlocutor for collusion: if you keep dropping into your exchanges 'like, you know', you are asking your listener to come halfway to understanding you, you're rolling over and showing your tummy to demonstrate willing, and if you end your sentence on an upward note, turning your opinion into a question in the manner of young New Yorkers and Australians, the hesitation and irresolution of your tone is a kind of small plea for reciprocal reassurance. *Magari* offers a vestige of an entreaty – a request for mercy or generosity – because it calls on someone beyond the speaker for protection or blessing.

As if, hopefully, I wish. It's interesting that the use of hopefully, standing in for 'I hope', has gained so much ground in recent times.

Magari – the word can also act to deflect something bad happening, and be used to mean 'even if' or 'despite': 'I'll wait for him, even if I have to stay here all night' (*'Lo aspetterò, magari dovessi restare qui tutta la notte'*). It may also convey melancholy over thwarted wishes: 'We were alone, if only he had come!' (*'Eravamo soli, magari fosse venuto!'*). It forestalls disappointment: 'In your dreams!'

In Egypt, where my parents moved in 1947, with me aged six months, I used to speak Arabic – in the limited way a child speaks – with my playmates at the Gezira Sporting Club and with Abdel and Mohammed in the kitchen, and my nanny. One word of Arabic that I haven't forgotten is *malesh* (ah well, never mind). Like *magari*, it's a trace of a culture of blessing and cursing, of actions to avert the evil eye. Both words seek to reinforce the wishfulness of the utterance, spread a little grace into the gloom and ingratiate us frail beings below with powerful destiny above. *Magari*, like *malesh*, is the stump of a beatitude. It performs a small act of self-defence: if the event in question lies in the future, the speaker verbally crosses fingers that something will take place. Touching wood also holds a dim, very dim and mostly forgotten memory trace of faith in higher powers, as it's likely that the wood is the relic of the true Cross, a talisman of power. If the speaker is looking back, the interjection adds a sense of fatality to the disappointment, because it broadens the horizons to include the heavens.

Magari defines the mood in which my mother Emilia Terzulli, known as Ilia – who, in June 1944, became Mrs Esmond Warner – set out on her journey to England to rejoin her husband. She was taking a chance and invoking fortune to walk with her on the road. Hopefully.

I

Two Diamond Rings

Two half-moon rings, one smaller than the other, but each made of five stones cut as Cushion Brilliants, still the most popular style for engagement rings, the stones graduated in size, and set in platinum, a silvery but untarnished metal which became fashionable for jewellery in the nineteenth century, and works better than gold to enhance the sparkle inside the stones, making the rays shoot this way and, like cloud particles in a quantum experiment, spring off the sloping facets of the bezel, the diamonds' hexagonal centre. Jewellers call the exposed top part the 'table', and it allows the sparkle to fire through the cut cone below, which they call the 'pavilion' of the gem. These angles are so key to a diamond's brilliance that mathematicians are still employed by companies like De Beers to calculate the angles and intensify the cut stones' lustre. It's a science that blossomed after the mines like Kimberley in South Africa were opened – and led the way to diamonds' popularity.

These two rings, brought to Italy for Ilia in 1944, after her engagement to my father, Lieutenant Colonel E.P. Warner, emitted light far beyond anything known to the miniaturist Nicholas Hilliard when he added a tiny diamond to the painting of a jewelled belt Queen Elizabeth I is wearing in one of his portraits. Nor would the diamond Postumus in *Cymbeline* had from his mother, which he gives to Imogen as a pledge of his love, have been as fiery as my mother's stones. Even with her hand at rest, the facets would wink kinetically and now and then, depending on the angle of the light, shoot tiny flares of green and indigo and flame.

The collector of stones, philosopher and writer Roger Caillois, used to scrutinise certain gems and agates he collected. Of a meteorite he wrote that after cutting and polishing it, 'Then there will appear and glitter different sparks of the geometry proper to the specimen: interlacings of triangles, imbricated polygons, a complex system of oblique and parallel lines . . . the only drawings that humans know that are not of this earth.' The lights deep inside the diamonds' translucence could likewise be drawings – not from the cosmos beyond this planet, but from inside it: a registry of the core settling and the earth's drawn breath frozen into silence.

≈

When my granny heard the news, at long last, of the engagement of her eldest son – Esmond was born in 1907 and getting on – she gave my mother these two diamond rings, and my mother wore them every day of her life, till the hoops on the inside became worn and so thin they seem made of wire. When you pick up the rings today, they've become featherweight, as if the stones were not stones at all or even frozen vodka (which they look like), but particles of light itself.

The two diamond rings were in a dish on my mother's dressing table when she died; along with her hairbrush and her glasses, they seem the most intimate of her possessions, the most saturated with her being when she was alive.

'My mother's name is Agnes,' Esmond told Ilia. 'But no one in the family uses that — not even Daddy. She's always been Mother Rat to us.'

At first his young southern Italian fiancée heard Esmond's pet name for his mother as Motherette, and imagined her small and neat — motherettish, like her own mother.

He'd landed in Italy at Salerno, with the 8th Army, after fighting in the desert campaign for so long that he began to feel at home in North Africa, most especially in Cairo, where the British — officers and squaddies — headed whenever they had leave. On 26 April 1943, Esmond wrote to his mother, 'Dear Mother Rat, Well here it is, North Africa '43, my life is almost here now, my friends, my work, my knowledge, CAIRO my 2nd home (if I could ever get there!) my Old friends of England ceased to write nearly, but many now out here, the spirit of 8th Army.'

'CAIRO my 2nd home': it was a premonition.

He frequented the bars and the nightspots, played cards and golf and tennis at Gezira Sporting Club and the other clubs, and he'd enjoyed roaming the bookshops around Ezbekieh Gardens, where he found drawerfuls of loose pages from travellers' tales from many countries. He liked these antiquarians' dreamy love of their stock, but saw, in a flash that would come back to him after the war, that they weren't businesslike about selling and displaying or even knowing what they had. He'd picked up some interesting things, he told his mother. Prints of the pyramids and Philae; of the obelisk in old Heliopolis.

Among the officers he made friends with during one of his periods of leave, was Major Max Harari. Max was born in Cairo, and like so many Cairenes, had the great advantage, in my father's eyes, that he spoke several languages, including Italian (probably because he was brought up by one of those nannies from Trieste who were so sought after by the grand Jewish families of Cairo and Alexandria).

Major Max Harari, on a mission. Asmara, Ethiopia, 1941.

In the spring of 1944, Max had recently come back from Ethiopia where he'd been fighting against a ruffianly band of Italian occupiers; their leader escaped but Max took his horse prisoner: in an extant photograph he looks spectacular on the huge grey soaring over a jump, but is chastised in the commentary: 'With his weight pitched forward, legs shooting backward and a tug on the horse's mouth for good measure, Major Harari, of the Irish Hussars, could have done with a little Italian cavalry schooling.'

Providentially, this glamorous friend was making a return trip to London and was entrusted to collect the diamond rings from Mother Rat and bring them back to Bari.

Max was tall, urbane, with thick, swept-back dark hair and an aquiline profile, in every way dashing; you'd think that Esmond's chosen go-between might have endangered rather than promoted his suit, as when Viola in *Twelfth Night*, wooing the beautiful Olivia on behalf of the lovesick duke, Orsino, finds to her dismay that Olivia's eyes light on her instead (cases of falling for the messengers may outstrip instances of killing them). But no, Max, one of the many enigmatic male charmers in my father's circle who later married well, also delivered to Ilia the heaps of tulle which Ilia had stipulated she wanted to make into her wedding dress. Esmond had been to Naples specially to comb the black market there and send back everything he could find – and afford – for the family. He kept writing to Ilia to keep them all up to date with his successes.

Tracking down caches of coffee and chocolate proved elementary, even if he had to dig deep in his wallet. But the fabric for her wedding dress, her wedding garland and her veil: that led him a wild dance in the dark tenements of Naples, the *bassi* where the only light and air comes in through the door on to the street.

But he managed, and she appears in the photographs in a gauzy aureole of the light shining material, ruched and gathered as only a very slender frame could bear without looking like the Michelin Man.

As it happens, Max presented no danger to Esmond: he wasn't my mother's type, too Latin, too suave, too Rhett Butler-ish and *rastaquouère*, not sufficiently languid, willowy, sensitive and 'distinguished-looking', unlike her preferred idol, Ashley Wilkes as played by Leslie Howard.

Max fulfilled his errand, and Ilia remained steadfast. Esmond was able to report home that Mother Rat's gift of her rings had been met with delight by the whole assembly of mother, aunts, sisters, friends and neighbours on the Via Calefati:

Easter Sunday 1944

To Daddy, MR and Betts [his sister]
By the photos you are thought great aristocrats, and by
your gifts millionaires, so look out for the standard we have
to live up to!!

But the engaged couple met with complications about the ceremony itself.

The *parroco* at the cathedral of San Nicola told my mother, 'I can't allow a marriage to a Protestant to take place in my church.'

This phrase signalled something else entirely, as Ilia understood. An Offerings Box stood by the door of the cathedral, although such discretion wasn't strictly necessary and she could have simply passed him a roll of notes. Ilia and her sisters had faith, but not in priests, not since two years before, when her eldest sister Nancy had miscarried twins, they had asked this same parish priest round to their flat to help them give the babies holy burial, and he had looked grave and, glancing at the little forms lying in a shoe box by Nancy's side where she lay in bed, shaken his head:

'They have not been baptised, so, *purtroppo*, it is not possible.'

He did not add that he regretted it, nor did he add anything to console the young mother and her family about that no man's land, limbo, where at least babies didn't burn as in hell.

Then he had drunk the coffee and taken the 1000-lire note which they had placed under the saucer.

For a while it seemed as if the wedding with the Englishman might not take place in a church at all, which would have made my mother unhappy and her mother extremely uneasy. But a family friend stepped in and offered the private oratory in his house. They were married there, with the Anglican padre signing the certificate, and a small crowd of children gathered in the bright sunshine looking in through the open double doors.

On 21 March 1944, writing to his parents in London, Esmond reassured them that his bride's Catholic faith would not be an impediment to her adjusting to life as his wife, and added how he envisaged their future together:

> I will tell you more of her family . . . I have often been to their flat in Bari – and they have nice friends of 'the professional classes' type. Ilia however (you know she is only 21) belongs to the new world, and her life will be mine, NOT her circle's.

∼∼∼

Diamonds' exceptional physical qualities, hardness, limpidness, luminosity, render them a major symbol of perfection, says my *Dictionary of Symbols*. But its authors then add, 'though their dazzle is not universally considered beneficial'. That caveat strikes home with me, for in spite of their sparkling fires, the diamonds on my mother's rings are chilly stones.

A friend once told me that she had met an astronaut who

had been out in space. She asked him whether he could smell the void. He answered, 'No, because we're sealed into our space suits when we leave the capsule.' Then, after a beat, he added, 'There's a moment, though, when the smell of space is still clinging to the suit when we come back inside.' My friend urged him on. After another pause, he said, 'It smells like banging two rocks together.'

The image brings up for me the remote, deep tempo to which the universe moves, with the iridescent fire concealed inside mineral hardness.

2

The Box Brownie

A Brownie Model C Camera. Patented in the USA, 1 February 1910.

The black metal box looks far lighter than it feels in the hand; its solid metal walls, covered in a crêpy, tooled leatherette, enclose a simple dark chamber, a compact body with six apertures, four of them round like eyes, the two others miniature rectilinear viewfinders; a small metal lever with a satisfying clunk still opens the shutter for just a split second, a wink you aren't sure you saw; a metal winder on the side, like the bobbin case on Ilia's Singer sewing machine, rolled up the exposed film on its spool inside. To carry the camera, there's a neat, real leather handle stamped 'BROWNIE', a name that echoed the name of the camera's designer, a certain Mr Brownell, but was soon intertwined with the brownies of the secret commonwealth and the trooping fairies: Eastman's cheap novelty was originally aimed at the family market, and especially the new child photographer, and brownies were the good, clever helpers of folklore (unlike many of their cousins, elves, imps, borrowers, pucks and goblins, who were mischief-makers). Soon after the arrival of the camera, girls in the Boy Scouts complained: they didn't want to be called 'Rosebuds', the name Baden Powell had given them. From 1914 they too were called Brownies instead.

The manufacturers called it the 'Brownie Box' but Esmond always said Box Brownie, and he had it with him in Italy and was still pointing it at us on family holidays in the 1960s, making memories of our being together, stork mother with her two fledglings side by side, images in which he, the photographer, is inevitably absent. The box is entirely bare and dark now, a theatre closed down for the duration. But back down the years, its fleeting winks caught many moments − new outfits, new places, new friends and old, Esmond's garden in bloom, adventures − and farewells.

~~~

After Esmond died in 1983, Ilia kept his things in trunks in her garage, including this camera and, among some papers, in an old cigar box, I found a small aluminium film canister. Inside two rolls of negative film were coiled around one another: the outside one turned out to be the first snapshots Esmond took after he met Ilia in early 1944 (the other roll, taken in Cairo in 1952, would take us too far ahead in their story).

My mother is standing in front of a jeep in a street in Bari, and Esmond's batman Prestridge (F.E. in the army records online, but I never heard his first name used) appears standing to attention, his bottom lip thrust up over his upper lip to push forward his chin determinedly; his cap is perched at an angle on his head. On my mother's other side stands Esmond's driver in his beret. The jeep is huge; the fender comes up to the elbow of the driver, and the bonnet reaches his shoulder. Many passers-by, all of them civilians, are caught

During the desert war, Major Esmond 'Plum' Warner, 1942.

in the wings of the picture: a young woman, very thin (wartime scarcity), is crossing the street with a smaller and rounder old lady, not so much plump as misshapen; both in black, both in clumsy shoes; the older woman is clutching some supplies to herself, supporting the bag almost tenderly. Another woman in black is striding past in the dappled shade under a line of mimosa trees which alternate with a row of the smaller, slenderer oleander trunks. Behind them the town is empty of all traffic, though from the shadows it must be around ten or eleven in the morning; or two or three in the afternoon. My mother – she too very thin – is holding a bunch of feathery white flowers – unidentifiable, but not orange or almond blossom, though judging from the long jacket she's wearing over a blouse and skirt, it was still early spring. March 1944. She is smiling, openly, warmly, clearly very happy.

In the next shot, my father is standing at ease, also smiling – perhaps my mother is taking this picture? A bicyclist is passing behind him, near a hand-lettered notice pinned up on the trunk of an oleander, announcing Holy Communion at St Augustine's in Bari, next to Area HQ: sung Eucharist at ten, matins at noon and evensong at seven. 8th Army have settled in, and the Anglican padre – who helped when Esmond wanted to marry a local girl – has taken charge of services.

Esmond, a staff officer in the Royal Fusiliers (London Branch), reached Bari before 3 December 1943, the day the harbour was bombed: a direct hit on ammunition ships caused a massive firestorm and great loss of life. The bombs also exploded a clandestine cargo of mustard gas – but this disaster, which caused terrible sickness in the town, was hushed up for years. 'I was carried through the air,' Esmond remembered. 'The blast lifted me up and dropped me down again, my eyes streaming, nasal passages on fire. It was the second time it happened to me – I was lucky, what! So near to copping it, but unhurt in Tripoli that time the Germans came in and bombed the harbour there too. But in Bari, it was worse – they took us by surprise. A huge raid just as we were unloading and the harbour was all lit up. And this time in Bari I lost my glasses. But I found them again, believe it or not, a hundred yards from where I came down. They were cracked but at least I could see something.'

Soon after this, he was deployed north with the army as it advanced up the peninsula.

On the arrival of the Allied troops, all four of the Terzulli sisters immediately volunteered to help the Allies, who were disoriented, especially as all the street signs had been destroyed. For most of the locals, including my mother's family, the Germans were an occupying power – until I was in my late teens, I never realised the Italians had at one time been on the enemy, Axis side. 'We were bicycling along in the country one day near our grandparents' farm,' my mother remembered, 'when some German troops came by in a truck and didn't slow down or stop and so we were forced off the road and when we fell into the ditch they rushed on and we saw them in the back laughing their heads off.'

~~~

Ilia was the youngest of four sisters in the family, with their widowed mother, living on next to nothing and the charity of an uncle. After their father Luigi Terzulli's premature death in 1931 at the age of 42, the younger daughters, Beatrice (Bice) and Ilia, my mother, stopped going to school. Ilia was 9 and Bice 11. Later, Ilia would explain this decision rather vaguely, 'The Fascist ways of doing things confused Mamma. She didn't like it, though I don't know why.' More importantly, she also remembered, 'We were known as *le Americane*, and Mussolini banned anything foreign, especially American. We had to hide the discs that *babbo*'d brought back from Chicago.' They still danced to them, clandestinely, learning from the lyrics: 'By the light of the silv'ry moon / I like to spoon . . .' and 'Picture me upon your knee / Just tea for two and two for tea . . . Can't you see how happy we will be?'

The three elder Terzulli girls had all been born in Chicago during the family's attempt to settle in the US. But in 1921, the family ran from the violent anti-immigrant and especially anti-Italian feelings that spread through the US in the wake of the trial of the Italian anarchists, Sacco and Vanzetti. My mother was born in Italy the following year, the only one in the family who did not have US citizenship.

Her next oldest sister, Bice, spoke the most English in the family, as of the four sisters she was the keenest learner and the most irrepressible. Annunziata and Purissima, the two older girls, remembered the language from their years in

Chicago. On the arrival of the Allies, they reverted to their American names, Nancy and Pat, but they were less voluble and forthcoming by nature. And Nancy, the only one who was married, was recovering from losing the twins. Ilia knew the words of some songs, and she had a fat anthology of English and American literature, packed with writers from Chaucer to Kipling.

The family of women needed money, and the British were grateful for any translation and interpretation. So the sisters took in work for four, and Bice did it. In the evenings, the family used to invite soldiers round to the flat; the men would gather around the girls' sparrow-boned, myopic mother who, like so many other widows in the town, wore the sad livery of her state, however bright the summer light or sultry the temperature.

At some point in the spring of 1944, Esmond was given his first leave, and returned to Bari; a friend suggested taking him to meet the charming and respectable Signora Terzulli and her daughters.

Several of the family's visitors wrote over the years to my mother recalling those days and the hospitality and miraculous beauty of the four Terzulli girls; one or two of them have also written to me, after piecing together that my mother must be the Ilia they had known. 'It was a haven . . . a home from home,' one remembered in a letter. 'We played records on the gramophone and your mother sang to the numbers; sometimes, we danced.'

A few days later, when Ilia was in their temporary offices, picking up some documents for translation, Esmond began introducing her to a fellow officer: 'Here's just the thing for you,' he said, laughing.

But my mother turned away from this new arrival and said to Esmond instead, 'But why not you?'

At least that is the family legend.

The odd thing is that I could imagine this, her looking at him, levelly because of their shared height, but with a slightly cocked head and mock raised eyebrows. 'Why not you?' And the possibility struck him to the heart, the words flying true from the bow of her lips.

Yes, it was very touching, she said, that he was looking to make a match for this penniless and fatherless waif and didn't think of himself as a candidate. But when she proposed herself, he could suddenly see himself in the role.

On his third or fourth visit to the family's apartment, they became engaged. He filled an airgraph letter to his parents, reported that on 27 February he had been promoted to lieutenant colonel and went on without a break to announce:

6 March '44

from Bari

I have much bigger news for you than any promotion though. I am engaged to be married to an Italian girl Elia Terzulli – she is only 21 – she works as a typist for our 'welfare'. She is tall and slim (5ft 8 and a half), dark-haired, enormous brown eyes (her Italian friends call her 'the Stars Look Down' after the Cronin novel) and she is as good as she is beautiful. She has been very strictly brought up, is the youngest of four very good-looking sisters (one, Nancy, like Marlene Dietrich!) and the pet of her family. She has a very bright intelligence and a very keen sense of humour. You would all love her, and her voice is a dream. The sad thing of my leaving 2 Dist[rict] is that I shall be (temporarily) separated from her.

Along the margin:

> Save up some jewellery for Elia. She wd 'set off' good
> things wonderfully.
>   Elia is also a <u>very good cook</u>!

After they'd become officially engaged he could now stay
close to her, at home with the family. But they had still never
been alone together (and he didn't yet know how she spelt
her name).

Writing from Naples where he had been assigned a new
job, Esmond told his parents:

16 March '44 (Naples)

> I am many miles from Elia whom I miss very much though
> I have only been <u>alone </u>with her 2 minutes in my life (that
> strata of Italian life is about 1885 I shd say for customs!)
>   If only the war will end soon and I can bring her home
> for you she will add at least another 5 years to your lives,
> her combination of spirit, vitality, and what a pleasure to
> look at, like a 2-yr-old filly now, 'rangy' NOT quite filled
> out! She has Lrd Birkenhead's qualifications of true
> breeding, apart from all else, beautiful hands, small feet
> and ankles, tall 5.8 and a half and a long slim neck! Black
> eyelashes are half an inch long and curl upwards in a
> sweep. In character she has much in common with 'Ju-Ju'
> aged 3, including that almost fierce possessiveness. (We
> have to be very patient as I consider marriage before the
> war over impossible.)

Ju-Ju was a pet, much loved, but a dog. And a filly, well, is a young pony, before growing into a mare, a mother horse. From *fille*, girl, daughter. Fillette, little girl, little woman, 'darling little woman', as I was always called by Esmond after I appeared.

Ilia would mind terribly, later, that Esmond took to calling her 'old thing' and 'Mummy' to her face, not only when referring to her in our company as was natural in presence of a woman's children.

Yet, all in all, 'filly' was preferable to Mummy.

But filly was something sporting, too, and he reported in another letter home that his suit had been egged on by a fellow officer and Master of Foxhounds of the Cottesmore Hunt, a good chum:

26 March '44

To Daddy
I may tell you when I was only courting Elia, Chatty Hilton-Green encouraged me a lot as he wanted us to be able to bring her to stay with him at Melton, where he guaranteed her a 'furore' (and I fear he's as good a judge of a 'filly' as of a hound or a horse!) Elia is the most thorough-bred-looking girl I ever saw and a lovely open character, although very <u>possessive</u> and jealous!!

The letter then runs on without a break (using up every bit of the airgraph) to describe climbing Vesuvius:

I have a charming adjutant here, Angus Collier lately of Seaforths, and he is very good to me. We went up the observatory on Vesuvius near the crater at the height of the eruption. The eruption has been amazing and serious. Much lava flow nearby, one town destroyed, ash thrown

hundreds of miles, one part one foot deep in heavy
clinker, my car completely bogged in it. I have had
rained over me a heavy clinker like grey gravel up to soft
balls bits, but much dust (read, our garden 2" deep). The
clinker has covered parts up to one foot. Accompanied by
a gale and a snowstorm. Tremendous rumbles, the crater
belching fire, smoke black and oily, thousands of feet
high, now an impenetrable fog. Words cannot describe
the conditions – It has given us quite a lot to do too. All
the above is an UNDERSTATEMENT! An unique experience.

Along the margin Esmond adds:

Do ask at Buck's for Chatty Hilton-Green – he is a great
chap and friend.

On 17 March 1944, Esmond wrote to give the news to Aunt
Dot and Uncle Basil Lubbock, addressing an envelope lined
with brown tissue and stamped 'Federazione Provinciale
Fascista Siracusa / Il Segretario Federale', with inside, thick
cream, watermarked writing paper headed 'Marchese Romeo
delle Torrazze Senatore del Regno'; this luxury has been annotated in my father's hand, 'captured in Sicily early on (Very
special this paper!)'. He repeats some of the description in his
letter to his parents, but adds that Ilia:

speaks English (only too devastatingly . . .) She is the
nearest thing to a Persian 'odalisque' I ever saw in reality. It
is a quite incredible piece of luck I sh'd find in wartorn
Italy what I always sought.

I don't fully grasp this rapid sequence of events, but I can now see that my mother's initiative played more of a part in their union than I had thought: in a diary entry many decades later, in 1989, six years after my father had died, she writes, in Italian: *'Io sono sempre stata la parte attiva nell'atto sessuale'* ('I have always been the active partner in the sexual act').

Was this really possible? At first reading I was disbelieving – shocked. It is difficult to think of one's mother in this way, of course.

But then, on reflection, the vivacity and charm she was so celebrated for, her refusal to allow tedium to take hold of a room or a gathering, her capacity to kindle the ashy embers of a dinner-table companion's moribund spirit into licking tongues of flame, all those ways of hers which were so life-enhancing and vivid, which I used to marvel at and, at the same time, revolt against as geisha-like ministrations to male authority, itself unearned, rotten and undeserving of her efforts, were interwoven with this active desire on which she acted – not only later when she knew she was unhappy and that Esmond and she were so profoundly unsuited to each other, but from the start, when she took the initiative as she said was her wont and proposed he should consider himself a candidate for her love. No, not only her love, for her *desire*. One of the most pejorative words in her vocabulary, alongside 'frump', was 'prude'. Ilia never could bear a prude.

~~~

The wedding, which took place in Bari on 25 June 1944, followed soon after the entry of Americans into Rome on 5 June and the liberation of the south, and Esmond was able to take Ilia on their honeymoon to some of the towns and cities on the cliffs above the Mediterranean on that western coast which she had never seen before.

Ilia, on her honeymoon, Villa Cimbrone, Ravello, June 1944.

They went to Ravello: the photographs show Ilia smiling as she peels an orange on the balcony of the Palumbo hotel, giving her new husband a candid, utterly convincing smile of happiness; shots of views – from the balcony of the ridged vineyards rising up to rocky scarps, crested with parasol pines; another snapshot later in the gardens of the Villa Cimbrone, Ilia gently caressing the ear of a gazelle, with behind her, rooftops covered in frills of terracotta tiles, windows inset with barley sugar columns, and pergolas on flat roofs. Confectionery, pasta cutting and architecture developed in Italy in a continuum, the shapes of sweets and cakes cut out in clay or flour to build churches and public buildings, houses and gardens.

Esmond had travelled the world ever since he was a babe in arms, he told her; before this beastly war, he'd toured Italy and seen more of her own country than she had; he would show her Venice too, one day, when peace returned. He'd travelled on to the Balkans and Albania in 1924, and before then, the family had been on long sea voyages, all the way to

Australia with his father on a cricket tour in 1911. She listened intently; she asked him to repeat words; she committed them to memory.

'One morning but not yet first light I heard a noise that I couldn't understand, though mind you I was a tiddlywink then who hadn't seen much. The noise brought me up on deck and we were drawing up to dock – it must have been Port Said, and everything but everything was black. Do you know why, *piccola?*'

Ilia shook her head.

'Because the ship was taking on coal, it was being filled up from the bilges to the gunwales with tons of it, bloody tons of it, to get us to . . . where do you think? Colombo!'

Colombo was where Esmond would get stuck in 1945, waiting for another boat to bring him home.

'And after Colombo, we'd steam on straight ahead – give or take a few bends – onward eventually to Sydney. Australia! Daddy was playing there, you see. His game, cricket. The game you don't have in Italy – not yet, anyway. Almost everywhere else plays it, where we British have set foot. It's not just a game, you see. It's the embodiment of what it means to be British. And Daddy has been knighted for his services to the game, in 1936 – the King himself dubbed him.' Esmond laughed, 'Whack, whack, with a sword, first one shoulder then the other.' He swished an imaginary blade through the air. 'Rise Sir Pelham!'

She was listening, carefully. Her English officer was laughing that hooting laugh of his, which misted his specs so he had to take them off and wipe them and mop his tearing eyes.

He collected himself. 'Where was I? Yes, going through the Canal. The deck, the lifeboats, the funnel, every fixture and fitting of the boat was covered in coal dust. And so was I within minutes. Panda eyes, my toes a mudlark's, and my nice white cotton pyjamas begrimed and seamed in soot!

'That sound I'd heard, that had woken up a sleeping boy in his hot cabin before dawn, was the roar of the coal pouring into the hold, and all around me lascars were mopping. They were swarming over the ship with buckets, dropping them down the other side of the boat from the wharf to fill them in the Canal and slosh the water over the decks.

'I'm telling you, those fellows knew a thing or two about work — before you could say Jack Robinson, the widow's shrouds that had wrapped the ship were gone. When Nanny found me, she was fit to explode 'cos there wasn't a sign left of the soot anywhere except on me! It was an apparition, I'm telling you, and I never forgot it.

'Then we set sail down the Canal and the ship seemed to float on the desert which stretched all a-shimmer around us and laid, shining, wide and flat, a silver path ahead like moonlight beaming on a calm sea. I ran the decks from stern to prow to look — the Suez Canal! It unfurls calmly level with the wide flat desert on both sides. This was it, and nobody'd thought to wake me to see it — I could have missed a bloody wonder of the world and who would have given a toss? Not Daddy, who cared only about wickets and scores. What a sight it was! What a triumph of raw human will! If I'd known the words then, I'd have howled out to that marvellous belt of silver that links us in Europe to Africa and to Asia "What a bloody piece of work is man!" We'd sliced through a continent to open the fast way east! To India, to China, and to Down Under, where Daddy and Mummy and I were headed. It was 1911 and the Canal wasn't old hat, not at all.

'The Canal has loomed pretty damn large in the desert campaign. Larger than the ship floating through the desert on either side of a small boy before that first World War. It was everywhere in our thinking. We fought to hold Cairo and Egypt because of it: it's the empire's coronary artery. The channel that keeps us in the style to which we're accustomed, *mia piccola*. Without it – well I can't imagine what life was like or what'd it be like, honest to God.'

~~~

Esmond went back and forth between duties in Naples and visits to Bari. Meanwhile, the parties at the Terzulli girls' flat continued in his absence: in 1993, a thriller writer, Bruce Munslow, who had also been in the 8th Army, wrote to me from Devon how he had never forgotten them:

> I was reading the interview with you . . . and I knew at once that your mother's name was Ilya [*sic*] . . . a beautiful Italian girl I met long ago . . . I went a few times to parties at Ilya's home – I think it was in the Via Calefati. Actually I think someone was on the lookout for a husband for young Beachi [*sic*] – for at least once I found myself along with her at night on the little balcony – and I remember her saying softly, '. . . but let us talk of loff, Bruce'. She pronounced my name 'Broooch'.
>
> I'm afraid I couldn't talk to her about loff, because I was already half in love with Ilya, whose husband was further north with his regiment. Apart from her not being free, I had no desire for an outraged colonel to come looking for me. However, I must have been alone with Ilya at least twice (which was hard to achieve with any Italian girl at that time) because I gave her a love poem I had composed . . .
>
> I remember another incident very clearly. There was to be a dance at the depot where I was stationed . . . Another chap asked if I was going . . . I thought I'd show him something and asked all three girls, Ilya, Nancy and Beachi to go with me, which they did. They were of a different class to the other girls at the dance and in their beautiful dresses looked absolutely stunning . . .

In August, Esmond was able to organise a ride for Ilia to join him, and they spent their first birthdays – they were born one day apart over a gap of fifteen years – in Ravello.

10 Sept 1944

Elia came over to stay at Ravello on 21st August and stayed till 29th – I was able to get away most nights and 3 days of her visit. She had with her also on leave from Bari my good friend 'Uncle' Harry Marley, who is kindness itself, brought her over in his car and took her back, and looked after her when I was at work. It was a great success, and we both loved our second honeymoon.

We had the same lovely room at our beloved 'Palumbo' – what a little Paradise Ravello is. Two or three others were over on leave from 2 Dist[rict] also, and for our birthday dinner party we sat down 10, and had a very gay evening, with an Italian band and singer going on very late for our special benefit – the Italian popular songs, especially the Neapolitan are very catchy and a good many of the boys know some of them well already. And we had of course the inevitable Lili Marleen with its nostalgia of desert days.

I had to go up to Rome for a conference on the 28th and was 'doing business with' as usual and stayed with my good friends of General Alex's HQ. Their mess in Rome was Musso's late villa, Torlonia, rather lovely, but pretty shabby now. They had a dance the night I was there – I wondered who else had danced in that salon in late years.

Two days later, they found themselves in Amalfi on the feast day of the town's patron saint, St Andrew the Apostle. The photos he took show the procession, with a huge silver effigy of the saint, pouring down the long steep flight of steps that leads up to the west door of the harlequin-patterned cathedral, with dozens of boys in white surplices carrying small vessels – probably censers, but too small to see exactly – and very, very tall candles. A whole peacock tail of robed prelates sweeps on behind them – the photograph is fuzzy (light has got into the camera) but I can count *twelve* of them, no less, in mitres very wide and shiny and tall, and they are stepping down two by two to accompany the saint who is enthroned and raised high on the shoulders of a cohort of *spallieri*; some of these bearers are also holding up, to shelter the statue, a fringed canopy on four poles pinnacled with complicated tasselled crowns: this whole machine is being manoeuvred down the steep flight. The thronging clerics in their finery are themselves flanked by officials in sashes and capes and ingenious hats (the Italians are endlessly inventive when it comes to millinery, as well as pasta and confectionery). You can just see the large knot of men heaving to under the relic, all of them in white robes with dark tabards – the vestments of a local confraternity, most likely, the one to which the God-fearing *borghesi* of the town all belong where they can do business in full trust of one another. These *spallieri* are as tightly packed together as a rugby scrum and it is indeed miraculous that even such concerted manpower could lift the colossal reliquary and carry it down the precipitous steps that descend for over fifty metres to the Piazza del Duomo. It's a feat, an ordeal, putting its citizens in danger in order to attain a collective high – at the bottom of the steps, the *festa* is beginning.

In the last of three photographs, the reliquary bust of the saint has almost completed the descent successfully, and the crowd is already relaxing in the piazza, the confraternals and priests hobnobbing, and the saint himself has come into closer view, and towers over the gathering like a colossal Buddha, like an enthroned Mughal emperor.

Ilia always went to Mass and prayed with fervour, and Esmond attended the services by her side during those few marvellous weeks they spent together. He watched her pray and was enchanted by her absorption. Every now and then, she'd give a small, parched cough – she had had TB when she was a child and the illness had shrunk her lungs, or at least her mother and her sisters thought it had and telling her so over and over gave her a sense of precariousness when she breathed, so that all unconsciously, she often gave this little dry sputter of a cough to open her lungs a little to expel the old air trapped in her tight passages and bring new oxygen to aerate her. The closeness of the deity and his mother, of the angels and saints in the church, made her feel this need, as Esmond realised, tenderly and protectively, when the incense misted the distance between them and the priest, who was turning around now to face them with the chalice held up theatrically in front of him, a host pinched between finger and thumb, offering Communion.

'Aren't you going to take Communion?' he whispered into the side of her face, which was still slightly curved downwards, absorbed in her missal, her lace veil the tint of mulberry juice against the deeper blackness of her loose curling hair. She turned, eyes wide and laughter in them: 'How could I, when you have given me so much chocolate for breakfast?' She did not express it quite in those words because her English came out in bits and pieces during those first weeks they spent together.

But she had said, as she laughed, something about chocolate.

～

In England, Frank Pakenham, Esmond's old school friend, for whom Esmond had fagged at Eton and who, on the death of his older brother in the war, was to become the famous campaigner Lord Longford, heard the news and wrote from his home in Oxford to congratulate him on marrying a Catholic and expressing his hopes that he would soon have a very large family:

1st July 1944

My dear Esmond . . . though you say you are sticking staunchly to your old Anglican heresy, just you wait and see! I don't want to crow too soon, which might have a 'putting-off' effect, but I have no fears now about your ultimate salvation.

Summing up 'News of old friends', he passed on that

Evelyn [Waugh] broke a bone in his leg learning to become a parachutist, and is now, I believe, preparing to escort or actually escorting journalists round the Second Front. He has also written the best part of a long novel. If any of his virulence against the 'brass hats' finds expression in print and makes its way past the Censor, I should expect this to prove his most entertaining satire since 'Decline and Fall'.

At one moment he was posted to a Divisional Headquarters and served as ADC [aide-de-camp] to the general. Freddy [Birkenhead] saw him off from White's fairly well oiled. He had a few drinks on the way, arrived thoroughly 'canned' and spilled the wine all over the general's trousers at dinner. Next morning the general dismissed him. 'No offence I hope Waugh, but can't have an ADC of mine getting "foxed" at dinner.' Evelyn, disliking the word 'foxed' almost as much as he disliked the general, 'You can hardly expect me, sir, to change the habits of a lifetime to suit your peculiarities.' Exit.

I could drivel on like this, Esmond, for a long time

because it seems to bring us closer together, but I must
stop in a moment . . .

Yrs affectionately,

Frank

PS Telephoning your mother to confirm your address . . .
I learnt that you are now married. <u>Marvellous</u> [underlined
seven times] Still more congratulations to <u>you both</u>. Now
for a family.

That family would eventually consist of my younger sister
Laura and myself, and Esmond would laugh heartily when I,
terrified he would burn in hell, begged him to convert.

Esmond loved Frank and went on loving him through
many vicissitudes and the marked difference in their interests
and status. There is no other word for the intense attention
my father paid to Frank's every word and deed; he was proud
he was his friend; he admired him, marvelled at him, mocked
him: Frank had 'gone over to Rome, and taken Elizabeth
with him'. Elizabeth Harman was the only 'undergraduette'
anyone at Oxford knew. Frank's faith, discovered and kindled
by the living saint Father Darcy, responsible for Evelyn
Waugh's conversion as well as Graham Greene's, was always
a source of utter perplexity and entertainment to Esmond,
who liked his friend chiefly for his worldly ambitions – and
successes. But Frank's new-found religion puzzled him less
than Frank's earlier defection from every tradition and allegiance of his class (Anglo-Irish plantocracy), when he became
a fervent socialist, serving in Attlee's government. Esmond
was not going to follow him down either of these crazy paths.
Instead, he snorted with laughter at his friend's idealistic
zeal.

In Amalfi on the day of the *patrono*'s feast, the priest
sounded like a caricature to Esmond because the Latin

Esmond first learned at his prep school was pronounced altogether differently. In Bari, the celebrant on the high altar, sweeping from side to side in his gleaming embroideries with a small boy following, censer and vials at the ready, pronounced the words as if they were in Italian – not the solid masonry edifice of Cicero and Tacitus that he'd declaimed at school. Ilia echoed the words of the Mass, and this too filled Esmond with a swelling tide of tenderness towards her – Roman Catholics certainly knew about the feminine virtues! In London, he'd had girlfriends who were for the most part the sisters of his old school chums, and later of his university friends, men he'd been at Oxford with and later in the Guards. There were sisters in the story, there always were. Sisters appeared when you went away for the weekend during term to stay with a friend at his family's, they carried golf clubs and ciggies, drove quickly and tossed their gear – tennis rackets in severe presses with wing nuts and screws at the corners, long cartons stamped with dressmakers' crests in azure and gold, in which the ballgown and the stole and the cocktail dress were lying between sheets of tissue waiting to leap out and enfold their mistress with encrusted ruffles, slippery rustling stuff, while the little strong box for Mummy's tiara which she was lending for the night, so sweet of her, was thrown on to the back seat as well. Then off, off down the lanes to the country house.

Penelope had been Esmond's most frequent companion. She was more eager to tuck her hair into a riding helmet than under a tiara, and she didn't have a car, but her brother Roger had, a Model T Ford which he willingly let Esmond borrow to squire his sister round. The Chetwodes, though connected to everyone, were short of the readies, like Esmond, but they had land, lots of it, thin shale somewhere with endless rain and midges; as chauffeur Esmond could make himself indispensable, and drove Penelope and her pony in its neat box to point-to-points where she grew flushed and glowing as she competed – never minding a fall, or a broken collarbone or crushed rib every now and then.

There was never a breath of romance; he'd wait outside the St John's Ambulance tent while they set her fracture, and he'd smoke anxiously until she reappeared, a bit wan, but grinning at her luck. What an adventure, oh what fun.

〜〜

When my mother prayed, she was always intent; when I used to go with her to Mass, I followed her in many different churches during my childhood, from the Nissen hut at RAF Oakington to the Dominicans in Cambridge where she liked Father Robert Pollock's sermons, and, last of all, Brompton Oratory in London, she was fully possessed by the service and its unfolding drama. Sometimes her lips moved; sometimes her eyes were closed; sometimes she gave that short dry cough that afflicted her all her life, but it didn't interrupt her absorption.

By then, my father never went with her, and in spite of his devotion to Frank, he never even flirted with conversion.

On their honeymoon, accompanying her, he took in the earnestness of his young wife with similar amusement:

> to MR and Betts
> . . . I went with Ilia to Mass in Ravello Cathedral where an
> old bishop (over 80) (and held up!) celebrated a solemn
> charade full of conjuring tricks, and looked like Uncle
> Auchie!

Meanwhile in London, Mother Rat, herself from Northern Irish Protestant stock, and his father 'Plum', whose father

the Attorney General of Trinidad has gone down in the
history books for the truly hostile environment for Catholics
he created, were a little anxious about the Italian girl's
allegiances.

21 March '44

To Daddy
Thank you very much for your charming letter ref. Elia –
your reactions are what I wd. expect, and I fear MR's are
too. I thought <u>true Christians</u> like MR believed in the
'indivisible Christian brotherhood of men' so <u>her</u> remarks
about foreigners amuse me, if it was NOT rather sad. Elia is
of course a RC – we only once discussed religion – I was
rather delighted to find that she barely knew there <u>were</u>
any other Christians except RCs!! But I have left her in no
doubt that I stand by the principles of the glorious revolution of 1688 and the Protestant Succession and 'down with
the Pope'! Poor darling that she should be considered
against a theological and dynastic background. I fear that
we who here have made the long trek from Alamein have
little time for this sort of thing, as Churchill has said
'good citizens are all nations and creeds'. The fact is
however that MR will, of all of you, be especially mad
about Elia (for Betts' information, accent on the E) as she
has a very Irish character, full of light and shade. I will tell
you more of her family . . .
    She is very worried you will think her 'NOT good
enough for me' when the facts are <u>very much the other way</u>,
and I say that most objectively.

This is where he goes on to write those words about her future
as his wife:

they [Ilia's family] have nice friends of 'the professional
classes' type. Elia however (you know she is only <u>21</u>)
belongs to the new world, and her life will be <u>mine</u>, NOT
her circle's.

Esmond was to leave the following Saturday for South East
Asia Command and another war front in Burma; in 1945,
with Esmond still in the Far East, my mother left Bari, carrying
a hatbox and a suitcase for London to meet her parents-in-law
and enter that new life.

It is disorienting hearing your father's voice from long ago,
sounding in the chamber of memory, and seeing your mother
then, before everything that was to happen. I can't help
flinching at the way he wrote about her — was it naiveté? Yet
he was raised to worldliness, far more than she. The world he
had lived in as an adult for nearly two decades — he turned
38 in 1945 — was a narrow anchorage of cards and cricket,
the school yard, the officers' mess, the house party, the supper
club. She was stepping into it:

Elia is a greyhound . . . [she] has the lightest step I ever
met.

Bruce Munslow, in the letter written so many decades after
the events he recalled, wondered 'how Ilya would fare in
England. She was rather like a delicate flower, not suitable I
thought for this climate.'

3

A Hatbox

Fifteen inches in diameter, seven inches deep, dark blue buckram laid on board, with a leather strap; some P&O stickers from later voyages, including a passage on the RMS *Strathaird* back to London. At this date, 1945, there are hats inside which Ilia has trimmed, including the lacy one made of straw with dark ribbons which she is wearing with a slightly self-conscious smile in the press photograph taken of her with her father-in-law Sir 'Plum' Warner, in the *Illustrated London News*; he is wearing morning dress, too, and looks Chaplinesque beside her tallness; they're standing outside the gates of Buckingham Palace with a small group of onlookers and guests arriving in 'morning dress' – grey top hats and tails.

~~~

The journey to London in 1945 was Ilia's first time travelling in an aeroplane. She was booked to fly to London from Rome soon after peace was declared in Europe in May; Esmond had sent her the plane ticket from Rome, a list of instructions on a piece of Palumbo writing paper he'd purloined, telling her how to send her box ahead, and then drawn her a map of a bewildering mesh of streets lying at different angles to the mansion block in South Kensington where his parents had a flat and would put her up until he returned. She had a seat overlooking part of the wing and the propeller, which as they trundled up to speed on the runway soon whirled into a diaphanous halo such as surrounds the Madonna in some of Raphael's paintings; Ilia looked through it, blinking to see if she could catch a glimpse of the vanes. 'Elica'. It was one of those words believers in the Duce's promises had called their children. Vita, Luce and, yes, Elica. Elica. She took out her pocket Italian–English dictionary: it said, 'screw'. Surely that wasn't quite right? Elica was the daughter of a Futurist, and he'd named her for a more glorious dream of machines.

Ilia with her father-in-law Plum (Sir Pelham Warner), about to attend the Royal Garden Party, July 1949.

Today's skies were clear blue. She saw islands beneath her; she knew the larger ones – Sardinia, Corsica – outcropped in the metal sea like uncut gemstones studding a Byzantine binding, and when she saw the smallest floating on its own she remembered the rock where the Count of Monte Cristo was persevering still with the Stone Age tools he'd shaped himself in order to . . . escape.

Surely, he could have then stepped out on to this sea, its glinting stretch of hammered aluminium offering him a land bridge to his new life, to freedom? But she was passing overhead, angelically, in a roar louder than any deity would ever make in order to reach air and light and England. Her *vita nuova*.

She'd read about Great Britain in a textbook about Europe by a local Pugliese professor: 'London is not beautiful,' he'd written, 'in the sense that our cities are beautiful . . .' So she wasn't altogether surprised as she rode the bus into London, and saw the war-damaged streets. As Esmond had told her to, she got off in the Cromwell Road; everyone would be helpful, he'd assured her. She was then to ask the way to the address he had written down for her.

'Say Pelham Street – just a coincidence, it's not actually called after him! It's in South Ken. – Kensington.'

She kept her pocket Italian–English dictionary in her handbag near her compact and lipstick, so she could always look up a word or a phrase; it even included useful information, on irregular verbs, weights and measures, species of fish; the volume so tiny it could fit into a matchbox.

A light rain wept on the windows of the bus and there was no countryside between the airport and her destination, only roads and more roads enclosed on both sides by houses, one or two with cars parked in the forecourt, and each house with a front door, all different; the people inside living in separation from their neighbours, maybe not even knowing them at all, a thing unimaginable, then, to someone who had grown up in apartment buildings which had evolved from fortresses and castles and monasteries and where everybody was packed together to form a colony, like the cooperative species, the smaller birds who flock, not the way of the single raptor who works and feeds alone.

The conductor, a cigarette tucked behind one ear, sat her down at the front near the driver, on the benches facing across the aisle, so he could keep an eye on her; he stowed the hatbox and her suitcase ('They'll be safe there, don't you fuss'), patted her on the shoulder and called her pet names – different from the ones Esmond used. This man with his wooden board where tickets were trapped like mice, was asking her all kinds of things she couldn't answer except with a smile.

'*Sir Pelham* – ah, I see, "Plum" Warner. Cricket's Grand Old Man, hmm. He's expecting you, is he, pet?'

'He is my father,' said Ilia.

'And I'm the Queen of Sheba.' Passengers behind him tittered. The conductor went on, with bright eyes, 'Your father! Well, love, that's a thing.' Then he winked.

She caught herself, and remembered, 'No, father-in-law.'

Passengers were taking a keen interest, now.

'Can we come too,' said one, laughing, 'and have a cup of tea with his nibs?'

It was awkward, not being able to grasp the mood through the unfamiliar words, but she smiled back and after thinking carefully, asked, 'How long until we come?'

'I'll let you know, pet, don't you fret.'

He helped her down off the bus platform, which made her anxious – she had grasped the hatbox, and she could feel the diamond rings tucked under her belt in their pouch, but her case was still in the compartment behind him. She was reluctant to get off before he handed it down to her – in Naples and in Rome far more meagre takings than her belongings were spread out on the pavements for sale or barter every night by the railway station and in the narrow streets off the main thoroughfares. But he did pass it down to her, with a cheery line she couldn't understand, except that she knew from his grin that he was wishing her well in a jocular spirit that carried a hint of disbelief.

Leaving the stop in the Cromwell Road in the direction the conductor had pointed her towards, she showed the address Esmond had written to a man sitting selling newspapers at the corner of a Tube station. He too chuckled and pointed onwards. Eventually, she found the low-lying redbrick mansion block in South Kensington. It was almost the only building left standing in that street and its surroundings: opposite a charred and cavernous hole where a bomb had hit.

The porter opened the door to her; he had one arm and limped. She showed him her letter. The fug of the mansion block came off his serge uniform, a fug made of the coal-fired air that lingered still from the wartime struggles against raw chill and damp, and the general stewed comforting frowsiness that, somewhat shocked, she came to know and recognise so clearly as the smell of England. Mouse droppings and rats' nests, suet and soot, cabbage and cabbage water, Worcestershire Sauce, lard, mustard, Marmite, chicory coffee; then the hoarded treasures, eked out one by one, rationed crumbs in cake and biscuit tins, caramel and fudge – she would always let her new in-laws have her portion of sweets; though she had a sweet tooth, she could do without.

This whiffiness of London startled her. She came from a country where white linen was hung out of the windows daily and mats too, to be beaten with a wicker fan; she was never to become accustomed to the sluttishness of her new countrymen and women – especially among the well-off and the well-born as she knew

Esmond to be from what he had said and also from the things he'd assumed they'd do together. But Mother Rat, she would soon discover, let her sleeves fall into the scummy dishwater when she tried to keep house on Doris's day off – like the worst slattern nobody would have kept for a day's work in Bari. But this was because Esmond's mother hadn't been brought up to know how to deal with a sink and had never learned since.

~~~

Doris was his mother's companion, Esmond had explained to Ilia the last time they were together at the Palumbo, when he was planning how she'd join him in London and they'd eventually be together again at last.

'Companion?' Ilia was puzzled.

'Well, it means she's really a maid, but a mainstay, what? Sort of family but not quite. She's a bit younger than Mother Rat,' he'd continued, and she would look after Ilia in London; Doris did everything for his parents – their household was small, now. There had been a time when they had a proper staff, but with the war, lean times had struck. He was vague. 'Gentlemen play cricket . . .' he began. 'It's not a real job. There's no money in it. Daddy turned a penny writing – anonymously at first – and now books pour out of him – mostly about his exploits, hah! He's quite up to praising his own prowess, you know. Daddy's been everything in cricket – manager of the England team, lots of heady times we had then, I'm telling you. But Daddy's also known to be a man of subtlety and subterfuge as well as a straight bat. He's the Talleyrand of cricket!

'He's not interested in anything else, though there's no money in it, as I say. And then, stocks, well, the war has made that bumpy, to put it mildly, what? It's the ways things are going. There'll be no more indoor staff for us.

Esmond, in a three-piece suit, with his father, Plum Warner,
Maidstone Cricket Week, 1911 or 1912.

'My sister Betsy,' he went on, 'we call her Betts. You'll get
on with her like a house on fire. She's married now to a naval
chap. She calls him Father Badger – he's a big fellow, you'll see.'

Badger: she asked him what it meant. He looked up the
word in the dictionary he carried. '*Tasso.*'

'Like the poet! I knew he has the name of the animal, but
I have only heard of them, never seen one.'

Esmond had fetched his shaving brush to show her, and
whisked it over her cheeks, then kissed her.

'As children,' he explained, 'we were all very fond of every
sort of animal. I had a pet rat, whom I called Scoot and kept in
the pocket of my blazer because at my prep school' – he was

speaking too fast for her, and her eyebrows, in slender arcs like swallow's wings, wrinkled in perplexity – 'my prep – preparatory – school was in the country and there were sheds where we were allowed to keep our pets and visit them after tea before homework and supper. You should have seen boys cuddling and cooing to their animals! People say men mock tears, but I know, I've seen grown men with rough manners singing together ballads of longing for home with the tears running down their cheeks – I tell you there were more fights broke out in the ranks about girls than about anything, and that was because every one of us – however knocked about and hardened the ranks might appear you know, each one was as soft as a newborn babe inside,' Esmond thumped his chest. 'There. Heart, you know. Heart. Home. If it struck one of them that someone was slighting his girl, that fellow was in for it, what? But I'm not surprised that feelings run so high about these matters because if you've been sent away from home, like me, and like everyone in England, you've seen boys curled up with homesickness as if it was dengue fever or malaria. But it made men of us. And the animals helped. We visited them and cuddled them, and they understood us.

'Of course, my brother John, he wasn't sent away to prep school.' Esmond touched Ilia's hand, tapped it on the back rather sharply, almost hurting her. 'Mother Rat kept him by her, she wanted one of her children at least with her at home, she said. So he went to a day school, in London, near my parents' flat. Lucky blighter.

'I used to take Scoot into lessons. She was as good as gold. Usually.' He laughed. 'But not always, of course.

'Then she got pneumonia. Rats are prone to pneumonia. Especially pet rats. After that I had another, but she wasn't a patch on Scoot. So I changed to ferrets – they were funny things, clever as monkeys, shimmying through anything. There was a gang of gippos used to come every summer to the village fair and lay on races: their ferrets poured themselves through pipes laid out side by side – the funniest thing you ever saw. We'd place bets.'

He looked up the word ferret in the dictionary: *'furetto'*.

'Furetti!' she frowned. 'They are very wild.' She snapped her teeth, to show. Hers were round and small, and overlapped unevenly; nothing like the fierce white needle-sharp spines of his ferrets.

'Oh, ferrets make terrific pets, once you learn how to handle them. They're bags of fun. But badgers are another thing. You can't keep badgers as pets, not badgers. Or at least I never heard of it.'

～～～

The porter called upstairs on the intercom and nodded at what he heard down the line from the flat above, then he began ushering her into the lift.

'Only one floor, but seeing you have luggage, Miss, your carriage awaits.' He swept an arm to beckon her in.

The lift was mahogany and brass with a leather seat that was somewhat cracked on the front edge, but luxury all the same and Ilia sat down on it, overwhelmed for a moment by the closeness of the air, the dimness of the light, her empty stomach. She had a tendency to faint; her sisters joked it was her height that caused it: she was so long and thin her blood couldn't always reach her head.

A thick rope ran through a hole in the lift floor and ceiling, and the porter with his one good arm hauled on it to set the wheel spinning below in the bottom of the shaft and they began to rise. As the doors of the first floor came in view, her escort hauled on a huge brass level to stall their ascent, and with a clunk and a rattle, pulled on the accordion pleated railings.

He stepped out with her and stood before the dark shiny front door well furnished with brass and, all around the knobs and letter box, halos in the wood varnish where the polishing of them had lifted the colour. She waited behind him.

'I can hear them coming, Miss,' he said to her reassuringly. And at that moment, the door opened, and there were the three of them: Mother Rat, and Daddy, and Doris in front, for it was she who had opened the door.

The porter was trundling her case with his one arm, with Ilia trying to take it from him and Daddy interposing himself between both of them and taking charge.

Then, after another few moments of confusion in the dark corridor, she was propelled into a larger room where the air was less stuffy, but heavy drapes hung at the windows and a lamp gave out a yellowish light.

'Come now, my dear,' said Mother Rat, settling down with a wheezy sigh in the soft cushions of a big sofa, 'how was your journey? I've flown to Le Touquet and Nice. But never as far away as Italy.' She smiled, a sweet dimpling smile that lit up her plump face and gave a glimpse of the young girl she once was, who had been slender and light as the feathers that sprang from her jewelled bandeau in her silver sequined dress and train when she was received at court with the debutantes of 1902, during the first year of Edward VII's reign, when, thank goodness, the annual ceremony had been held, in spite of a movement to defer it a year in honour of the dead queen.

To Ilia's eyes, Motherette was not entirely rat-like, she saw with some relief, as her teeth were small and blunt and brown; she was wide and squat and soft, and swaddled in fur wraps, even though the flat was very warm, Ilia felt; she was so rounded and bundled in softness that she reminded her more of the baby owl, a fluffy ball of down, which she had once found on the ground outside the chapel of San

Corrado's, near her grandparents' farm in Ruvo di Puglia, where she and her sisters used to go sometimes in the summer. The nestling had fallen from the eaves, and she knocked on the door of the priest's house to hand it to the housekeeper for her to give it back to the owls who nested there year after year.

But Motherette's eyes had nothing of an owl's gig-lamp soulfulness: with an unfocused mild vacancy, they invited sentimental complicity and laughter. Although at five foot five she was in fact taller than anyone in Ilia's own family (apart from herself), her mother-in-law appeared diminutive, with glazed brown eyes and small dry hands which plucked at her to sit back beside her on the sofa. Ilia perched on the edge, unsure of how she would extricate herself if she fell into its soft folds, and she twisted round awkwardly, her long thin legs tight together, to face her mother-in-law.

The room was crowded with furniture, she noticed; and all of it was covered in ornaments: vases, silver knick-knacks, china animals, clocks, one very tall another small on the mantelpiece (they both chimed, at different times); carpets and drapes; cushions and pelmeted curtains. Some of the things must have been wedding gifts, from that amazing haul that greeted the returning hero of the Ashes when he married the young Agnes Blyth, before she became Mother Rat. 'You wouldn't believe how famous they were! Nearly six hundred presents, I swear,' Esmond had told her. 'You wait till you see the ledger – red morocco – with all of 'em entered in black ink copperplate!' It was plain to Ilia their circumstances had shrunk. They now seemed very squashed in among all their possessions, as if they had outgrown the bed, the chair, the table of the golden haze of childhood.

Ilia, emblazoned with a W for her new name, London, 1945.

'My lamb,' said Mother Rat, 'would you like some tea? Doris . . .' She reached for a small china bell that stood on the whatnot beside the sofa and tinkled it. 'Doris?' Before Doris appeared, Mother Rat consulted the watch on her wrist. 'No, my love, no, it's time for a drink, isn't it?' She tinkled again for Doris, and when Doris came, tapped Ilia fondly on her hand, and then said, 'And my dear Daddy, what would you like?'

Ilia's father-in-law had not yet spoken, but had been sitting quietly, the newspaper opened in front of him at the desk in the corner of the room. His build was surprisingly slight for such a sportsman, she noticed.

He now spoke, with a quick, shy smile that showed small, even and very white teeth: 'I'll have a cup of tea.'

Doris went down the corridor, with Sir Pelham following.

'Would you like to wash, my lambkin?' asked Mother Rat. 'You don't look as if you do.' She scanned Ilia's suit. 'That looks a fine piece of dressmaking, did you make it yourself, you clever girl? Esmond said you were quite a needlewoman.' She paused, looking her over and eyeing Ilia's hands. 'Where're the half-moons, my dear girl? The diamonds I sent you? If you're keeping 'em hidden, no need any more, now you're here.' Ilia hadn't yet tuned her ear to her mother-in-law's delivery and was trying to find words to reply to phrases that sounded very rapid and indistinct. 'Perhaps you'd like to see your room? Doris'll show you, when she comes back.' Mother Rat was slumped; she seemed exhausted by her sociability, and Ilia felt the heat of her closeness on the sofa, and the smell of the furs, powder and a faded old violet scent from a bottle, and other things, best not thought about too clearly.

She said, carefully, that she was very happy to meet her at last. Then, her tongue feeling clumsy as a wooden clapper, she asked if there was news from Esmond.

'Oh, he's now stuck in Ceylon,' said Mother Rat. 'It's a bloody nuisance, altogether. Doris!'

Doris was on her way, pushing a tea trolley in front of her with practised speed.

'Doris dear, turn on the wireless, so we can hear the news. And pour me a little glass, there's a love.'

Swiftly behind the trolley came Sir Pelham, carrying a long wooden implement in his hand.

'This, my dear girl,' he said to Ilia, 'is the way you'll become one of us.'

He stood squarely on the rug in front of her, placed the bat between his knees and stooped over it, looking at her keenly as if taking aim. 'A Bokhara's not a bouncy pitch, and best not to bowl in here.' He gestured towards the glass-fronted bookcases, closing in on the crush in the room. 'But come and stand beside me and have a go at swinging your bat!'

On the sofa, Mother Rat was giggling softly: 'He's dead

keen to get the gels to play, you know. Thinks ladies' cricket is the coming thing. Has been writing all about it and stirring up lots of trouble!' She sounded cheerful as she sipped from her little glass. 'Go on, my dear, never refuse a gentleman's offer to teach you something you don't know. And now that you're in England, you might as well know how to play! Esmond will be so pleased. When he gets home.'

From under the sofa, in between her feet, she began rummaging.

Plum patted Ilia on the shoulder and said, 'Only two rules in life, that's all you need. Keep a straight bat. And your eye on the ball.'

~~~

As she began to learn the customs of the house, she would stay in her room and arrange her things; sometimes, she'd read from the few books in the suitcase that had been stowed in the hold.

She began to sense when it was time for her to emerge and join Mother Rat in the sitting room by the radio, where Sir Pelham (she never called him Plum) would join them from his office at the *Cricketer* in time for the evening news, which she kept hoping would bring the end of the war in the East and hasten Esmond's return. She began to help Doris in the kitchen, and found the chute from which the stink rose, like the fumes from the steaming compost heap tucked into the distant and shaded corner of a field on her grandparents' farm. There were no plastic bags then, so any leavings were scraped off the plates and tipped down into the building's ample digestive tract. It was puzzling that here in South Kensington, with in-laws who were going to take her to meet the King at Buckingham Palace – and the silver-framed photograph on a side table in their drawing room, showing Plum, strolling along beside the smiling monarch on a cricket field somewhere,

seemed to bear out this promise – that in this capital of the
great empire of the British, rubbish was dropped straight into
a hole in the kitchen wall. The mouth of the chute was a kind
of trap with a shutter that split horizontally in two like the
face of a ventriloquist's manikin and gave a glimpse of a dark
gullet, streaked and smeared by the passage of rubbish now
growing fluffy patches of verdigris mould.

Vegetable rot and worse exhaled from the depths: below,
Doris reassured her, were dustbins which caught the rubbish
as it fell, and dustmen came in from the East End with ponies
and carts to shovel it and carry it away.

Ilia worried about the state of the basement; it was clear
that Mother Rat didn't understand about rats at all. Or about
other *creature* which she and her mother and her sisters used
to battle with daily, for they were aware of the things that
happened down in the *bassi* where the wretched inhabitants
couldn't air their rooms or their bedding or their bodies or
anything, but roosted in the dust and the dark like fungus.
At home, she and her sisters and Sabina the maid mopped
the uncarpeted floors every day, and hung cloths and coverlets
and linen and rugs and mats out on the balcony or the roof
and beat anything that could provide shelter hard with a
broom stick to expel all the eggs of any mites or fleas or
mosquitoes or flies or . . . In the villages, the walls were
limed; in the city streets, trees stood wearing stockings of
whitewash, too. Without this drumming of rugs, shaking out
of linen, scrubbing and washing of floors and furniture, there'd
be gummy eyes and groaning guts, fevers and agues, swell-
ings, pustules . . . the blind look of beggars, fits of shivering
and yellow skin of malaria victims, the raised purple welts
on their exposed limbs beside the tarry tin where a few coins
sadly glinted.

But here in London in late summer, the flat was close and

musty like damp felt, and the kitchen was greasy and stale,
yet she mustn't open the windows, Doris said, with a shudder,
to let in draughts. Besides, there was the problem of soot.

'There's no point, my lambkin,' she said, 'if you open just
a chink, the smuts'll fall black on everything.'

～

Doris slept in a narrow room off the kitchen near the chute and
when there were guests, and she'd finished busying about the
sink and the larder, she sat there on the bed, tracking the results
of the races in the evening paper, and doing sums in the margins.
Ilia left the sitting room to join Doris there, because she wanted
to practise her English, and Doris, who wore a very fine net
over her curls, was patient and precise. When Mother Rat had
visitors, Ilia felt she couldn't interrupt the conversation to ask
for explanation. But when the family was alone, Doris took off
her apron, which she had embroidered in simple chain stitch
with buttercups and daisies, and joined them in the sitting
room to listen to the news and the bulletins about the war.

'She's the one who goes down to the betting shop, what!'
Esmond had told her. 'When Mother Rat's rung up her bookie
once already that day but wants just another flutter before a
particular race, you know, when a filly's form's caught her eye.
Or a number.'

'She wins?' asked Ilia.

Esmond put his finger to his lips and rolled his eyes. 'Best
not to ask, old girl!'

'She could ask me,' said Ilia, 'I'm good at guessing lottery
numbers – the old men in the local café the *circolo* would ask
me to think of one for them. I'm lucky.'

'You've certainly changed my luck, baby,' said Esmond.

While they waited for him to return from the war in the
East, Ilia was given the spare room, which was larger than

Doris's room, but mostly filled with a wardrobe in which Esmond had left his clothes from his bachelor days after he'd had to let go the flat he'd rented in Mount Street once war was declared and he'd joined up. It had a little washbasin with running water, hot and cold, brownish at first from the tap, but clear after a while. But even London water, Ilia thought not wanting to be ungrateful, smelled sooty.

'When Esmond comes home, he'll be looking for somewhere for you to live, my lamb, but in the meantime, you can stay here, and he'll go to the club.'

Ilia wanted to ask about this arrangement, and her expression prompted her mother-in-law to explain.

'He'll put up at the club because the room's too small for you both.'

Ilia's alarm was clear, and Mother Rat went on, gently, 'You see, dear girl, it's a gentlemen's club, and ladies aren't allowed.' She giggled. 'That's the point of them, really. Chaps getting on with things.'

Doris was less alarming altogether, and she'd listen to Ilia read out from the labels on kitchen stuff, on the sink, and from the shelves in the larder, to practise pronouncing English correctly. On the blade of a knife: 'Sheffield steel Master Cutlers Hiram Wilde & Son'. She picked up a picture tin and read out: 'Peek Frean biscuits & cakes'. The box was oddly heavy, full of odd keys, screws, buttons, bits and bobs.

'No real biscuits these days,' Doris said mournfully. 'Might as well chew on cardboard.'

Another gaily printed tin stood beside it: 'Mackintosh's Quality Street'. Ilia sounded the words carefully: 'Toffees – Luxury Assortment'. More words seemed closer to Italian, now, than when she'd tried to read *Romeo & Juliet* in English. She picked it up; the tin was light and empty. In the picture an old-fashioned couple, the woman in a poke bonnet and ribbons, holding the arm of a tall Hussar-style officer in a braided shako, were looking in at a quaint bow window where a box of toffees was displayed with the same picture on the lid, so that they were looking at themselves looking.

She exclaimed and Doris groaned aloud, and cried out, clasping her water-roughened hands over the front tab of her apron, 'Don't, don't! Oh, what would I give for a Quality Street toffee! For the Purple One with the big Brazil nut inside! Or for the Gooseberry Cream! Or a Mint, or a Malt! Oh, my dear, they used to come with lovely crinkled and rustling coloured wrappers, silver inside, translucent outside! It's the worst thing about the beastly war – no sweets! Honestly, the Blitz was fun compared to this dearth. I know people died – God save their souls – but what I'd give for a toffee! I'd throttle a German with my bare hands. I'd pick up two of them and knock their heads together.' She was howling and roaring. 'And we still can't have a single one . . . when we're being told that the war here in Europe is over! Hell's bells!'

Hell's bells. Ilia stored Doris's words in her mental phrase-book, to surprise Esmond with when he came back.

Doris was right about the smuts. Ilia tugged the stuck window open in her room one morning that Indian summer, and found specks scattered all over the bedclothes. The greasy-dusty smell, which came off the bombsite opposite the block of flats and clung to her hair when she came in from a walk to the shops, had now penetrated the heavy blackout drapes on her windows. They could be taken down, now, she thought, the war was over.

Every Monday, a great clatter of hooves outside and the creak of the wooden wagon rose to the first-floor flat and the tightly closed windows were no barrier to the sounds as the coalman, a figure in negative with his blue eyes whorled in white and the rest of him soot-dusted all over, hoisted the sack on to his back and swung it upside down to empty into the coal-hole to the basement. Down the lumps tumbled, like a hailstorm pelting, into the same underworld where the rubbish gathered, and the sooty smell of the glinting fuel fused with the lardy leavings of the mansion block's inhabitants and built up into the rich thick London fug of a density and a danger that, Ilia thought, would have worried the troglodytes of the Matera slums.

Soot, radiating out from Pelham Street, South Kensington. Soot, cinders, potash, coal – burning in furnaces the length and breadth of the country; smoking up chimneys in their millions; plumes of smut-laden smoke unfurling thickly through the murk. Not scarlet, not purple, not pink, the empire's bloodstream ran mineral black, sweated out dusky as a rook's gleaming plumage, carrying power and know-how and the standards of civilisation and the code of conduct of the English gentleman far and wide, fanning out in tributaries across the world, touching her, Ilia, where she was growing up by the sea in Italy, and bringing back – what? – the whole world to the family table, to the city street: one day when the war's long aftershock was spent, there would once again be overflowing supplies of tea, rubber, coffee, chocolate, gutta-percha, rubies, parrots, lignum vitae, juniper berries, cotton pyjamas and silk dressing gowns, iron ore, copper, magnesium, manganese, tin, phosphorus, sugar, diamonds – and toffees. The coal wouldn't be burned any more, it would be replaced by cleaner fuels, smokeless, or so they were supposed to be, and, in the far distant future, the mines would be closed down in scenes of ugly police action, but the exchange of goods and their abundance in the interim would have been unstoppable, multifariousness beyond imagining, stretching ahead into the future of her old age, which Ilia could not yet envisage. She would never fail to remember that in 1945 none of this had looked likely or possible. In the small spare room at Mother Rat's, where she heard the silence from the sitting room between her in-laws, and waited for some breach in its walls to happen so she could come out of her room and join them without horrible awkwardness as to where to put herself, or for Doris to knock and announce that it was time for dinner, with Esmond still away and no news of his return, she could not be confident that she knew what was going to happen to her.

~~~

Eventually the news came that the *Queen Mary* had docked in Colombo to pick up the troops; the demobbed men bagged corners of the dance floor to set up camp, while the officers like Esmond took it in turns in the bunks in the first-class cabins, and relished the showers. There were hundreds perhaps thousands of soldiers on board and when they finally reached Southampton, they were all too late, whatever their rank or skills, too late for finding places to live in the bombed towns and cities, too late for finding work, too late for finding fuel and food – and women.

But Esmond was married, and at long last, he arrived home in time for Christmas 1945.

4

Some Books She
Brought With Her

A clutch of miscellaneous titles published over the whole
span of the Italian Fascist Republic included the First
World War weepie, *Cuore*, by the much-loved, bestselling
Edmondo de Amicis; an anthology of English – and American
– literature; a standard Italian edition of several Shakespeare
plays – the ones set in Italy dominate; a textbook about Europe
stitched and falling apart (in later years, when she had a bookplate designed, she added it opposite the title page). Throughout,
many greyscale photographs – sawmills, tulip fields, green-
houses; lakes, fjords, deltas; wonders of the old world (Cologne
Cathedral; the Alcazar); high points of modern ingenuity in
nations allied with Italy (the high ironwork bridge at Porto;
the covered market in Hamburg; Albanian petrol refineries);
diagrams and maps, including one which shows lines of Italian
shipping in the region, with Rome as its hub. The author
Carmelo Colamonico, a geography professor, has little good to

say of 'Gran Bretagna'. Not a single British city appears under 'Northern Europe', but only an Irish *abitazione*: a hovel for a colleen Cinderella, described with brief, pitying hauteur. The second chapter, 'The Mediterranean and Italy', shows signs of attentive – approving? disapproving? – reading, with many little inked crosses and pencil underlinings of passages in which the professor complacently surveys the pervasive influence of *Italianità* through the region – as well as Libya, the new Roman Empire is expanding to Albania, Malta, the Balkans, Tunisia, Morocco, Corsica . . . The map is coloured in – not pink, the livery of the British – but imperial purple. There's a vigorous black cross against this paragraph.

She also brought with her a picture book about the Italian royal family; a bound copy of fables by popular sage and troubadour Trilussa; and a large linen-bound volume called *What Will People Say?* by the cartoonist Giuseppe Novello.

~~~

In 1945, when my mother left Bari for the first time, these were among the books from her life as an Italian girl which she sent with her trunk to London. The harvest, going back so many decades, is meagre and often odd – a scrape of historical DNA. She and her sisters were learning from these pages: the textbook came out in Year XIX of the Fascist state, when the Duce looked poised to fulfil his vision of a renewed imperial Rome, embracing Mare Nostrum, our sea, east to west, and it presents an unselfconscious Italian Fascist programme. In 1941 there were only three years to go before the liberation of southern Italy, including Puglia. Yet the victory of the Allies, which would bring Esmond to Bari, was still barely imaginable, then.

Colamonico complains that France and England have considered the Mediterranean their territory during recent decades;

bitterly he lists their military installations, their warehouses, and their disregard for the local inhabitants' health and economic advancement. England's influence in North Africa and Egypt must be resisted: Libya figures as the key to power in the region, the crucial bridgehead offering Italy the chance of wresting control of the Suez Canal to the east and of Upper Egypt to the south.

For much of the time when the young Ilia was first reading these books, the Germans and the Italians were winning the war: Rommel was advancing unstoppably, it seemed, across North Africa towards Egypt. In Cairo, in 1942, the British began evacuating all non-Egyptian nationals who were on the Allies' side. George Seferis, the Greek poet and future Nobel Prize-winner, was in his twenties, working in the diplomatic service, and had fled to Cairo after the Italians had taken over in Athens and forced the Greek government into exile; in his diary, he catches the growing fears among inhabitants of Cairo as the German army moved triumphantly towards the city. Seferis and his wife were ordered to leave; they joined the chaotic exodus fleeing eastwards across the Canal. They crossed it on a bridge of barges and waited for a train. It was July, the heat was infernal, and there was no food, little water and no news as to their destination – it would turn out to be Jerusalem.

Seferis' day-by-day account conveys the utter disarray of the situation. He sees 'an elderly woman, huddled to one side, talking to a friend from Alexandria. She was crying loudly.'

He begins talking to her – their language in common is French.

'"I'm quite strong," she said, "but my body can't take any more."'

Seferis sat down beside her.

'"Are you French?" I asked her.

'"No," she said, *"je suis italienne antifasciste."'*

She then tells him that she was married to a Fascist, someone who knew the leaders of the Fascist movement personally.

'"But I could never understand why they did the awful things they did,"' she goes on.

Her brother was also against the Fascists, like herself. But she had left her daughter behind, with her young children.

The reported conversation ends, '"Oh what an awful thing . . ."'

Later, when the ghastly, terrifying flight has come to a temporary rest in Jerusalem, Seferis confides his despair: 'Here in the Middle East, as it's called, we're sinking all the time. We're not people anymore, we're exiles. But we don't share the same exile; there are as many conditions of exile as there are of us. We're the crew of a ship that's gone down, each one fighting for his life, each one separately, astride his own piece of flotsam.'

Colamonico must have been putting the finishing touches to his 1941 textbook just before the long assault of the Germans and Italians on the port of Tobruk began, in what became a grinding and terrible protracted siege and a critical turning point in the Second World War: the Allies, by managing to hold the town, at last prevented Rommel's advance on Egypt and cut off easier German access to supplies of oil there, and to the granary of Cairo. For grim long days and weeks and months Tobruk was perseveringly defended by Australians and then by Czechs and Poles and British troops who took over. Decisive relief came when the 8th Army, marching from the west, joined the defenders. By the end, the siege had lasted over seven months.

~~

Esmond Warner, at this stage a major, was driving east along the shore in his jeep. En route to Tobruk, he would pick up a piece of the entablature of the temple at Leptis Magna; it was used as a doorstop at home for years and now does the same job in my sitting room.

Spoils of war: now a doorstop.

In the desert, he became a keen botaniser, as time hung heavy between battles. His Collins handbook (1937) is marked with dates of discoveries and find-spots: campanula growing on a crumbling wall in a village near Carthage; asphodel rising among the stones in the ruins of a Roman temple: the new buds on the plants' branching candelabra throbbing with bees, the older spears heavy with the full-blown blossoms exhaling their perfume and dripping with honey. 'I would rather be a slave, than live this eternity of nothing,' so said Achilles, turning on his heel and striding away through the fields of asphodel. Esmond was remembering, muttering the words to himself, surprised that Homer thought these tough spikes of blossom would grow in the dark of the underworld. He had a 'green thumb' and prided himself on it, keeping pots of seedlings with him in his billets.

HQ North Africa District

I made a tour of East Algeria, amazingly varied country,
some like England, green (partridge and snipe) and very
well-farmed and watered country, near the coast and inland
eventually SAHARA. I stayed the night at BISKRA ('Garden
of Allah'!) . . . the edge of the desert is a mass of birds,
carrion-crows, desert chats, goldfinches! And many sorts of
larks especially . . . I collected (with roots) some wild irises
from near Zavarye which I now have in pots outside my
window on the flat roof. Lovely mauve flower with yellow
tongue. Where I took them from the hillside was a mass, a
lovely sight. I brought my seedlings from Italy; they seem
to have stood the sea voyage and the new warmer climate
all right.

The Allies were beginning to turn the fortunes of war in the
course of the Western Desert campaign and other battles but in
1941 their landings in Sicily in July 1943, their advances onto
the mainland and the consequent liberation of southern Italy,
which would bring my father to Bari to marry my mother, were
not yet in sight, so hard-won were the Allied gains and so bitter
the fighting on the ground and in the air.

In Tuscany, during this same phase of the war, Iris Origo
and her husband were taking in refugees – mostly children
– and they also gave food and shelter to passing partisans, to
lone British troops and officers who had lost their regiments,
and to defectors from the various Italian armies, which in the
ghastly chaos of the defeat were struggling on in the cause of
a bewildering number of different parties: in June 1943 Italy
rejected Mussolini's government and the alliance with Germany,
but then split into different factions, one still fascist under
Badoglio and fighting the British and the Americans. In her

journal, *War in Val D'Orcia*, Origo reports from day to day with steady, understated calm on the unpredictable shifts that each piece of news or passing official brings, as the threats rise and fall and they negotiate their preservation, waiting in anguish for news of the war.

I imagine Ilia reading or hearing the news during this time of unbearable tensions, destruction and foreboding, when the British were fighting Italians all along that Mediterranean coast of North Africa, when the siege of Tobruk went on and on and on, and afterwards, when the Italians suffered terrible casualties, and thousands were also taken prisoner.

Esmond, writing to his parents, reported from the field:

> HQ Tripolitania
> M[iddle] E[ast] F[orce]
> 26 April '43

> I am ageing myself a little . . . Have seen a lot of prisoners
> we've taken 1000s lately as you know. I thought they all
> looked rather nice boys especially the Germans, who are
> very English-looking and all so fit and have all, Italians and
> Germans, been through the same experiences as we have. It
> is all the fault of their wicked governments – I hate the
> whole bloody thing and yet you can't deny that it brings
> out the best qualities of the survivors. I know after the war
> I'll feel more in common with a desert soldier of the 'other
> side' than with some of our own crowd.

Few signs of Ilia's further interest in Colamonico's textbook surface, until we reach some underlinings in pencil, only the second time they occur. They mark comments on the English:

Old customs and old practices of every kind, old formulae
from the time of the Normans, are maintained in public
and in private life: the civil and penal codes are nothing
but an undigested mass of examples and sentences accumu-
lated over centuries. This conservative spirit, like respect for
law and abhorrence of lies, which have been so much
vaunted as the English character, is demonstrated more by
not violating the form and the letter than by a spirit of
substance.

Colamonico goes on with steady scorn: 'The Englishman is
not industrious, nor thrifty; on the contrary, he has a curious
tendency to idleness, to free-spending his money, and is a lover
of living it up.' Most significantly, he remarks, 'The English
countryside has been defined, not without reason, as a single
park made and kept for lords.'

Wavering pencil underscores these phrases – my mother's
hand? I shivered a bit at these schoolmasterish remarks; I
glimpsed the junketing in Cairo during the war so joyfully
reported in my father's letters home. I see Donald Maclean,
first secretary at the Embassy, during a long rout of a night,
brawling and flailing, breaking a friend's arm, smashing up a
girl's flat and hitting the *bawab* – the doorman – who was
trying to restrain him. And Maclean a closet communist, too,
supposed to love equality and the workers – before he disappeared, to resurface in Moscow, alongside Kim Philby and
Guy Burgess. Maclean, a key diplomat in British Middle
Eastern policy, was one of the Cambridge spies. And Esmond,
who was idle and free-spending (when he could be) and fond
of living it up, who glowed when he was included in *Burke's
Landed Gentry* and would so like to have owned hundreds more
pleasant acres of his own.

Ironies load the pages of Ilia's schoolbook; as in a Greek

play the oracles keep being fulfilled but in a contrary direction to the sense the historian intended, as if the god of time were laughing up his sleeve or capering with mischievous glee. For as Colamonico was writing and Ilia reading, the vision of Africa Orientale Italiana was under attacks that would prove terminal.

Ilia's forlorn and battered picture book about the House of Savoy came out in 1937 when my mother was fifteen. It hosannahs the ruling dynasty and hails the King of Italy as Emperor of Ethiopia, provides a full genealogy and includes photographs of all the popinjay princelings, fulsomely captioned with their new dukedoms. It would be comic if it weren't all so horrible. Maresciallo Badoglio also appears – as Duke of Addis Abeba; Mussolini displays his medals as *'fondatore d'impero'*.

Two years before, Mussolini had ordered the invasion of Ethiopia in a war of extreme bombing, including the use of chemical weapons.

Ilia always remembered how everyone at home in Bari rejoiced at the great victory over the Ethiopians, and she could still sing the troops' marching song, *'Facetta nera, bell' Abissinia . . .'*, the ambiguous, eroticised anthem of an imperial war. She also remained a loyal monarchist, switching later to admire the English Crown, while following the news of the fallen fortunes of the Italian dynasty – especially the women – in the pages of *Oggi*, the photo-magazine that Esmond subscribed to for her, which arrived every week with fascinating chronicles of heartache, film stars and car crashes, and exciting hopes of love – and its disappointments: when Princess Fawzia, the sister of King Faruq, returned from Tehran in 1948 after the failure of her marriage to the shah, her beautiful face, set off by furs and jewels and lipstick, filled page after page, alongside the latest miracles at Lourdes, bleeding statues of the Virgin Mary, the canonisation of Maria Goretti, and Pope Pius XII in snowy white robes feeding the lambs in the Vatican gardens.

The collected Trilussa offers a different perspective: he wrote in Romanesco, the dialect of Rome, was a cynic and an aphorist, who told acerbic squibs against bureaucracy and made up tart animal tales of cunning wheezes against raw power. Ilia liked proverbs, and went on collecting them all her life, amused by differences between English and Italian versions of the same thought: in later life, she published a selection called *You Can't Get Blood Out of a Turnip* ('*Non si cava sangue di una rapa*').

In Trilussa's work Ilia has marked up some lines: '*la prima speranza è sempre quella / d'esser capito da una donna bella*' ('our first hope is always / to find a beautiful woman who understands').

Beauty was hard currency, it was my mother's capital, she was discovering as she read, and it was all come and go, just like harvests and stocks. She also underlined a story poem, 'La Pupazza' ('The Great Big Dolly'). Trilussa recalls how he secretly took out his sister's gorgeous china windup doll from its original box and:

La squartai come un pollo, poverella . . .
D'allora in poi, se vedo una ragazza
Che guarda e che sospira,
Benanche me ce sento un tira-tira
Nun me posso scorda' de la pupazza.

(I quartered her like a chicken, poor little thing . . .
Ever since then, if I see a girl
Who looks around her and sighs,
Even though I feel my heartstrings tug
I can't forget that great big dolly.)

Was Trilussa giving himself a warning here? Or others? There were clearly dangers to being beautiful. He's owning up to something shameful in himself, and the alarm he sounds makes my pulse quicken, too, but out of fear. These were the battle lines drawn around my mother and her contemporaries, the real dangers which stifled girls who grew up in that wartime world. In 1954, a monument was set up to the writer in Rome, with his jaunty portrait bust – tipped hat, waxed moustaches – in the square in Trastevere named after him.

In *What Will People Say?* Novello spares nobody's lumps and bumps, awkward limbs, grimaces, tics and vanities, but above all he has a keen eye for social anxieties of every kind: here are pathetic pretensions to gentility skewered, venal humiliations and triumphs, scroungers, hypocrites, exploiters and gluttons lording it over anyone prone to shrink and sink. Wives, former wet nurses, family maids, female friends – women in general are a blight. 'Small Consolations' shows a man sitting stiffly and shyly surrounded by women who are exchanging knowing glances. The caption goes, 'Her intimate friends, to whom Maria had wanted to introduce her fiancé, have already discovered that he has bow legs, a lisp and two gold teeth.' Another drawing shows a woman in an empty stadium, sitting alone with her head sunk in gloom. It's captioned 'After the rape of the Sabines: the one who wasn't' – a joke so much of its time that it puts the lie to that favourite conservative maxim *plus ça change.*

Though the cartoonist is never openly political – the petty day-to-day human comedy is his theme – he captures the casual, bullying atmosphere of the years under Fascism. He had served in the Alpine corps during the first war and was to join it again in the second; yet when, after being taken prisoner, he was offered release on condition he joined the Fascist party, he refused, and so remained in German camps till 1945.

The poison in which his barbs are dipped was distilled far longer ago than Mussolini's reign, and it drips on long after through Silvio Berlusconi's bunga-bunga world and Matteo Salvini's exclusionary nationalist *Italianità*. Novello pokes at the numerous ways *fare figura* – striking a dash, keeping up appearances – drove people down blind alleys and false turnings; the imperative not to lose face dominated his part of Italy – Milan – and was keener still in the south of Italy. It could lead to florid displays of generosity and admirable courage in hardship, but it also exacerbated the terrible crushing conventions that Novello scorns without mercy.

This is another of my mother's carefully preserved mementoes that gives me a cold shudder of recognition, because learning to anticipate how others see you was taught early, to boys and girls, but more especially girls, and not only in Italy before the war. It wasn't an ethical ideal, but a call to masks and camouflage, to conscious moulding in the mirror of others' responses. To make a good impression – *fare figura*. And that *figura*, that impression, was coordinated by social expectations and values. Breeding. Money. Looks. And – style. Style that comes with breeding, money and looks. Facebook profiles, Instagram boasts, aren't a diabolical contemporary invention; they merely transpose into the tentacular sphere of the virtual the same social requirement, to anticipate what others might think. In some ways it's surprising Mark Zuckerberg doesn't have an Italian background, because the evening *passeggiata*, when the citizens of Bari, or Palermo, or Messina, or Reggio, take to the evening air and stroll the main streets or the *lungomare* in the cool of the gathering night, required self-styling, self-fashioning, self-projection – *fare figura* in the eyes of others was parading a self-portrait to invite admiration and envy, prevent negative comment, ensure likes, thumbs up, not dislikes, thumbs down. A greetings card I found among Ilia's papers shows a pair of young women in tight-waisted full-skirted Dior-style dresses and neatly perched hats stepping out and saying, 'Let's go out and judge some people.' Sometimes, my mother would sit with one girlfriend and number all the bones of another, remarking, 'She's got thick ankles, poor old thing. There's no disguising them.' They'd laugh together about the size of someone's bottom and the slouch of another's shoulders and how another was letting herself go. I remember how, during my overplump childhood, she wouldn't exactly comment directly but would reassure me: 'Plain girls are much more likely to be happy.' One time – I was 17 – Ilia was talking and laughing along these lines with a friend of mine, and they were getting on so famously as they dissected bodies – this one scraggy, that one lumpy, some were beanpoles (poor things) and others frumps, some were a bit whiskery ('Someone should tell her'), prudes and bores. On that occasion, I was overcome by such a storm of tears, rage, and self-consciousness at my own shortcomings that I flew at my friend to shut her up. But it was really my mother I hated for judging people so harshly, and no doubt harbouring thoughts that I didn't come up to scratch either.

5

A Bundle of German Marks

The wad of notes turned up in the steamer trunk with MCC stickers which stood in the garage, covered in spiders' webs and filled with memorabilia of Plum's cricketing triumphs, of the tours to Australia when he brought back the Ashes – the first time, in 1903–4, and then again, in 1911–12, though on that tour he became too ill to play. The packet is bulky, the notes squeezed into a strong envelope, made of paper stiffened by fibre, and addressed to P.F. Warner, Esq. It's registered, with blue pencil streaks pretending to be string and a crusty wax scarlet seal – a trace of the blood pact, memories of battles won, like the frogging on Hussars' uniform, those decorative mementoes of victims' bones. The envelope has been opened at some point, but the notes inside are pristine: 41,000 German marks in denominations of 100, printed in 1920 in Berlin with on one side the Bamberg Rider in his Prince Valiant hairdo contemplating his own mirror image. The following year, 1921, according to several postmarks, my grandfather's bank manager informed him he would be deducting £10 from his account for the purchase he had ordered.

The wad of cash from Weimar has a desolate, orphaned air: that wild inflation that sped the German government's collapse, Hitler's rise, the annexation of the Sudetenland, Kristallnacht, the invasion of Belgium, the defeat of France, and on and on to the end of Palestine and to so many other ills that plague the world today – this loss of value was well under way, until you needed absurd heaps of those same notes to buy a needle and thread.

There can never have come that moment for trading them in for sterling or Egyptian pounds at a favourable rate. I remember in Phnom Penh, after the regime fell, the banknotes with Pol Pot's portrait were being used as scrap paper, to twist around a dozen joss sticks, a bunch of lemon grass, a peck of black tea. Online now, in the flourishing market in antique banknotes, this stash of pre-First World War marks is still worthless.

Neither Plum nor my father had sound hunches.

~~~

Many of Esmond's letters to his father, during the campaign in North Africa, ask Plum to buy this currency or that and it seemed that such speculation was a bond between them, spurred on in part by m'tutor, C.M. (Cyril Mowbray) Wells, who offered tips for stocks and shares, bonds and bills on a regular basis. Wells, who was born in 1871, played rugby for England from 1892 to 1897 and cricket at county level under Plum as his captain, could recite by heart the *Odes* of Horace and even the whole of *Paradise Lost* – or so it was said – spent over thirty years as a housemaster at Eton and taught classics there, especially that rarefied skill, Greek prose and verse composition. If he liked a line someone produced, he'd reach into a pocket, saying 'Have a small diamond' and hand the boy something – something imaginary.

Wells was one of those Victorian/Edwardian heroic

Englishmen of a certain class and background whom we meet in the rolls of the dead in the First World War, but, like Plum, he was too old to fight. After trouble with his knees put an end to his glories on the pitch and in the field, he strove in other spheres: stamp collecting (perhaps remembering Plum's cricketing youth, he specialised in the Caribbean), connoisseurship of port and wine, and heroic angling – landing what strikes a reader today as shocking piles of the beautiful creatures, hundreds and hundreds of salmon every year on fishing trips to Norway (in the year he turned 80, he caught his eightieth salmon weighing over forty pounds).

The two sportsmen remained very close: he would later bring both Warner boys, Esmond and his brother John, into his house at Eton. After his death in 1963, *The Times* published a letter from another pupil, who asserted that at Eton, 'no one in his time had a deeper influence'. It was there my father developed a fatal sense of, and a fatal yearning for, most favoured status.

Lytton Strachey's barbed portraits of Wells' contemporaries, Virginia Woolf's rebellious bitterness against their insouciant privileges, haunt this figure from Esmond's youth: in 1926 Wells published – privately – an anthology of favourite pieces, rendered into Greek on the opposite page to the original. Suckling, Baudelaire, Tennyson, Shelley are mixed in with cuttings: leaders from *The Times*, General Blanco's revanchist manifesto from Havana, an epitaph for Outside Porter's 'little collie' Nellie, and a notice from 'a morning paper' – 'MARY. Waited three hours for you at the appointed place, until questioned by a suspicious policeman. If this is the price of love, it is too heavy a one for me to pay. Good-bye. POTTS.'

The book's front cover is engraved in gold leaf, with a hexagonal podium set with an octagonal desk, which appears to be lifting off on a sheaf of rays: sacred geometry in flight.

Wells was the family Tiresias. The Eton Ramblers

end-of-year newsletter in 1963 remarks that CMW was known as 'Bummy, affectionately, and for visible reasons' (I never heard my father call him so).

The Warners were living just downriver from Eton in Datchet, and Esmond's intensive correspondence begins when he was seven and sent away to board at Stanmore Park:

'Dear Mother I forgot to say in my leter to ask you for sum jan and fruit. Send sum onginges and aples and sum pares and sum kinds of jam. Lots of love you Esmond'.

The constant flow falters during his time at Eton only because he was seeing his parents every weekend. The letters I've inherited start up again from the army's Staff College at Camberley, two or three times a week before he goes overseas and thereafter even more frequently. Throughout, he keeps passing on Wells' financial prophecies. Mother Rat was known to like a flutter, but it turns out, which I never suspected, that quiet, trim, soft-spoken Plum was into currency speculation, egged on by Wells. He passed on the habit – the hope? – to his son, for Esmond in his letters home from the desert reports tips from his old tutor from school. In June 1945, m'tutor wrote (the letter had caught up with Esmond in August): 'I am staying at my flat, wh. is barely habitable owing to enemy action.'

He was, however, enjoying some fine wines laid down before the war. He passed on news of his latest windfall in the currency markets, urging Esmond to buy South African gold as soon as the government allowed it: 'I think you might buy a few more Blyvoors, & perhaps Crowns. I am only telling you this because I know you're interested. But if you see a good profit anywhere, take it – in my opinion, though a good broker friend always says, "hang on". Our expected boomlet has not yet developed.' He signed off, 'Cura ut valeas' ('Take care that you may flourish').

One of the obituaries of Wells (in the Salmon and Trout Magazine, May 1964) commented: 'His sound judgement as an investor enabled him to supplement his salary and later, a very small pension.'

This teacher, born thirty years before Victoria's reign came to an end, stoked my father's values, his striving, and his whole outlook. My father went on seeing him throughout Wells' life and went to his last birthday lunch – his ninety-second: 'Dinner at UUC, 7 p.m. in ordinaries', Wells commanded.

~~~

Esmond's devotion to his old schoolmaster and his institution never diminished. The Latin tags he'd learned from Wells stuck and he pronounced them in the now superseded English way, with W sounds for Vs and the vowels very strange: 'Odi profanum vulgum et arceo,' he would declaim. When asked to translate, he told me, with an aggressive chuckle, 'I loathe the vulgar crowd and I shun them.' When debutantes stopped being presented at court and a top hat was no longer de rigueur at Royal Ascot, he'd sigh, 'Eheu fugaces.' Neither disdain nor melancholy suited him – he was a congenial, sociable man, 'clubbable' in his own parlance.

In their last exchange of letters, Esmond is still reminiscing about winning the house colours, which were also there in the trunk in the garage, a heap of ragged silk ribbons. But the bond meant more than friendship: it fastened Esmond to a certain spot, where 'people like us' belonged and followed certain pursuits. As in a musical score marked 'Repeat', the melodies my father heard as a boy kept him humming happily along, long after the instruments were no longer tuned according to current temperament and the playing style was changing.

6

Brogues

The shoes are deep brown leather all over, inner and outer soles likewise, made by hand in 1945, by Peal & Co., a dynasty of cobblers stretching back at least to 1791 or even – it's sometimes claimed – to 1565, who showed at both the Great Exhibition of 1851 and the Festival of Britain a century later, and stopped trading only in 1965. Ilia was fitted in the premises at 487 Oxford Street, part of an elegant run of Victorian Arts and Crafts buildings of dressed red granite mixed with red brick, on the original Grosvenor estate, which developed that part of London in the 1880s. (A fussy glass and steel complex now occupies the site next to Bond Street Tube station.) She called them her brogues, though they're not as chunky as today's fashion requires, nor are they sufficiently pounced with a tracery of holes, 'broguing'. The box in which she kept them was in her wardrobe when she died, still with their wooden shoe trees, numbered 289643 and wrapped in tissue paper. Fine cracks in the leather have appeared where it came under stress from the swelling joint of her big toe, but otherwise, though they are now over seventy years old, they still look almost new.

~~

When Esmond finally disembarked at Southampton, Ilia was waiting for him in the flat in South Ken with his parents. She was thin, even thinner than she had been when she first appeared beside his jeep with her sisters and they offered their services. A dragonfly, her hair flickering with iridescence, her complexion full of light – he could lift her as easily as a little child. '*Mia piccina*', he called her, '*angelino mio*', '*bella ragazza*' as well as '*piccola*' – he learned the phrases (he was a quick study at languages) and whispered them till she squirmed.

As soon as he could, perhaps for a late twenty-second birthday present, he took her to be fitted for a pair of the celebrated Peal's bespoke brogues; his young Italian wife was to have the best of English classic design, sturdier by far than a glass slipper, but as clear an expression of his hopes for his bride and her status.

'We'll have a last made,' Esmond declared the first week that they were reunited in England. 'It is a model of your foot,' he added, when Ilia's face showed she didn't understand. He loved instructing her; letting her into his familiar world; showing her the ropes. 'If we're to live in the country, you'll need a good sturdy pair of walking shoes.' He imagined the pair of them standing on a lawn, a rose-wreathed house behind them, and the slope of land – the Chilterns? the Quantocks? – rising up gently to an English sky, where sweet fluffy clouds wafted.

They went to Peal's, and Ilia's feet were measured. Esmond picked out the style: lace-up brogues in a dark chestnut. 'When we go for country walks,' he said, 'these will be perfect.'

She had walked to her grandparents' farm with her mother and her sisters after the local carter had dropped them off but had never gone out for a country walk as such; she had no concept of healthy exercise in the English style of the constitutional. They used to join the daily *passeggiata* in town every evening; the breeze off the sea lifted summer headaches and refreshed tired limbs, but its purposes were not otherwise therapeutic: the strollers had other things on their mind, and walking was a way of airing them, of talking and gossiping and eyeing other families' children as they grew, testing the current trend in hemlines or lapels or hat-brim breadth, and sizing up neighbours and rivals. Even during the prelude to the war and during the whole extensive fighting, this kind of walk remained vital to the town. The shoes Ilia wore then were locally made by a shoemaker too, but on account of her height (her nickname was la Giraffa), they were flat-soled pumps and she wore them with white socks, as stockings did not become available again until the Americans came in 1944.

Peal's clients were the big celebrities of the day – Humphrey Bogart! Marlene Dietrich! Fred Astaire! The Duke of Windsor and his lady! Each customer was measured, and the findings entered in a series of ledgers known as the 'Feet Books'. The bespoke shoemakers then modelled a wooden last to be used to make the shoe; this effigy was numbered with the client's personal number to be kept in the firm's store for use the next time a new pair was ordered. The lasts were known as 'bananas' because the Peals favoured a curved outer edge and a straight inner edge, a shape peculiar to their tradition, not used by rivals in Jermyn Street and elsewhere in the custom trades of London.

Ilia realised the seriousness of the gift Esmond was making, as the Peal's family fitter, wearing a grey-beige overall with a tape measure around his neck, knelt in front of the young woman this English soldier had returned with and drew the outline of her left foot and then her right on the paper he had asked her to stand on.

The fitter was cheerful, leaning around her as he exclaimed at the state of things and the future that lay ahead, when she would be putting on this elegant handcrafted pair of shoes, not the piebald tasselled kind that the Duke of Windsor fancied, but a plain flat lace-up with ten-point criss-crossed lacing and a short tongue.

How did Esmond pay for the brogues? It wasn't a question of cash, though he wasn't particularly flush, because any shoes were an extravagance in the immediate post-war period, when rationing was at its most stringent: a mingy twenty-four coupons a year were allowed for clothing, compared to sixty-six during the war itself; the ticket price made no difference, so those with funds could buy far better quality for the same outlay of coupons. A pair of women's shoes required five coupons – men's needed seven. This may have been an echo of an old system of pricing shoes: by the size of the foot and the amount of leather. But it may also have given men's styles more cachet.

The Peal brogue is a woman's version of a man's shoe, and the style has made a very strong return in the last few years, filling the fashion pages and the windows of shoe shops from Bond Street to Madison Avenue, favoured by urban professionals, especially young women. But in the 1940s, when Ilia was fitted, it announced her life to come in the English countryside, her formal enrolment in the world of the squirearchy, hunting, going to the point-to-point, the harriers, the beagles, the open-gardens scheme, the charity fête. During the war, the princesses Elizabeth and Margaret had worn just such lace-ups to review the Girl Guides, to launch ships. Ilia knew none of this when her narrow foot was measured – size 5½ but the left slightly longer than the right – though she understood that she would no longer be stepping out of a summer evening, arm in arm with her sisters and cousins in their strappy cork-soled high sandals, to swing down the *lungomare* in Bari, let alone squeezing the warm wet sand under her bare feet by the Adriatic near the harbour of the city where she grew up. The brogues would walk her safely on turf and moorland and through woodland and along riverbanks where the trout twinked to the surface for water boatmen and flies, and take her striding across winter fields where the pheasants whirred up, a flurry of gorgeous feathers against the unrelenting grey; the brogues would plant her on – they would *transplant* her to – British soil.

The word 'brogue' now means strong lace-up footwear with decorative pouncing or perforations, but its earliest recorded meaning, dating to 1537, seems very distant now and rather a surprise: 'an escheat; a fraud, a trick'. Escheat is the common law that decrees that when someone dies intestate, the Crown can take their property. Severed inheritance is implied here. Almost 250 years later, this sense had not yet faded; with a cheeky rhyme, Robert Burns attributed such devices to the Devil: 'Then you, ye auld, snick-drawing dog! / Ye came to Paradise *incog*. / An' play'd on man a cursed brogue.'

However, by the time Burns was writing, brogue also commonly described 'a rude kind of shoe made of untanned hide', worn in the 'wilder parts' of Ireland and Scotland.

The dictionary's earliest example for brogue meaning footwear (1587) came into use when the word still meant a fraud; the entry suggests it might be related to 'breeches' and recall the rough leggings worn by Irish peasants and Scottish Highlanders. They could rise to the knee and above, and were often used as waders by fishermen. During his journey through the Highlands Dr Johnson shows detailed curiosity about local – national – dress; it had been banned after the Jacobite uprising of 1745, but he noted it was still occasionally seen in all its splendour. He first saw brogues on Skye: 'a kind of artless shoes, stitched with thongs so loosely that though they

defend the foot from stones, they do not exclude water'. Each
man made a pair for himself, he recorded, as a 'domestick art
. . . as the wife made an apron', using rawhide with the fur
side in, and dyed with juice of tormentil. That was 1773;
later, in 1825, another observer commented even more warmly
that 'for real elegance there was nothing to beat the women
of St Kilda: their menfolk might wear simple brogues, but
they themselves had shoes of gannets' skins, and were said to
look like "feathered Mercuries"' – so this rough home-made
tack could translate a labourer into a nymph, a shepherd into
a dweller in Arcadia. Brogues were brimful of the spirit of
Romanticism, nostalgia for the wilderness, passion for the
elsewheres and the beyonds, for heath and moorland, cliff and
crag, cataract and glade, for wuthering heights and long
drifting walks through the night, as when Dorothy Wordsworth
set out, with her brother William and her brother-in-law
Coleridge, to watch the moon rise over the Severn.

Country as home ground; country as native place: such shoes
belong to the soil, are worn by men – and women – of the soil,
and the word itself gathers up associations with their state: in
Gaelic, brogue also means 'sorrow' and 'brog', sorrowful. Of
course Esmond, when he presented my mother with this gift,
didn't reflect on all these resonances, but the shoes speak of them.

~~~

At some point in the Victorian era, this kind of shoe – and its
regional name – travelled south and as it did so it began moving
up the social scale. It belongs with R.S. Surtees's genial stories
in *Mr Sponge's Sporting Tour* (1853) which was one of Esmond's
favourite books, bringing out chuckles of pleasure as he exam-
ined the detail in John Leech's sprightly illustrations. Brogues
shod the English landed gentry and their betters as they went
about their identifying pastimes: huntin', shootin' and fishin'.

The fashion for the brogue started well before then, however, and the impetus came from the craze for Scotland that Queen Victoria and Albert spurred on when they began to spend time at Balmoral, and wore tartan and papered the walls with it, went trout-fishing and deer-stalking and turned these activities, once necessary means of getting food, into defining upper-class leisure. Brogues began their social ascent as hunting became entertainment. Animals large and small, and every kind of bird and fish to be found the length and breadth of the globe (and the empire), were slaughtered by the thousands, some of them beheaded to be stuffed and mounted, others mummified whole, their pelts and plumes adorning the hats and figures of expensive women, or displayed in glass domes or rectangular vitrines, hung in serried phalanxes on the walls of Sandringham and Balmoral, and in the shooting lodges and hunting lodges and country retreats, the domestic interiors of these pleasant refuges now become vast animal mausolea, where the large sad eyes of quarry look down glassily on the company enjoying themselves below, and their towering racks of antlers or marvellous scimitar horns scythe and thrust hopelessly into the air above the jollity.

It's a general rule of fashion that designers plunder the slums for its styles, and photographers like to seek out graffiti-spattered rust-belt ruins to set off luxuries whose cost would help repay the debts of a small nation state. Brogues were similarly imported to the upper echelons and as they did so, they crossed the gender divide (even when they weren't made of gannet pelts). They added point to the newly admired boyish silhouette of the iconic 1920s gel, a tennis player and a golf champion, a huntswoman and a showjumper, an Olympian or Miss Joan Hunter Dunn ('Oh! would I were her racket press'd / With hard excitement to her breast . . .').

All this chimed with Esmond who was such chums with

Penelope Chetwode, who went and ran off with 'that Dutchman Betjeman'. Her brother Roger had been in the Bullingdon with him and they'd motored through Europe together in Roger's Model T Ford the summer of 1927, and both played bridge for Oxford against Cambridge and later, in Berlin, and won silver cigarette boxes and ashtrays (Esmond's trophies were stolen in a burglary in the 1970s). Penelope would inspire Evelyn Waugh's novel *Helena* (1950), which the author proclaimed his favourite, when the young heroine dreams of riding her pony to a furious lather while the court bards of her father, Old King Cole, sing interminably of his people's glorious history. Penelope was horsey all her life – unlike some young women she didn't grow out of it, and she exuded that throaty, careless androgyny that Esmond seems to have found powerfully attractive. He shared other interests with the Betjemans, too, the characteristic pursuits of the tribe – the niceties of snobbery, parish churches, clerihews, droll epitaphs.

Golf and croquet also rose in popularity – for both sexes – from the latter part of Victoria's reign into the 1920s when Esmond began going out and about with his much more handsome and well-heeled friends, and they too required sensible and appropriate footwear. In the last panel of his *Bilderatlas*, Aby Warburg identified a photograph of a female golfer in full swing as the latter-day reincarnation of the striding Nympha of antiquity. Again, it was brogues – made to slightly different patterns and ornamental punctures traced in the leather, variations in the lacing and the soles – that were worn to saunter on the green and stride across the course or walk around the hoops on the croquet lawn.

During my father's pre-war days games of many different kinds were central to the country house weekends that he spent with the chums he'd made at school and at Oxford; some of the time was spent drinking and playing cards and billiards and chess, but mostly they liked being out of doors. Steeplechasing, fly fishing, race meets and riding to hounds, beagling – and even otter hunting – helped along by flasks of cherry brandy, kept them busy. He'd play a round of golf now and then when he was still an undergraduate at Oxford and go to the races whenever he could. The Dublin Horse Trials were a fixture in the social calendar, with parties in the houses of the Anglo-Irish – these were still flourishing in spite of the new Republic and the burnings. He also went up to London to the supper clubs now and then (he developed a tendresse for a singer or two – especially for 'The Incomparable Hildegarde, the Queen of the Supper Clubs' in London's Mayfair in the 1920s and 30s). When I was quite young, he'd point out his friends in the photograph of the Bullingdon Club, all in white tie, against the soot-scarred wall of Peckwater Quad; several of them look portly, aged before their time. He'd tell me about them, later, when many of them were dead: 'Tore out his tubes in a fit of DTs,' he'd say of one; 'Shot his brains out,' of another. It was the difficulty at the core of his whole being that he'd hung around with this crowd because of his father's fame, when he didn't belong, and hadn't the money for it, either. Roger Chetwode, his dear old friend, had been killed early on in the war.

Later, during the war itself, any chance he got for furlough, he'd go to Cairo because, at Gezira Sporting Club on the island of Zamalek in the middle of the Nile, there was a splendid golf course and racetrack and courts for squash and tennis. That's when he wrote to his mother, during the North Africa campaign, 'CAIRO my 2nd home.'

None of this – not the golf or the clerihews, the point-to-points or the parish churches' furniture – ever became part of my mother's brogue. Such leisure pursuits weren't known to Ilia growing up in Bari, an ancient town surrounded by the most gnarled and magnificent olive groves in Europe. Men with rifles ranged the countryside as the songbirds winged their way south, dovecotes were as common as sheepfolds, and in Rome and Naples, races, sometimes in trotting calèches, were held – often unofficially. But the golf course, in a terrain where there were no great rivers like the Nile or the Thames, and scant rainfall, was as yet unknown. And besides, unmarried girls of the town did not hunt or shoot.

When Ilia was given that pair of brogues made to her unique measurements, she understood their elegance and the craft that went into making them, but they were not her kind of shoe, and never became so.

The lasts, which Peal & Co. made for each customer, do not have toes, just the shape of each foot. They are more like shoe trees, or the feet of dolls and puppets, which are also usually made in a single block – their footwear is a vital part of the costume that changes a generic wooden body into a particular character, into Angelica or Orlando.

The symbolism of shoes isn't identical to the symbolism of the footprint, the prime index that someone was once there: Jesus' footprints are displayed in the Chapel of the Ascension, Jerusalem, imprinted side by side on the rock he was standing on when he went up to heaven, and another pair appear on a stone in the church of Domine Quo Vadis in Rome, from the time Jesus appeared there to St Peter. Most famously of all, Robinson Crusoe knows he is not alone when he finds Friday's single print on the sand. Shoes play a vital role in self-fashioning or transformation, whereas the footprint touches the ground without mediation. A brogue likewise establishes connection with a certain stretch of ground or site, but as an article of dress that covers up the naked foot, it belongs to a costume or a livery, part of a chosen role – or an assigned one.

Those bespoke brogues were my father's way of saying Ilia Terzulli was now an Englishwoman.

When she entered the mess in the summer of 1944, soon after they were married, the men in there looked up and there was a catch of breath and a jolt as if the film of ongoing time that was slotting through the projector had snagged and stopped. Esmond and Ilia had just returned from their honeymoon, and a woman was an unusual sight in the officers' quarters. She was smiling gaily because at this point in her life she was young and happy. She wasn't yet wearing any livery of her adopted country, but still dressed in the Italian fashion, a swinging skirt of heavy blue slub silk with buttons down the front which she had made herself as her going-away outfit from the bale Max Harari had specially brought back from Cairo to Bari as a wedding gift. But when she stood there beside Esmond, who was beaming with pride and happiness, a fellow officer shouted angrily, 'What's that bint doing in here?'

Esmond replied, 'I'll have you know, sir, this *bint* is Mrs Warner.'

'Bint' is Arabic, and means simply girl or in a surname, daughter (as in Fatima bint Muhammad, the Prophet's daughter). But among British soldiers in Egypt during the First World War or even before, it came closer to trollop.

The insult rankled, recurring in Esmond's letters home like a hole in a tooth which he kept tonguing to soothe, to no avail.

～～～

Brogue, as in a country accent, intonation and idiom, doesn't have any identifiable connection with a certain kind of shoe. At least the makers of the *OED* hesitate to name one. The usage arrives later – the first instance given is from 1705

– and they concede that the link might have arisen because the same people who wore brogues – the Irish and the Scots – spoke that way. Country garments, country speech. One etymological dictionary surmises: 'Or perhaps it is from Old Irish *barrog*, "a hold" (on the tongue).' It resonates with 'broad' and 'broken', too, though these are coincidences. The literary scholar Kathryn Sutherland, a native speaker, suggests that leave-takings are perhaps cause for sadness, as when someone sets out on a journey, shod for the hardships en route. She also catches an echo of 'clog' ('A thick piece of wood; block . . . Anything that impedes' and finally, 'a wooden-soled shoe'). In *Coriolanus*, Volumnia cries out, 'I would the gods had nothing else to do / But to confirm my curses! . . . / it would unclog my heart / Of what lies heavy to't.' Shakespeare, as ever writing close to and with the body, segues from what trammels the feet, like a clog or a brogue, to speak of what weighs on the spirit or the heart. But the inference must be that a brogue clogs the tongue of folk who are also trammelled by heavy soil and heavy footwear, and that such speech is a sorrow – to them (it marks out the unfortunate and the oppressed), and even, perhaps, to us, on the receiving end of this rough language.

Not all the quotations supplied by the dictionary are pejorative, and brogue is often described as charming, lilting and seductive. I never could hear my mother's accent in English, but a friend tells me: 'She spoke in a declamatory, emphatic way with a wonderful Italian intonation, somewhere between a tinkle and a vibrato.'

The term hasn't wandered far from Ireland or Scotland, and it conveys that language is a particular kind of music, not only a sign system on the page or a structure of grammar. A brogue is also a tune, a pattern of sounds and intonation ('ah, the tune of Imogen!', exclaims Posthumus in *Cymbeline* when he hears her ranting – before he sees her). Yet a brogue isn't a foreign accent, not exactly: it can be a way of speaking your own tongue, a marker of region and class, not foreignness. The Irish writer Colm Tóibín recently recalled that when his grandfather was arrested for his part in the Easter Rising, he was sent to prison in Wales, and found to his surprise – his dismay? – that the guards were all Welsh-speakers, while the Irish prisoners all spoke English.

What could be the connection between a brogue on the foot and sounds in the ear and on the tongue? Oddly, shoes have a tongue, as if cobblers imagined they could speak – Charlie Chaplin, the tramp down on his uppers, makes them do so in his marvellous silent routines when he makes the bread rolls dance like shoes, and eats his boot, twirling the laces like spaghetti; Jan Švankmajer, too, the Czech surrealist and film-maker, has animated shoes as wide-open cannibal mouths. I'd claim there's a deeper affinity between the way you're shod and the way you talk and who you are   that a brogue is a mark of identity, a sign of tribal belonging and origin, it is the way you say the words in the country of words that you come from. It could be synonymous with 'mother tongue' except that it doesn't assume that affiliation runs through blood or the female line; it substitutes that Romantic wilderness – ground, bog, fen, marsh, scarp, turf – for the symbol of the motherland. Its homophonous link to the rude shoe for the wilder parts of Ireland and Scotland nudges its meaning towards place, not kin: the way you speak tells where you come from, which might cohere with your folks, your family including your mother, but not only. It's always possible to be fluent in the semantics and syntax of a language, but very rarely can you lose that trace and texture and intonation of your own. Your brogue places you, and it can be used against you – as in the Book of Judges (12:6) when Gileadites guarding a bridge asked all who wanted to cross to say the word 'shibboleth' and put to death anyone who couldn't pronounce the *sh* sound – resulting in 42,000 dead Ephraimites.

~~~

My mother Ilia Terzulli put on her brogues that first year of her marriage when she was at the beginning of the process of acquiring English. But is it possible to learn a brogue and sound like a native the way you can be fitted for tribal footwear? She became completely fluent in the language of her new place of belonging – the language of her daughters – and she soon began to write and think and even dream in English, Italian returning as the default only when she played cards, cast off stitches when knitting, and prayed. But her tune – and the dance of her gestures – were always identifiably Italian, and southern Italian at that.

The shoes were my mother's proof of membership, a swipe card, a badge which gained her entrance to a certain way of life – a certain caste, if you like. Like a way of saying things, they located her. The brogues fitted snugly and gave her grounding in her new home; they expressed her English husband's designs on her and her acceptance at this stage of the freedom she had achieved from the Fascist-stricken, wartorn Italy of her whole life until she left. They marked a rite of passage, a kind of initiation into a class, into a tribe, into a new place of belonging, just as Cinderella's foot uniquely matched the glass slipper which would transform her fate.

In the course of her life, her Italian receded, though later she began teaching it, with great success, at a crammer's for O and A level. When she went back to Italy for holidays younger people congratulated her on her perfect command of the language – theirs had moved on. Her delivery had become old-fashioned, the Italian equivalent of Celia Johnson's English in *Brief Encounter*. But her English reverberated to the notes of the native place she had left behind, as she reviewed and recalled her story and made up new ways of telling it.

Her crafted Peal's brogues, sitting so quietly in her cupboard, toe-to-heel kissing, were a kind of trick, a disguise; her under-ear speech always remembered her earlier home.

7

Nasturtium Sandwiches

A 'New World' Regulo-Controlled Radiation gas cooker (1929), cast iron, enamelled in blue and white speckle; set on four tall prongs as if it needed to clear floodwater; comes with *The Radiation Cookery Book* (18th edition, January 1935), its pages turned down at the corners at dishes which were just about possible during rationing – recipes for cooking nose-to-tail: tongue; ears; gizzards; cheeks; trotters; hodge-podge ('half a pound of scrag end of neck of mutton, quarter of a pound of dried peas or beans, a pound of potatoes'); head cheese; brain sauce (method: wash the brain in salt water, and skin. Tie in muslin, place in cold water and boil for ten minutes. Chop finely and add to half a pint of parsley sauce). Ilia has turned down a corner on: drop scones, Bath buns, butter icing (made with marg.), treacle sponge, jam puffs, Yorkshire pudding, and marmalade.

Mrs Warner was beginning to cook *all'inglese* and learning the words to match.

In November 1945, Joan Colville, an old chum of Esmond's from before the war, offered him a cottage with its own generous garden, in fertile farming country near Aylesbury – a tenant's tied accommodation on her land which was, by a stroke of luck, not needed. Ilia was finding that Esmond had a bewildering number of these chums in the circles he wanted her to move in now, and these English friends were all connected in a great cat's cradle of families across a patchwork quilt of countryside: they shot rabbits and hares, ran with beagles, and discussed keeping birds off raspberry canes and sweet peas and blackfly off nasturtium plants. They had names like Eulalie and Violet, and surnames like Buckmaster and Trefusis. To Ilia's eyes, Eulalie looked severe and mannish, whereas Violet was pale and elegant, with a past that wasn't ever fully aired but, whenever she appeared, started tremors of excitement through the company. Joan held a special place in Esmond's affections, yet without any quiver of attraction, Ilia assured herself, as Joan was sporting, good with animals, and a mother duck with many vigorous children. She was also sandy-haired and freckled, as Esmond had been before the war, when his nickname, to some of his oldest friends, was 'Red'. Joan was the sister of 'Grandy', who was one of those English *signori* her school textbook had talked about, and had his own island, Jersey, which was really in France; it happened he was also married to an Italian, Bianca.

In the album Ilia began keeping, under a snapshot of the small square brick house, Ilia wrote 'our first home' in white pencil on the black paper. She's holding on to Esmond's arm, and is wearing the pair of country brogues. Her husband was back in his own country after five years in North Africa, Italy, India, Ceylon and Burma, and he had strong ideas about how they should live and wanted to pass them on. He was attached to the pre-war decade, like a ship in a picture from a great polar adventure when winter sets in and the pack ice closes round it, holding it tight and lifting it, as if the desire to move forward could take it only upwards, into a zone of dreams.

～～～

That first winter of 1945–6 when she lay in bed to keep warm, she could hear the frost scritching in the beams of the cottage at night, and in the mornings, the windows would be diapered in lace on the inside as well as the outside, as if determined to intensify the privacy of their bedroom and prevent the sparrows, finches and tits who fed from the bacon rinds Esmond scattered on the path from fluttering up and looking in at them. Tits and robins and finches pecked through the bottle tops of the milk, which was delivered every morning, their beaks acting like a stylus on a clay tablet, piercing the gold tops above all for the soft yellow crust of cream inside. Then the snowdrifts grew too deep for the milk cart to get through. As the cold took hold in January 1946, they filled the two hot-water bottles they had and cuddled up tightly; but Esmond could not sleep for worry that the local mechanic, Mr Farrar, might be unable to start the car and fail to get through the snowfall to give him a lift to the station as arranged, and then Esmond would miss the train to London, where, searching for work, he was in conversation with numerous old friends about possibilities.

In a letter to his parents in London, he wrote, 'There is no need for a refrigerator here now – the larder is so cold that everything solidifies on top.'

～～～

Before the war he'd only toyed with this profession and that, never sticking to them for long – the Guards, the law, the stock exchange, the cigarette firm of Wills & Co. where he'd done a stint as a salesman – none of this had held his interest. The war had come as a godsend, Mother Rat said. It presented a solution to his drifting and idleness, party-going and card-playing. He'd jumped at the chance to go to Camberley and train; they'd put him in intelligence after he'd shown such aptitude at organising inter-regimental matches – chess as well as bridge. 'Not much to it, you know,' he said as he scanned the satisfactory scores for the three rubbers in the little book where he was keeping them neatly in pencil. 'Just a matter of counting to thirteen. But few can do it, few indeed!' he suddenly guffawed.

Now, he was nearly 40, and married. Although Ilia was as tall as he was, she was so slight, nothing to her but light and air and the rainbow dazzle in her black hair and bright face, and that winter she shivered and when she hugged him, she was trying to protect herself from the tooth of the winter. There wasn't much fuel in England either and there were limits to what Esmond could ask of his chums. The victory of the socialist government had come as a shock, and he didn't see it as offering him much, in spite of the visions conjured by his old friend from school, Frank Pakenham, who now had taken up his Cabinet post.

Armed with some cookbooks Mother Rat had passed on ('I've never been much of a cook, my lamb, so no loss to me – Es is quite a dab hand, though, so I'm sure you'll do better with 'em than me!'), Ilia began trying out English recipes with such ingredients as she could lay her hands on in the post-war scarcity. Esmond mourned the days of butter and cream, the 'blonde' sauces and 'brunette' sauces of his gallivanting youth.

Joan or her daughter Sally and young Robin or all of them together in a gaggle would often bring round eggs from the farm, and sometimes an old hen whose laying days were done. Sally and Robin shot rabbits, too, and the family lent Esmond a gun and he'd go after wood pigeon, but he complained the scrawny scraps weren't worth the trouble of plucking. Ilia paid close attention to their visits: the family was her principal conduit to the new world she found herself in.

One afternoon, when Sally and Robin were back from school for the Christmas holidays, they came round with some 'goodies': a pot of strawberry jam Joan had made, and a jug of cream, covered with a bead-trimmed hanky; Robin lifted it up and stuck his finger in, his eyes dancing mischievously as he sucked it.

'Oh Robin, you're a disgusting greedy-guts,' scolded Sally. But nobody seemed to mind very much.

Ilia noted this insouciance, and she recognised it as a privilege, worn very lightly, unconsciously, by Joan and families like Joan's who really could do as they wanted. Ilia, by contrast, had always had to watch out to know the rules and, usually, keep to them.

She was often on her own. Learning to drive had been out of the question for a young woman of her means in Italy (in the pages of *Oggi*, female film stars appeared at the wheel of fabulous cars), and when Joan or another friend or neighbour came round to check she was coping, she could communicate only falteringly and was no company at all. She applied herself eagerly to adapting, to mastering his country's ways. She knew she was the youngest daughter of a widow of no means from a stricken region of a defeated nation and a vainglorious regime and needed to prove her usefulness. She enjoyed the novel processes and methods in the same way she had enjoyed helping her mother, when they had prepared a dish of *lasagne alla ricotta* and taken it round to the baker's to cook in his oven. She had her own stove now. The gas travelled down a tube from a replaceable cylinder that stood under the sink; it was too heavy for her to lift on her own when it needed to be changed; Farrar would deliver the replacement, and Esmond liked to keep another in the shed, like a tyre. 'The secret of success,' he'd say.

'That's how we won the war. Spare parts – and we had 'em. *They* didn't. And we had 'em because every time one of us saw a piece of machinery buried in sand, we dismantled it and took every bit that had any life in it. The army teaches foresight,' he'd say, as he trundled the spare gas into the garden shed.

She studied the spurts of the gas flames, garlanding each burner in flickering blue petals. Then she'd see something of home that would pierce her: the flames were chrysanthemums, spiky globes picked to offer to the dead, and wound into the wreath on her father's coffin, just over a decade ago when everything changed, because after he died from the bullet that had lived inside him since the duel he'd fought in his youth which had finally got to his brain, their uncle Sandro made them leave the cool airy apartment on the *piano nobile* in the palazzo; it had always belonged to him anyway. They moved to the smaller top-floor rooms in the Via Calefati; and when Zio Sandro came to tea, her mother told them to pinch their cheeks and look happy, otherwise he might not continue to help them.

In the previous apartment in the palazzo, the reception room had a marble floor and was wide enough for her to dance with her father who, like her, loved to dance, and they put on the records from America he had brought back, very quietly, as the Duce had banned foreign music. She put her feet on his so she could step exactly with him: '*Mio fagiolino*,' he said, tripping deftly to the foxtrot, keeping her close so she could smell his delicious mixture of tobacco and vanilla pomade. She was the tallest of his children because, it was said, they'd given her injections to strengthen her bones.

That winter, Esmond also introduced her to Horlicks. He would heat Carnation condensed milk from the little tin, mix in the beige powder, and watch with satisfaction when she sipped it and found she liked it.

'Just what the doctor ordered,' he said, contentedly. 'That'll put some flesh on your bones. My bird. My little bird-boned darling, my *piccola*.'

There was also Ovaltine, but she never liked it as much. And cocoa. Cocoa she developed a taste for.

The hot drinks helped through her first winter in England; the one that followed, when I was born, saw temperatures sink to well below freezing and stay there; it is still the harshest winter on record.

Esmond liked his food fiery; he encouraged her to follow suit. Travelling on the continent had opened his eyes to the idea of cuisine, and he was a keen brewer of consommés and glazes, but his palate always tended to strong, hot flavours. He wanted what he ate to explode on the palate. He went on living up to his boyhood nickname long after he lost the 'golden red curls' that his first passport included under the term 'peculiarities'. Inside he liked to be aflame, too, it seemed. Of course, spices helped to conserve provisions in the climates where he'd been fighting – North Africa, the subcontinent – and before then, they'd been the only way to liven up the insipid stodge offered at school. 'Condiments' pepped it up: Tabasco, HP Sauce, Worcestershire Sauce, mustard, horseradish, chutney, and Patum Peperium. 'The Gentleman's Relish' was 'established', it says on the chunky ceramic pot, during the first decade of Victoria's reign; scenes of cricket or sailing or other pastimes are sometimes painted on the lid, images taken from fine art (photography had not yet been discovered).

When you unseal the tight lid, the paste inside smells sharp and super-fishy, for it's mortared chiefly of salted anchovy in a little milk and butter, with a pinch of oats. The recipe is still meant to be a secret, but if you could eat a firework, this would be it. When spread thickly, Patum Peperium has a bracing effect, as if potash or gunpowder had been pounded with spices and then set alight; the mixture explodes against the roof of your mouth and the cavities of your nose and eye sockets.

The solid paperweight-like pot of waxy white china cooled and contained the fiery mixture and was kept in the fridge or, that winter, in the larder; its pepperiness was part of the male mystique that clung to the very idea of the English gentleman, and connected him to faraway places where his forebears and his peers were powerful and where strong measures were needed to prevent goods from rot and decay: the anchovies in the paste are blended with powders from the four quarters, cinnamon and pepper, nutmeg and its bark, cayenne and ginger – if you took aim at a map of the world and threw darts to land on the countries where these grow you would be marking out the contours of imperial power, Spanish, Portuguese and Dutch to start with, then French and British, the latter hewing close to their colonies – till they were out of time before they realised it; before Esmond knew it.

The kick of the spread was not merely gentlemanly, it was manly, and dealing with hot flavours was a trial of strength which Esmond enjoyed – though I remember an occasion much much later, in the 1960s, when we went for an Indian in London – Indian restaurants still a novelty then – and he ordered a vindaloo . . . and seized the water jug and tipped it over his head, and even that wasn't enough.

To Ilia, Patum Peperium in its heavy sealed pot reminded her of cosmetics beyond the reach of her purse, like the precious salve that Santa Maria Maddalena lavished on Jesus' dusty feet from her jar. Phials and bottles of similar satisfying weight and glassy smoothness contained caviare and other expensive stuffs like night cream, which should be used frugally, though Mary Magdalene splashed about the contents of her jar – 'she spilled her spikenard', the very best variety from Gilead.

Ilia did of course try this fiery relish, and she tried to like it, and she grew to tolerate it. Esmond on the other hand did not quite spread it 'sparingly', as recommended on the pot, but he did indeed relish it, especially on crumpets where it functioned like a sprinkling of salt and pepper. He showed her how to prong the spongy cushions on to a toasting fork, as he had done for Frank when he fagged for him at Eton, and hold them against the fire, where thin blue flames hissed as they licked up through three pillars of fossil skeletons and kindled them to a soft coral glow. No pasta in Bari came close to the mushroom texture of an English crumpet.

Butter, which her husband longed to melt on them, came in the basket Joan and the children brought them that Christmas. Along with a whole goose. 'An actual goose!' Esmond exulted. He was able to render the bones to make meat jelly, essential for the rich sauces of pre-war France he pined for. But Ilia was not used to cook with butter, and olive oil was not to be had, not in Buckinghamshire in 1946.

~~~

Many years into the future, when Esmond had become the director of the bookshop Bowes & Bowes in Cambridge, he unexpectedly bumped into Max Harari in King's Parade: Max, then working for Wildenstein's, the art dealers, had come to visit the Fitzwilliam Museum – confidentially – about an Old Master entrusted to him by the owner's family to find a home.

'My dear old boy!' cried Esmond at the sight of his best man. 'Come back to the house with me now and see Ilia – oh do, it's been too long! She would love to see you to say hello. And stay to tea or a drink . . . have you time? I'll run you there and back to the station . . . Com'n, do say you will.'

When she opened the door, Max saw she was as tall and

slender as ever, but the young Italian in the Dior imitation full skirts was now wearing a light tweed pair of trousers, with a soft blue shirt and gamekeeper's warm waistcoat, and a scarf knotted round her neck; her brogues completed her perfect country-gentry camouflage. They greeted each other in Italian then, switching to English, she waved him into the drawing room where the fire was lit and said, 'I was about to toast some crumpets – does that appeal?'

~~~

At the beginning of their life together, Ilia would fry Esmond two eggs in margarine each morning, but her stomach began to churn at the sign of melting grease, as that winter, my mother found she was expecting – me – 'expecting' being the idiom in use then (the now pervasive 'pregnant' sounded medically brutal in 1946; 'contraception' likewise harsh – Ilia always said, 'taking precautions'). She could do less cooking but worked at her sewing machine, another wedding present, a second-hand but marvellous Singer, with a lever at knee height on the right, which you pressed against with your thigh, and the whole delicately tooled black, gold and silvered steel device, descendant of the automata made by eighteenth-century clockmakers and jewellers, could be folded down out of sight into an elegant table on tall fluted art deco legs. Esmond sang her praises to his mother, especially for the thrift that they demonstrated.

7 Jan '46
from Avon House,
Dorton, Aylesbury

To MR
Ilia sewing . . . curtains and her new black dress for London.

Once spring was on its way and the cold was loosening its grip, Esmond began planting vegetables and flowers, scattering seed Joan gave him from her kitchen garden into trays he put on the south-facing window ledges of their cottage. In the garden, he pegged out a square patch of ground, dug it over, and planted it with potatoes, three kinds of beans (runner, broad and dwarf), onions, radishes, carrots, strawberry plants, mint and borage, thyme and angelica.

As the warmth began to rise, he pricked out the flower seedlings in the garden, and by early summer, the fragile azure trumpets of morning glory were opening up to the sunshine and ramping up the trellises he'd put up, the orange and red caps and bells of nasturtium blazed as they tumbled from the pots, the pale veins threading the luminous light green of their lily pad leaves, like a chameleon's skin.

Nasturtium was another excellent ingredient, he told her, a peppery pick-me-up. The flower's seed pods were draw-purses packed with tangy seeds, and the plant's leaves were sharp, too, deliciously spicy, especially when newly unfolded and tender. '*Nas-tortuere*,' Esmond would chuckle, 'nose-twisters,' as he took a bite and sniffed on the hit. But they were best, he said, in sandwiches, between thin slices of the whitest bread – no oil. Perhaps buttered, but if no butter was to be had, no matter.

The flowers could also be eaten, but they didn't go up your nose the way the leaves did. She would pick some leaves and make a neat stack of finger sandwiches on the glass tazza, with pale green showing in a fine thread, like buttonhole embroidery, and the retroussé bonnet of a bright flower on top to warn any visitors – Joan or Sally or Robin – who, seeing the green filling, would think it was cucumber and find the fizz up their nose a bit of shock.

Mint and borage took off by the compost heap he'd started: vital ingredients, he told her, for a treat to come that summer, a drink that Esmond and his mother loved to mix in summertime: Pimm's No. 1. This also required squash and water from the siphon in a jug which Esmond then crammed full of sprigs from the plants. Borage was hairy and scratchy, and its blue flowers attracted bees, very good for the rest of the garden, he said, for pollinating the orchard where there were apples and plums. Borage seemed to Ilia rather thistly, something a donkey might nibble, and its Italian name wasn't in her dictionary.

Horseradish was much less appealing to look at than borage, but an important stimulant, too. He taught her how to shred the long, tough root and then pound it into a paste; he heaped this onto the side of plate. 'Adds a hit to a cold cut,' he would say. It was another fiery relish, marbled and gleaming, and was sometimes replaced by a blazing yellow dollop of mustard. He showed her how to mix the powder from the small oblong yellow tin, adding water till it became a paste. 'Stuff that comes in a tube's no damn good. But never make up more than we need,' he'd instruct her, ''cos mustard won't hold its flavour long.' With a tiny silver ladle, he'd scoop the bright ooze from the blue glass vessel set in a silver pot, like serving thick soup at a dolls' tea party.

She was also learning about drinks. She had never drunk spirits. They'd sometimes had wine on the table in Bari, but her mother and her sisters had no taste for it. Now, she became used to the English daily ritual, as her husband and his chums drank before and after meals, and in different rooms besides the one in which the table was laid for eating, and they set to talking into the night over their drinks, laughing more and more loudly, passing the port and the liqueurs.

Esmond had unrivalled access to supplies of drink through his mother, because her father Henry Blyth had been a partner in Gilbey & Son, wine importers, merchants, distillers of gin, and even though he was long dead, Mother Rat still had connections and relatives in the firm. Its cellars, much depleted by the difficulties of sea journeys and imports from the Mediterranean during the war, still held such quantities of tipple that Esmond's mother had not been stinted, and nor was her son, once he had returned to England.

Ilia also began to learn the customary sequence of drinks in the evening (and sometimes, if there were people for lunch, in the morning): first, sherry or Madeira, a special brand called Rainwater. Or they might have a mixed drink: her husband sighed nostalgically for the cocktails he had enjoyed before the war. They were restricted in variety in the immediate aftermath, even for Esmond's mother. But gin was available, and was mixed with Schweppes tonic water, with its whiff of juniper, like the scrub under the olive groves that danced in columns, their twisted branches extended towards one another, as soon as you reached the outskirts of Bari or Molfetta or Ruvo di Puglia. Esmond had a cordial he liked to add to the mixture: it resembled a *rosolio* such as stood, crimson, green, golden-yellow and translucent, on the glass shelves in the cafés in Bari, and it stained the drink with a cloudy veil of rose-pink from only three drops.

Angostura bitters tasted spicy, not sweet. Like many of the tastes she was learning to acquire, its name had not formed part of her sisters' English vocabulary, because it did not appear in American popular songs: 'Angostura' almost sounded Italian, but when she said so, Esmond told her that it was named after some plant that grew on an island in the Caribbean, 'where the chaps make fine cricketers, what?'

The flavours and customs she was learning belonged, like Angostura bitters, to an untried zone of her taste buds: it needed training to appreciate bitterness. Yet they did not only tend to bitterness; they tended to sweet dewiness as well, originating in the tropical colonies of the empire or recalling the enterprise required to rule, the games, the horses, the conviviality. But she didn't sort them in her mind according to this common property at the time that she was first becoming acquainted with her husband's tastes.

After the pink gin and the other refreshments, she learned that different wines accompanied food, usually a hock with the first course, and a claret for the main dish. But this sequence was complicated, as sherry could be brought into the dining room and even splashed into the soup. For the pudding course, another wine, a sticky syrupy kind, might be served on very special occasions, and for this, tiny glass chalices were produced from the cabinet Esmond had designed himself, in walnut, with bowed legs and lion's claws in imitation of a Chippendale card table. But he'd added a cupboard, three shelves and veneered doors. He was proud of the piece when it arrived from the cabinetmakers' at the flat in Mount Street in 1932; the whorls on the doors showed four aureoled sections through what must have been a magnificent large tree; they looked like a colossal butterfly's ocelli, guarding the drinks inside the cabinet. It would become the centrepiece of the drawing room of every house he lived in. He would use the high bottom shelf of the cabinet as a bar, and keep a tea towel, a corkscrew, and a dish for corks and other tools, and would mix the drinks with his back to the room and turn to hand friends their orders with the doors still open behind him, showing the array of bottles and glasses inside. It was his hearth, the hub of his activities as an Englishman in his castle.

For the cheese course, at which appeared remote cousins of the *provolone*, *scamorza* and *gorgonzola* of her childhood, they would revert to the claret or even change to an older burgundy; then, after the meal, when she and the wives or any other female guests would leave Esmond and the old boys together, he'd bring out from his cabinet the heavy decanters of port and brandy and a different kind of Madeira, all of them labelled with silver tags, and she would take the women to their bedroom so they could tidy themselves and 'spend a penny', and some of them would smoke, and she'd offer them a 'long drink': there weren't any liqueurs yet in the period immediately after the war, though in later years, the same cabinet would be full of the glittering flasks of green and yellow and purple-pink and crystalline fluids, lethal, alchemical and almost phosphorescent. My sister Laura and I would enjoy bashing ice cubes wrapped in a tea towel till they were in smithereens and then making crème de menthe frappé; Ilia's favourite was Cointreau on ice. 'And what's your poison?' she would ask, in a cheerful tone.

A 'long drink' was made from something that came from a bottle, mixed with fizz from a siphon that was fun to squirt into the yellowy green of Rose's lime juice, or the bright chemical orange and lemon of the squash concentrates, all of them also kept in the drinks cabinet. But none of these juices tasted of fruit as Ilia thought of it, of the oranges and lemons that you could pick all year round from the sweet waxy trees, with their sticky, heady blossom, which stood in tubs on the balcony of their apartment in her home town or downstairs in the central courtyard, or, sometimes, even grew in the street.

Of all the different flavours and experiences, this particular estrangement made her feel the most intense homesickness.

These pleasures of the English way of life and the English table made Eno's 'Fruit Salts' a necessary tonic – a necessary purge? – every morning. 'Where Britain Rules All Are Free', the makers proclaimed.

Esmond would tear a corner of the sachet, tip the salts into water, and pause while it spurted up in miniature geysers. The trick was to drink it down so the sparkling, purifying fission would continue inside him, deep down in the claret-curdled and Stilton-and-port-enriched guts. The powder – the fruit part citric acid, the fizz plain bicarbonate of soda – never quite dissolved;

over the years, the bathroom tooth mug developed a crusty rim like the lips of a fumarole in the volcanic beds around Naples.

Ilia never dosed herself with Eno's; it always seemed to her something for men to take, especially Englishmen abroad. The need to keep blood pure is stressed on the labels, where the dangers of foreign parts are invoked, accompanied by passionate testimonials about the protection the mixture gives from disease and impurity, which were collected from army personnel and colonial servants from the empire, who wrote in from postings in Spanish Town, Jamaica, to commend the potion.

From similar far distant places also came Bay Rum, a clear liquid from a square glass bottle which was burnished red, like a copper beech, and announced the ingredients were all natural – bay leaves, cloves, a touch of friar's balsam, ground with a pestle, with bergamot added for the high notes; apothecaries had perfected it for centuries, to act as a venerable skin stimulant, and when you unscrewed the gilt stopper, the scent of it was redolent of spice islands, tobacco plantations, perfumes on the trade winds from the West Indies, where it was first concocted in the mid-eighteenth century. It was a spirit essence for reviving tired spirits. Esmond used to buy it at Trumper's, the barbers in Curzon Street, or sometimes at D.R. Harris's on St James's Street.

It was from Trumper's that Esmond had acquired, with money Mother Rat gave him for his 21st birthday, a pair of twin mahogany brushes with his initials on them. This was a time when he had a lot more hair, golden red and curly; he'd pour some of the barber's special preparation into the palm of his left hand before patting it into his hair; then he'd take up the brushes, one in each hand, and attack his head with vigorous strokes. Bay Rum was a rub, and a 'scalp stimulant', though nobody mentioned baldness.

Bay Rum was familiar to Ilia, being a version of hair lotions used by barbers in her home town, and to smooth a lotion of this sort on to your hair to keep it sleek was a local custom. But her husband's preferred version smelled different from the pomades her father and other men in her youth had used to train their moustaches as well as control their hair. Bay Rum was not hair oil, she learned. Hair oil was foreign, and attracted malign comments (greasy, sleazy, caddish, vulgar). Bay Rum was clean and manly and tonic. Nothing suspect about it. He'd missed having it during the war, he told her, and one afternoon he came back glowing from London with a bottle from his barber's, recently delivered at the docks, he'd been informed.

~~~

Through all the talk and the meals and the drinks rang the laughing voice of her husband. Laughter was Esmond's chief mark of identity, the fingerprint of his very being, the signature of his iris. It exploded and cascaded throughout his life, reverberating through the bodies of his parents and siblings, friends, and, later, of his wife Ilia and his daughters. As a little girl, I always knew where to find him: I'd follow the laughter that shook him and the ground beneath him. It was tempestuous, and the pitch and volume were extreme, out of scale with whatever had given him cause to laugh. 'What, what?' he'd repeat at the end of the explosion, inviting the company to join in.

The memory of a triumphant bridge game at Camberley, which had cleaned out his fellow trainee officers as well as their instructor, might be the immediate cause for an explosion of merriment. Or the thought of someone's brilliant coup in the campaign; or a fabulous bottle of champagne found in a cellar in Cairo one evening. There was *joie de vivre* in the matter of it, but the undertow pulled in its wake carried many other passions. My father's wild guffaw, the very seal of the roaring English gentleman, didn't pack hurt and frustration at first. But its unsettling force rose from the twisted energies of his desires, and

demanded acquiescence, forcing the like response on his companions as he laughed. The laugh was a bid for authority and it was
light and free when opportunities stood before him; when they
didn't, it began to alter. It rarely flew from one listener to another:
as with the game of bridge at which he had shown his true and
indeed admirable powers of concentration, acuity, and calculation
of odds on the placement of the cards, Esmond did not always
know when to laugh. Or that he was asking too much of his
companions, when he demanded they find their own discomfiture
or defeat funny. He had been schooled in this strain of humour.
Laughter at others' expense was part of his upbringing, but he
never realised it was the mainspring of his jollity.

Ilia would learn to join in, later. She began to laugh like
her husband as part of her ways of fitting in with the new
life in England, and then in the best British circles in Egypt.
But not uproariously, since she was always more 'ladylike' (as
he would have put it), but long after her husband was dead,
she would jaw a peal of laughter, a bit hoarsely for she never
had much breath or power in her voice, and she too was not
conscious that this hilarity was utterly mirthless.

Esmond's laugh lived on in her society manners, but in her
case, unlike his, it didn't connect to deeper turmoil. Sometimes,
a friend or a new acquaintance would glimpse this, beyond the
surface joviality which made Esmond such 'capital company',
and the glimpse would cause alarm, for it revealed a dreadful
unhealed wound inside the hearty, boisterous Englishman.

It was the laugh that his employees would hear, and they
would pause in their work of taking stock of new deliveries,
or entering new orders in the ledgers, or moving towards the
van with a pile of newspapers. They would be arrested in
mid-task for a short while, captured by the long-cured confident blast of Esmond Warner's origins that resonated in rings
from the peal, and they felt secure even as they shook their

heads at his exuberance. But the waves widening out in circles from the burst of laughter from the Englishman struck others differently, especially later. For many of Ilia's friends, her husband's loud jolliness made them wonder on her account how she coped. For the locals who would rise up against British authority in Egypt, this hilarity hallmarked the hated rulers' spirit, spilling out on the terraces of the clubs where they gathered and roistered in the evenings and the hotel ballrooms where they danced at night. For Ilia herself, Esmond's laugh eventually signalled all her grief – and his.

But that first year of their marriage, Esmond appreciated how quickly and gamely she was learning his ways. He realised, though, that his protectiveness was failing; he couldn't find work. He thought, especially during the harshest temperatures that winter, that she might even die of the country he had brought her to.

~~

Marina's christening, December 1946, St Aloysius Church, Oxford: Antonia Fraser, second from left; Frank Pakenham, back row, right; Violet Trefusis in front of him, and Mother Rat, to her right; EPW, second from right.

In November 1946, I was born; the christening took place before Christmas in Oxford at the Catholic church of St Aloysius, as Frank, who was my godfather, was then living in the city (he had stood for Parliament there, but failed; he was now Permanent Under-Secretary for War in the new peacetime government, and would hold various other posts, none for long. Other chums came – several of them also godparents, regardless of belief, and in spite of fuel shortages. They're all in the photos: Eulalie Buckmaster motored in from Moreton Morrell, looking severe in her understated expensive clothes; all the Colvilles; and four of Frank and Elizabeth's eight children, including his eldest daughter, the future historian Antonia Fraser, who'd just left the Dragon prep school, where she'd been one of the very few girls. Violet Trefusis' luminous oval face and slender legs are visible even in that squash – she looks demure, though the model for Virginia Woolf's dashing Russian Princess Sasha in *Orlando* had just finished her *roman-à-clef* about her long love affair with Vita Sackville-West (she wrote *Broderie anglaise* in French for reasons of discretion – all thrown to the winds by Vita's son Nigel Nicolson when he published *Portrait of a Marriage* in 1973, to the delighted scandal of readers). Violet hadn't wanted to be left out of the party, my father told me, and had demanded to be a godmother, too. I never saw her again. I regret this now, but when I was studying in Florence, where Violet lived in the beautiful surroundings of the Villa Ombrellino on Bellosguardo from 1947 till her death in 1972, I was determined to strike out on my own, without using family connections.

Esmond's friends had rallied round for the christening: 'What a distinguished but dowdy crowd,' remarked my sister Laura. 'And Mother Rat looks exactly like a Giles granny.' They were happy for him – and perhaps surprised. Ilia stands out, smiling from under the dotted veil wound on a witty, conical hat.

~~~

That winter, Esmond's thoughts began turning to the south, to somewhere Ilia would feel at home and thrive, where he could live again in the style he was used to, where he could take her and the baby, and they could have oranges and lemons again from the tree, a card game or two, laughter over cocktails. Remembering how he had loved Cairo during the war, how he had thought of Cairo as his home, he hit upon a plan. Cairo would remind her of the bustle of Bari, it would be bathed in sunlight and swept by soft breezes off the Nile the way the sea wind lifted off the Adriatic at dawn and coolly breathed through her family's apartment once the shutters were opened to let it flow from the balcony into the bedrooms. But Bari was ruined now, ravaged by the old regime and the war, and the Americans there were being duped by gangsters so everything was still being laid waste.

Whereas Cairo, Cairo was unscathed.

In 1946, his laughter still rang out, cheerful and genuine; it sprang from the hopes and the excitement that lay before them as they decided to move to Cairo, where the plan was, he would open a bookshop.

Postscript

One evening, after they had joined the Colvilles for dinner, and had walked back down the lane that separated the house from the cottage they'd been given at a peppercorn rent, Ilia had gone upstairs to the bathroom to get undressed for bed, and found she was missing her rings. She was in the habit of taking them off for the night and leaving them in a porcelain dish by the basin, but they were no longer on her finger. She looked again; she could not believe they were missing.

In the bathroom, stuck fast to the floor, she stood whimpering until Esmond called out to her, 'Anything the matter, baby?'

When nothing happened, he coaxed, 'I think I'll need to wash too quite soon.'

She slipped the bolt and faced him, trembling.

'I knew I should have had them adjusted!' she cried.

The summer night had been cool when they came home and her finger was slender. She shouldn't have risked wearing them outside, but they made her feel, when in the company of people like the Colvilles in their own house on their own land, able to play her part as Mrs Warner.

She was in despair; she wanted to go out again into the night, retrace their steps along the way that very minute in the dark, search the hedgerows with Esmond's field torch, call on their friends regardless of the hour, beseech them to look around where the rings might have slipped off her finger.

'When you took off your gloves,' he said. 'Look inside them.'

He didn't seem very perturbed. Not like her.

'But I would have noticed,' she wailed, 'if I hadn't had them during the meal, I know I would have noticed.'

She was pleading to hunt for them, but Esmond was too tired, he said, and he had to be up early to get to London. Besides, they'd see next to nothing even with the torch.

'Don't worry baby – they'll turn up. Somebody will see 'em, that's the virtue of sparkling.'

She was incredulous at his equanimity. 'But . . .' she began.

She was crying at her folly. How idiotic and vain of her to wear diamonds to go out in the country lanes. Joan Colville, even though she was formally a Lady, never wore anything like that – her shirts were frayed, and the cat had pulled threads in her cardigans, and there were dog hairs everywhere on her clothes and the furniture and carpets. She was always commenting on Ilia's elegance, and anyway, diamonds didn't really go with the new walking shoes Esmond had had made for her or with her new hacking jacket of good tweed, the cloth that gives meaning to the phrase dyed-in-the-wool, which he had also bought her for life in England; incongruous and foolish, too, for the rings were gone.

The loss was a dreadful omen. The diamonds were the warrant of her escape into a new security, a kind of passport worn in full sight, a proof of new identity, family, position and value. And they had been his mother's; that counted as a token of entry, to be shown at doors that would previously have been closed. The wedding band, the sapphire engagement ring – they were pledges of Esmond's love and their union. But the diamonds, which were so large, so many, and which had caused such surprise and joy among her family at the sudden leap of her prospects, they were gone.

Her entire life, till her arrival in England, had known little else but scarcity and graft. Those years of government by the henchmen the Duce appointed to sustain the regime in the south, brought a daily struggle to elude official embezzlers and pilferers, to watch out for the street vendors who'd slide a thumb on to the edge of the bowl on the scales. Even the parish priest wouldn't add a prayer to the suffrages at Mass without a bribe. Not to speak of the police. She would always remember this side of her Italian youth. She hadn't ever known things otherwise.

She wanted to believe him, but such an outcome defied her every experience of life and other people.

But that is indeed how it turned out, the very next day. A neighbour walking down the lane nearby saw something winking in the pale low morning light slanting through the hedge, and picked up one diamond ring, and then, a little further on, another. He (or she – the story is missing fine detail) can't have driven to the police station because petrol rationing in those years was severe. But whoever it was brought the rings to the local bobby, and when my father, on his way back from London, came in to the police station to report the loss, the constable asked him for some material details to prove that he was indeed the rightful claimant, gave him a form to sign, and a small envelope with the diamond rings inside. He probably added his good wishes for the couple's life ahead.

It is easy to see this as a lost era of ideal innocence, of

honesty, of trust. For my mother the episode took on mythical status, conveying all that she had gained when she left an Italy ravaged by Fascism and factions and fighting, and adopted Englishness. 'Never ever in Italy would anyone give back a gift from heaven,' she'd say. 'They would have just thanked fate and run to exchange it for money – and the jewellers would have asked no questions. It was more than your life was worth to ask questions. Besides, if you had taken such a thing to the police, they would have had you in the cells before you could say Jack Robinson.' (She'd picked up the local idiom very quickly.)

My father went into Ogden's in the Burlington Arcade to have the rings tightened, and the assistant lent him the right instrument to use to measure Ilia's finger: a cluster of brass rings in different sizes on a tapered rule. Ilia's half-moons could then be fitted exactly, and she would wear them every day of her life without fear of them slipping off again.

PART II

1947

to Egypt

8

King Faruq's Bookplate

Bookplate of King Faruq, designed in 1936, the year of his coronation, when he was 16, tall and slim with a small moustache and a charming face, often wearing uniform with epaulettes and braid, many splendid jewelled decorations, and a tarbush on his head. He was the first ruler of Egypt to be a native speaker of Arabic, and from the start he vowed he would bring his people out of poverty and ignorance and spread education throughout the country. The image he chose for the bookplate for his library in the Abdin Palace shows his swirly *tughra* with a coronet, set above a printing press. This emblem of modernity is being operated by a sheikh, white-bearded, pale-skinned, in old-style Ottoman-era turban and belted gown, with the more recently built grandiloquent Raf'al Mosque and the city of Cairo on the skyline in the background; the sheikh is handing a book hot off the press, it seems, to a fellah, who is thin, darker-skinned, and covered in a shift; the labourer is kneeling beside his plough, which is being drawn by a pair of oxen. The *mise-en-scène* proclaims the young king's enlightenment lineage, going back to the first publishing press set up in Egypt, in the Bulaq district of Cairo, under the auspices of his dynasty's founder and Faruq's great-grandfather, Muhammad Ali. The scene suggests the book is a copy of the Qur'an, but it is not specified, and the young king was pious but not strenuously so, respectful of local tradition but a moderniser. His reign was secular in tone, too much so for many of his subjects. Or so it would turn out.

The figure of honest toil is receiving the unnamed book with a gesture that speaks of surprise and gratitude.

King Faruq's bookplate, 1936.

∽

December 1946.

'Cairo is the greatest city of Europe that isn't in Europe, not Europe proper,' Esmond told the partners of W.H. Smith's. He knew William 'Billy' Smith himself, 3rd Viscount Hambledon, the owner of the family firm, as they'd been at school together; Billy had been badly wounded in the war, and so handed over the business to Michael Hornby, another friend (chiefly through shared cricketing interests); Michael had recently become vice-chairman. There were others present at the table in the boardroom – David Smith, Billy's younger brother, whom Esmond knew less well and wasn't sure how he stood with him. He'd come up on the train to see them at their headquarters at Strand House on the south bank of the Thames and put the case for a branch of the bookshop in the Middle East, either in Palestine or Egypt.

'Cairo's escaped the ravages of the war,' he was saying, 'it's prosperous and growing more so. It's under British rule – well, not quite – it used to be a Protectorate. But since 1936 there's a treaty which gives the locals more, you know, independence. We're still in charge, just not so openly – and it's as cosmopolitan a city as you could ever wish. Even during the height of the campaign, before Monty turned our fortunes round, Cairo was flourishing. There was everything to be had – such delicious grub, you can't imagine! Like pictures from out of *A Thousand and One Nights*! And wines from cellars lavishly stocked before the fighting, and department stores overflowing with luxuries – and other things. With necessities that have become luxuries to us. They're paltry there! As for the people! You know about Alexandria, and the Greeks and Italians and Armenians, the sophistication of them all; well, Cairo has become the place for that now. Some Arabs are grand and mix with us, but mostly we'd be providing for the French-speaking locals, the *gratin*, you know, and the rich Jews, what!'

'Stationery,' said Michael Hornby. 'They'll love our stationery.' He was a genial, courtly figure, one of those high-bred Englishmen who walk on long legs like a pair of shears, his sharpest angles of elbow and shoulder sheathed in understated suits custom-made for his height. A topiary-perfect moustache, as worn later by Anthony Eden and his successor Harold Macmillan, was trimmed just to clear his upper lip. (Michael knew both future PMs, through what Ilia learned was called 'the old-boy network'.)

'Yes, indeed. Fine papers, die-stamped, engraved headings, lined envelopes – just the thing. There's no limit to the snob-appeal where the rich Egyptian world is concerned! And books,' Esmond added, 'don't underestimate the demand for books. They are great readers but their bookshops are, shall we say,' he paused, 'when it comes to business methods, not quite *au courant*.' He chuckled, as he remembered fondly the scene in the book market around Ezbekieh Gardens where the stalls and kiosks were heaped higgledy-piggledy, regardless of genre. 'Mind you, schools and colleges are still going strong and more are springing up. Foreign universities and training colleges. Schools of law and languages.

'The young king's keen as mustard – he's had a bookplate made, don't you know, with one of those stick-thin fellahin wretches down by his plough in a furrow while a schoolmas-terly type hands him a . . . book!' Esmond was laughing, but he felt for the fellahin, he really did. 'Don't think Faruq himself reads much, but there's a palace librarian, a fine chap, came across him one time at an Embassy do.

'It's clear the king knows the country's got to be educated, and we're the ones to do it. We have the know-how, have done so for centuries. But everyone else is at it, too, especially the French – Egypt's got a long history with France, so we need to make our move, what? Now that the war is over at last and we've licked the Germans. Our lot's been in with a chance for a long time, alongside the Roman Catholics of course, who can still teach us a thing or two when it comes to schools. Though some of them aren't bad chaps. It's a veritable salma-gundi of Christian sects! All busily saving the souls of the locals. And they all need books.'

'We already have outlets in those parts – in education, as you say,' Michael waved vaguely. 'We supply them directly. Not sure we wouldn't raise a few hackles.'

'We could deal with them in person. Think of the advantage in that – for them. No posting. No complicated paperwork and correspondence. Esmond would organise distribution, wouldn't you, old boy?' This was David Smith, the younger brother – at least his tone wasn't sceptical.

'Newspapers, too. To the clubs and hotels – no waiting for *The Times* and the *Telegraph* to arrive on the boat and then from Alex by train.' Esmond was revving up.

'*The Times* is delivered by air, surely?' David, again.

'We'd have it sent in bulk by air and we'd get it out to Shepheard's Hotel and the Turf Club and the Auberge des Pyramides that evening.

'Cairo would be first base. We'd branch out.' Esmond spread a map on the table – he was still in the desert, making strategy. He tapped it: 'It'd be our bridgehead to the south, to the Sudan.'

'Also under British rule – well, governorship.' Michael was supporting the idea.

'Used to be called "Protection",' said David.

'Our man Lampson, not to be trifled with.' Esmond was feeling happy with the direction of the meeting.

'He's gone. I believe. Sent east,' Michael added. 'Japan it is, I heard. There's another chap in Cairo now.'

'Still, plenty of potential within reach. Linked by railway.'

'The Levant!'

'And plenty of places of education in Africa, too!'

'What an opportunity!'

'To the East, too – think of Palestine,' Esmond's hopes were rising. 'Palestine is also wide open – a splendid people, highly educated, eager to stock up on the books necessary for advancement.'

'A stone's throw, too, from Port Said just around the corner . . . Esmond would organise a network of contacts, wouldn't you, old boy?' Michael was looking at him encouragingly.

'Yes, absolutely. Yes, sir!' Esmond made a sharp salute and threw back his shoulders.

The gathering was silent, reflecting on the prospects, and Esmond was uneasy until Billy spoke: 'Well, I think it's a capital idea,' he said, full of smiles. 'The firm's operated in the Middle East before, you know. In the first war, we were selling books and papers to the troops from a bivouac in the desert. So I'm game. Off with you then, Michael, go with Esmond to Egypt! Have a shufti. Don't linger too long and succumb altogether to the delights of the Orient! We need you back here promptly to give us a full account,' he nodded around the room and lifted his walking stick to point to his brother and other board members. 'We're all agreed, aren't we, that Michael and Esmond are to travel out to Cairo with a view to establishing Cairo House, the first overseas branch of the bookselling, newspaper distribution and stationery operation of the firm?'

A frozen sky slid up to the windows of the boardroom, and from the lightlessness, it might have been the close of day rather than eleven-thirty in the morning. Streaks of yesterday's grey sleet dimmed the glass, but it softened the view of the pits and holes, the fanged ruins and smoke-scorched damage to the city outside. Inside the boardroom the assembled members saw none of this. Instead there appeared in their mind's eye camels loaded with panniers packed with *English for Beginners*, the latest novels by Evelyn Waugh, Henry Green, Elizabeth Bowen, and the memoirs of generals and diplomats from the recent history-making epochal events; branches of the family firm were opening their doors in Jerusalem and Beirut, Amman and Damascus, Khartoum, Entebbe and Nairobi, as well as Cairo; there would be trains carrying English literature and English journals, leader writers' and news reports; railway warehouses stacked with cartons en route to institutions all over the continent and the Middle East. The populations were ready for expanding their horizons through knowledge, the knowledge contained in books written by the most prolific and energetic publishing nation in the world – even beside the French, the English reigned supreme. The nation had invented the idea of men of letters, and fostered them, because someone like Billy's grandfather had understood that it's no good leaving books to be found by themselves, any more than it was sufficient to people's needs to leave literature and knowledge to manuscripts alone. Printing had to be invented. Publishing, too, and what were printing and publishing without bookselling?

Without distribution? Without bookshops?

~~~

Drop coloured ink into a glass of water and watch the curls and rills flow through the transparent liquid; they could be the tendrils of a passion-fruit vine, twisting this way and that against the light resistance of the air; drip in another shade, suspended in a denser oil medium, and then pour it out into a flat tray and let the different hues swirl. Marbling allows distinctiveness within a perpetual commingling and holds off complete dissolving of one element into another. When Esmond haunted the many bookstalls during his periods of leave in the capital, he'd picked up stuff that focused on Egypt, its flora and fauna, curiosities and antiquities; fine-grained photographs of antiquities, and many volumes which came with tooled bindings and marbled endpapers. Privately, Esmond knew he wouldn't be trading only in textbooks for English learners but keep a cabinet of fine printings for customers who shared his interests. Michael would appreciate this side of the business, he knew, though it wouldn't bring in much profit. After all, he was the son of the mastermind of bookselling, the great bibliophile St John Hornby, and knew a thing or two about fine book production.

Cosmopolitan Cairo saw the locals mixing and matching their dress, combining *afrangi* or foreign/European items of costume with *baladi* or home-grown styles, a Westerner's jacket or coat, button boots and a turban or fez, shoes and socks from Paris or London worn under the traditional *galabiyya* . . . *Afrangi* comes from the old term for Europeans, Franks, a term that goes back to the Normans from northern France who were called Franks in Sicily and Outremer: in other words, these Europeans were the descendants and connections of the Normandy family of the Hauteville, who produced William the Conqueror as well as the rulers of Outremer, whose kinsmen also subdued the Arab emirs in Sicily in the twelfth century. The root gives other terms that have travelled and taken hold far and wide: in India successive waves of invaders are called Firanji and even as far away from France as Polynesia, the connection persists, always enveloped in a suspect miasma, in spite of its embedded claim to freedom, honesty, openness – frankness, *franchise*.

This cosmopolitan eclecticism of modern Egypt – the historian Nancy Reynolds calls it 'morseling', a kind of marbling, a swirl of disparate elements; she sees a continuum between the morselled look adopted by modernising Egyptians and their whole way of living through the changes to their society. Faruq's Egypt wasn't especially religious; it had a constitution and a parliament, was very powerful in the region, and had ambitions to use that authority to lead. But from the point of view of the locals, post-war Egypt was still held hostage by the British, whose high-handedness was embodied by HM's representative, Sir Miles Lampson. A giant of a man, he had notoriously forced his favoured candidate for prime minister and government on the King in February 1942, by surrounding the Abdin Palace with tanks; the public humiliation of the ruler did not help British dreams of peaceful coexistence. By 1947, although signs of the young king's future dissipation and undoing were starting, Faruq was not yet loathed. But nobody told Michael Hornby and Esmond Warner about the depths of this state of tension everywhere in Egypt and beyond, or perhaps they were warned and chose not to hear, during those encouraging soundings they made about the potential of a new book business in Cairo.

9

The Rankers' Club Bridge Book

A calf-bound set of score cards, printed by Asprey & Co. Ltd, with an inscription in fountain pen on the flyleaf:

Rankers' Club, Oxford. The club was founded sometime in 1929 but it was not until May 10th that this book was purchased on which date the undersigned original members were present.
Esmond Warner President
[Earl of] Ava Secretary
Charles Mitchell Exec. Sec.
Robin Mount
Herbert Sheftel [known as Buzzie] (Bell-Hop)

The original foundation of the Club should provide a fertile ground for historical research. The used pages have been torn out along the perforated margins provided so the stakes of the bridge games, the winnings and losses of the players, remain unknown.

~~~

The seaplane was listing on the scummy water of the harbour at Marseilles; like an oversized buoy which larger craft had collided with, it looked dented and lopsided and Esmond wouldn't have been surprised if it had boomed out a sad knell. They were due to set off for Malta, but there wasn't enough fuel to reach the island, where some passengers were putting off, and others, bound for Cairo, were to join the vessel. Esmond was hoping for some local wine, too: Malta had access to better supplies than the south of France, as they had found to their great disappointment.

The pale February sunshine of the Riviera bathed them luxuriously after the bitter spell of the winter in England, and Esmond felt he was in luck to be headed for Egypt to reconnoitre. Michael had seen a chance to escape the dismal mood back home where everything was in short supply and everyone seemed to be winded. It was moot whether trade outside England in a part of the world that was so unsettled and divided would be a sound business prospect, but Michael had the streak of adventure necessary to the making of fortunes and Esmond's reminiscences of wartime Cairo caught Michael's imagination.

The wreckage at home meant that after the initial surge of triumph and the relief at an end to the fighting, victory tasted strangely like its opposite. It gave shape to vague ambitions that the victory could bring about a new time, and that a new world was in the making. Besides, in the bleak beginning of 1947 running down to the south of France with a view to crossing the Mediterranean was almost like a jaunt from the old days before the war.

But, for the time being, they were stalled in Marseilles, in mounting exasperation, while the seaplane company were trying to extract supplies of fuel from the dealers in the unmarked entrepôts behind the harbour. A fussed official assured the English gentlemen and the rest of the passengers, who were assembled waiting in the departure shed or sitting it out on capstans on the wharf, that it wouldn't be long – someone had talked of a large new shipment and they had contacts; it was promised by someone close to the chain of command (the informant waggled a finger to his nose, tapping knowingly, grinning) and the barrels would soon be rolling towards them down the quay and the process of filling the plane's tanks could begin.

'How about a game of something to while away the hours?' Esmond suggested. 'Piquet? Just the pair of us – or if we can rustle up a game of four?' He looked over their fellow passengers waiting with suitcases here and there in the boatyard that gave on to the pontoons where the seaplane was moored. 'We might at least get a hand of rummy, what do you say?'

Michael agreed that there was clearly time enough for Esmond to go in search of a pack of cards in the streets behind the harbour. 'Try and find some more of those ciggies, too, old boy – while you're at it.'

Esmond had French, acquired in the casinos and on the golf courses of Le Touquet, Biarritz, Monte Carlo and Nice before the war, and more lately primed with Levantine elements from furloughs in Cairo during the desert campaign.

'Ah, we'll be well supplied in that quarter when we reach Cairo, don't worry, what!' Esmond set off along the quayside, his old pink sun-faded sailing hat squashed on his head, though the sun was mild and sweet overhead. But he didn't want the tips of his ears scorched, as had happened excruciatingly in North Africa and even later in Italy when he'd driven about with Prestridge in the open jeep trying to match the map to the lie of the land where every single identifying signpost or landmark had been torn out by the retreating Germans. Then Ilia had appeared with her sisters and they'd tried out their English – their American – on the British who'd arrived and helped them find their bearings. Ilia, who was now in the country in England, shivering, with the new baby . . .

When Esmond was gone to look for a pack of cards, Michael Hornby perched his briefcase on his knees and began composing his first report to his chairman, who would have come too, having given his approval to the recce. But his doctors wouldn't allow him to travel – he hadn't recovered from the shrapnel that exploded beside him, spattering him from his face to his feet, and indeed, though nobody admitted it aloud, Michael knew that Billy was dying (as indeed he did, about a year after the Cairo branch opened). Michael began by inquiring with genuine sympathy after Billy's health: 'Dear Old Boy, I feel so guilty, that I am sitting here in the sun. I hope you will take a rest and come south as soon as practicable; it would do you so much good. Esmond is terrific company and has gone on the trail of a pack of cards . . . We are waiting to embark for Cairo but there is no fuel here either, and we shall see how long we have to wait. Still, it is very pleasant, I fear, to be out of England.'

When they at last reached Cairo, Michael wrote a fourteen-page letter to his chairman:

Shepheard's Hotel

13.2.47

My dear Billy

We have now been here three days & I feel there is enough to tell to write you an interim report. You will have heard of our exasperating delay at Marseilles. 4 days of suspended anima-tion when one could never look far enough ahead to make any plans as every minute one was hoping to get away. About the only ray of sunshine was finding Raymond de T.[rafford] there the day before we left! He is living in Paris now & was in Marseilles trying to bring off a deal in surplus anti-gas capes

& jerrycans! We spent an amusing evening with him, & he
regaled us with some very frank reminiscences of his sojourn
in Maidstone and Parkhurst. Our fellow passengers were a
very motley collection, but a strong 'esprit de corps' developed
among us & we all found out each other's life history.

   We eventually left Marseilles at lunchtime on Monday,
had tea at Malta & flew straight on from there arriving here
at 2.30 a.m. – the flying was very smooth & pleasant &
there is really something rather romantic about such a
'magic carpet' sort of journey.

Is it priggish of me, now, more than seventy years on, to quail
at the thought of that amusing evening with Raymond de
Trafford, star soak of Happy Valley in Kenya in the 1920s?
He'd been in prison because in 1939, drunk as a lord (that
phrase!), he'd killed a man in a car crash, but was even more
notorious because his lover Alice de Janzé shot him – and
then turned the gun on herself – after he told her they couldn't
marry because his parents had threatened to disinherit him if
he did. She missed her aim in both cases, and he gained yet
more notoriety when he spoke in her defence at the trial for
his attempted murder. Did my father laugh with that big
laugh of his as this member of the old Irish peerage, the
embodiment of the flagrantly louche high life, entertained the
becalmed party bound for Cairo with his jailbird adventures?
   Michael Hornby's wife Nicole was partly Dutch; she equalled
his height and racehorse legginess, which made her look
Dietrich-like, and manly. She was a plantswoman, strong and
gaunt, who strode about in a ragged canvas hat, snipping here
and there with her secateurs at her prize-winning herbaceous
border. She was also a fine seamstress, perhaps a kind of lace-
maker in the Dutch tradition, and when she met Ilia in 1947
for the first time, while their husbands were laying plans, they

were left together and Nic showed her guest how to smock baby clothes. Her nimble embroidery came as a surprise, bringing to mind a sailor knitting. But Ilia liked sewing baby clothes – blue and green covered the chance of a boy, and she made a romper suit from a light voile cotton printed with peacock feather design, stitched in contrasting colours around the collar and the hem, with a tucked panel of smocking in red and green and brown embroidery thread, elasticated.

[From Michael Hornby,
13 February 1947, cont.]

Cairo simply beggars description. There is the real boom-town atmosphere with sleek, gleaming brand-new American cars gliding by in their thousands, the streets blazing with neon lights at night, the shops bulging with everything the mind can conceive & the food unbelievable & half the price of Paris or Brussels. The climate is perfection, like an ideal fine day, but always a cool breeze. It makes one feel such a cad when one reads of more fuel cuts at home. The flowers & flowering trees are lovely. Roses, anthuriums, stocks, sweet peas, bougainvillea, & lots of things I don't know the name of all in full flower.

Now having made your mouth water, I must get to business.

They had been very busy meeting people, starting with the British Embassy, then bankers, then local businessmen; they went about it thoroughly as they tested out the prospects for a booksellers. It's likely they consulted Robin Furness, an old Middle Eastern hand, who'd had many jobs – he'd been the Oriental Secretary in the Embassy and then began teaching at Fuad I University, but settled on the British Council (Thomas Hodgkin writing from Palestine in 1935 described him as 'a pleasant and gallant rather devilish old rake' – Robin and his wife Joy would become friends, and Mary, their daughter, later my playfellow at Gezira Sporting Club). These contacts confirmed continuing tensions between the British and the Egyptians and between the many Egyptian parties themselves but they made light of them, and while Michael and Esmond were in the city, the king's 27th birthday was celebrated in the streets and passed without incident: this was reassuring. The people they consulted were happy to encourage them: the times were right for such a venture. The British pre-eminence in world trade, and Egyptian need, dominated these conversations: they could not do without us, rang out the confident voices for going ahead.

[From Michael Hornby,
13 February 1947, cont.]

In my opinion, based on all I have heard, though there are probably difficult times ahead for the next year or so, they are developing so quickly on the line of Western civilisation that they <u>cannot</u> do without us & our professors, our techni- cians or our books. Also, on the purely commercial view we are their best customers & they must therefore trade with us, apart from the fact that they have enormous sterling credits which will remain on paper if they do not buy our goods.

This sound of British expansionism, familiar once again in the Brexit years, which rings so loudly among antagonists of the European Union, was accompanied by a strategy which once more figures strongly, as Michael Hornby and my father called in on the British Council and other representatives of English culture:

We have seen a good deal of the British Council people – all a first-class type – and they are naturally very struck

with the idea of our opening here, as we could back them
up strongly in trying to promote the distribution of the
right type of book and periodical. Their policy is more and
more to spread the gospel through the ordinary commercial
channels and not through free distribution . . . Under the
aegis of the British Council comes the British Institute,
which directs a number of educational and cultural
networks which actually has 1,200 Egyptian students from
the age of 18 upwards who attend class there & are
prepared for examinations etc. We had some very good talks
there and are seeing the chief educational book buyer
tomorrow. The field for educational books both here and
throughout the Middle East ought to be enormous.

He was still wary, however. But, by the third day in Cairo,
Esmond had won him over: 'Esmond is a splendid companion,
very intelligent and quick, excellent company, and he makes
a first-rate impression on everyone we meet. Practically every
word he said to me at home has been corroborated by what I
have heard here, and I think he had sized up the situation
wonderfully accurately.'

W. H. Smith and Son,   Cairo House,   1948.

W.H. Smith & Son, Cairo House, Sikket el-Fadl, Cairo.

My father had settled on renting **premises, in the heart of downtown**, in one of the small side streets off one of the elegant radiating avenues from Ismailia Square, unofficially known, since the 1919 uprising, as Tahrir Square; with lotus-bud topknots on each corner, it was a square, two-storey, modern concrete building with a basement; the overall look was authentic oriental art deco, recalling the craze for Assyrian-Theban-Ancient-Egyptian style of the old Carreras cigarette factory, that North London temple to the Egyptian cat goddess Bastet, but not as vast or as brightly painted.

The building at 3 Sikket el-Fadl, in downtown Cairo, was the property of a member of the great Adès family, who would give the booksellers from London a fair price.

Esmond Warner's telegraphic address was to be 'Bookman, Cairo'.

10

The Cemetery at Rayol

Cap Nègre rises up, impregnably, it seems, at the western end of the long smooth sickle of the beach at Cavalière where on a calm morning, the Mediterranean laps in scallops of aqua and pearl. The time we went there on holiday one summer, my father would take me for a swim before breakfast; we were staying in the Grand Hotel Moriaz which gave directly on to the beach from the hotel dining room, which stood on decking in the sand, and was shaded by slatted reeds. But that sea isn't tranquil and in August storms can churn the waves to a fury as they had done ten years earlier during the Allies' landings the length of this shore. To the east, towards Saint-Tropez and Cannes and the Riviera, scissored limestone cliffs plunge their footholds in the sea, and small pebbly coves provide deep anchorage – this is, after all, the Côte d'Azur! – and another sandy beach, smaller but still popular with bathers and yachtsmen curves under the linked villages of Rayol and Le Canadel. Midnight on the turn of 14 August 1944: Operation Dragoon was to secure the Mediterranean ports. The original plan was timed to coincide with the D-Day landings in Normandy in June, but the Allies' resources were stretched beyond any possibility of providing this pincer support. So the assault was delayed till later that summer, and the generals then chose the soaring bluff of Cap Nègre for one of the approaches, because they reckoned – rightly – that the enemy would discount any attempt to scale it. But scale it they did, the troops of the Free French, put together by the US, Britain and the French resistance. After the troops landed in their thousands along the more westerly beaches, intense fighting broke out, between the Germans in occupation and the Allies, with local *résistants* appearing out of the *maquis* to lend their support. In the hand-to-hand fighting in the villages and on the road, many died.

I found myself back in the area around forty years later, because I had a dear friend, Rick Mather, who was an architect and had bought a 1930s villa on the coast road between Rayol and Cavalière, with a grand view of the sea sweeping from the domaine on a headland to the east to Cap Nègre to the west. I used to go for a walk into the village and began to notice memorials of different sizes and grandeur on the beaches and punctuating the coast road; they mark what is now called the Chemin de la Libération. I recognised the place, experiencing that eerie sense of time folding up against itself and bringing back my child self, turning me into my own revenant. My father had chosen to come here for our first family holiday in France after we left Egypt. In the heat of the summer, Ilia liked to go somewhere to sunbathe and swim – she had after all been brought up in Bari, which sits on a long wide beach on the Adriatic coast. But Esmond, a former redhead, couldn't take the sun, so if he weren't to be horribly burned, he had to swim before the sun's heat took hold. He then liked to spend the day wandering about, sun hat on his head, guidebook and field glasses in hand. Historic sites attracted him.

One day, on my way back from the boulangerie, I noticed a small enclosure set a little way back from the road, the flag of the République hoisted rather woebegonely above it; there, in a gravel-strewn plot, thirteen small graves are lined up like the tucked-up beds in a dorm. Approaching, the inscriptions became legible. First, three French officers:

Texier, Noel – *Adjutant-chef*
Moyet, Jean – *Sergent*
Guillemot, Eugène – *Sergent-chef*

Then four '*soldats*':

Poussard, Serge
Beaulieu, Pierre
Jouvenceau, Marcel
Pancrazi, Jacques

Their tombs are marked by crosses. But beside them, three graves carry the ogive steles typical of Muslim tombs, inscribed under the sickle moon and star of Islam:

Benachenhou, Ghouti – *Caporal*
Aksouri, Mihoud – *Soldat*
Abdesselem, Ben Ali – *Soldat*

All died 15 August 1944. Three more men were killed the following day:

Lemaire, André
Nardeaux, René
Vallauris, Gaston

The main monumental stone, at the entrance, reads: 'In this necropolis the bodies lie at rest of the first French combatants coming from Africa who fell on the soil of Provence for the liberation of France.'

An information sheet, sun-faded under cracked plastic, provides the history: on this very spot, in hand-to-hand fighting, these men were killed, one of them the first to die on French soil in the campaign that helped liberate the country. They were Les Commandos d'Afrique, the specialist amphibian troops of the French army, and many of them – for example, the Senegalese famous for their *tirailleurs*, or sharp-shooters – were colonial subjects, and formed a major part of the forces de Gaulle raised for the Free French from the full extent of the French Empire, just as the Allies did in the First and Second World Wars. From all over the African continent, they joined up; as well as from the Antilles, or French Caribbean, the Ile de la Réunion, Mauritius, and so on.

The cemetery at Rayol is an inconspicuous memorial, all the more impressive for the story it alludes to so elliptically. When Frantz Fanon, in the French *département* d'Outre-Mer of Martinique – therefore a *citoyen*, not a colonial subject – joined up to fight for France, he was one of thousands whose contribution to the Allied cause was vital. The same can be said about the British armies and their colonial forces: from Canada, India, the Caribbean . . . Iris Origo, keeping her vivid notes about how she and her household survived the war, learnt in the summer of 1944 that the Allies had broken through and were approaching to liberate them. She was disappointed, she admits in her journal (and did not edit for publication), to hear that they were 'coloured'.

Perhaps it was because Plum, Esmond's father, was born and raised in Trinidad, and learned the game he loved among the people of the island, that Esmond would not have been surprised at all at the intertwining of history.

Along the same coastal road, D559, there rises a steepling shard, built of brick, where it takes a big bend on a high point above the beach at Rayol. The plaque adds an important detail: 'You who pass by remember the volunteers of the group of Commandos of Africa who disembarked on the soil of the fatherland at midnight on 14 August 1944, and whose bodies mark this coast of Provence.'

The fresh detail is that the troops were volunteers.

These liberators of Europe suffered when, in the aftermath of independence movements, they found their former allegiance stigmatised them; if they consequently left their own countries for France or Britain to escape ostracism, they found they often met with a hostile reception in those countries; this has not much diminished.

Though Esmond was such a thoroughgoing example of old-school-tie connections, he understood these historical bonds, from his experiences during the war and his life before then. To some extent, his falling in love with Ilia cohered with the trust he felt in foreignness.

He turned to Cairo for these reasons, but his experiences there were to change him.

A Bill of Lading

S ilver Antique Furniture and Original Paintings
The Property of Mr and Mrs E.P. Warner
To be sent from England to Egypt

According to the shippers, fourteen boxes were sent to Cairo
in the spring of 1947. Esmond had found a splendid flat, on
the top floor of Soliman House, a ten-storey modern block
with art deco ornaments, wrought-iron fittings and jutting
rounded balconies in Cairo-style Streamline Moderne; from
the front it looked out towards the Qasr al-Nil bridge with
its Pharaonic guardian lions and tall pillar lanterns, and over
the river to downtown and the grand department stores, the
hotels and bars, and the Mouski, Cairo's overflowing bazaar.
From the back you could see the green spread of Gezira
Sporting Club. The building is still there, at 10, Sharia el
Gezirah, the road that runs along the river on the eastern side
of the island of Zamalek.

The shippers' inventory lists items thought necessary and appropriate for setting up a home in a distant place where certain standards had to be kept up, and includes silver and silver plate – lots of it: dredgers and ewers and cream jugs and small 'muffineers'. The first entry reads: '13 silver inkstands, 1 broken'. It then continues:

snuffers
a punch ladle
paperknives (7)
sealing wax holders
pincushions and tea strainers
a snuff case
a bridge box
wine labels (12)
tea caddies
silver button hook and shoe lift
combination tantalus frames

The last entry reads '2 doz cheese, and 2 doz table knives'.

Esmond has checked the insurers' inventory on a separate document, and here and there added an item. He was setting up in a certain style, a style that breathes the spirit of the tribe as strongly as a potlatch copper or a Tepik mask. The insurance list specifies:

6 very large pistol grip knives valued at £10.0.0
1 marrow scoop £1.15.0
1 taper stick (George I) £20.0.0
1 plated grape scissors £1.0.0
4 decanters for port and sherry

The tantalus was for locking up bottles so 'the staff can't tipple'. Esmond also shipped from London the drinks cabinet in walnut veneer that he'd designed himself. With the carpets and furniture, the whole shipment was valued at £1,393, a surprising sum for someone who, like Esmond, considered himself penniless.

~~~

More than a heap of tableware, more than a young married couple's first property, was bundled up in those fourteen parcels: a way of life, a class and its expectations, a man and his self-image, a handbook of social conventions, a moment in history, and an identikit portrait of my father. It flooded me – still floods me – with conflicted feelings: somewhere between amazement at how things were and how they have changed, embarrassment at the assumptions behind that journey into Egypt, and of course a sharp sense of absurdity and pathos. These were the goods of his people, to keep him moored to home ground while he was abroad.

Was Esmond thinking of trading in some of these items included in the bill of lading? The quantities of silver do seem excessive. Given his interest in 'things', and his connoisseurship in furniture, prints and antiquities, perhaps he'd started dealing in antiques and imagined he might continue on the side, alongside books and stationery in the new branch of W.H. Smith's. Or perhaps he imagined silverware might be used to barter, as had often been necessary in the chaotic conditions in bombed cities with defeated inhabitants during the war? Or were these stray wedding presents sent to Plum and Mother Rat by friends, on hearing the news of their eldest son's long-awaited marriage?

The list remains mute.

Esmond had bought some more stuff for the flat at the Mouski: several Persian and Turkish rugs, curly-framed gilded mirrors, brass trays engraved with paisley *butis* and scalloped edges; a brass coffee pot with a toucan bill for a spout; little ruby glasses, also gilded and flowery, for drinking tea; a bronze sculpture of a crane eating a snake twined round its legs. Two 'Nubians', polychrome figures with ebony skin in green harem trousers and short crimson jackets, holding up lamps with a vigorous twist of their torsos, would add a touch of local colour. He ordered a dressing table and stool for my mother; it had bulky, rounded drawers, made of some kind of heavy yellow wood like the hide of a camel; she would drape it in pink spotted tulle over a heavier satin underskirt, with braiding and a frill to define the kidney-shaped contour of the tabletop. It's a piece made to look machine-tooled and modern; but it is handmade, each of the drawers being slightly different so that you have to put them back in the right order. There were also many views of Egypt to be hung on the walls of the Zamalek flat, picturesque Victorian prints by travellers and archaeologists of the ruins and the pyramids and Old Cairo, which Esmond was to search out from antiquarians in the city: Roman pillars, drowned temples, dhows like drawn bows on the Nile, colossal fallen gods of stone, camel trains, the dappled light under the screens in the suq, the desert dotted with tiny figures of herdsmen in the shade of ancient monuments with their animals.

The bill of lading reveals that my mother had no such effects. When she arrived in London alone after the war, with her hatbox and the dresses she had made herself and a handful of books, she brought next to nothing.

There were no snuffboxes or grape scissors or marrow scoops or combination tantalus frames in Puglia – or at least not in her family's flat in Bari. Her world is absent from this list.

PART III

in Cairo

1947-49

Malesh

alesh: English doesn't have a precise equivalent for this word, which would be sighed with eyes lifted heavenwards, a fatalistic shrug of the shoulders, or slow spreading of the hands. The term implies weariness and acceptance, but no bitterness, rather a certain degree of voluptuous surrender to fate. It's an Arabic word, but it also perpetuates an orientalist stereotype, because it's associated with languor and drift. It's not *tant pis*, which carries a tinge of devil may-care and sour grapes; even the English versions of *tant pis* – 'never mind', 'oh well', 'that's how it goes', 'more's the pity' – have an awkward, even fustian feel, close to 'alas!' – the latter's use in English, always in invisible quotation marks, often sounds like archaic hyperbole, too extreme to be truly meant. *Malesh* has ironic overtones too – sometimes speakers are only pretending that all lies in the lap of the gods, and that they have no control over events or their outcome.

It's almost interchangeable with *inshallah* but *inshallah* is more trusting and pious and expresses a hope for better things. Both terms echo the Italian uses of *magari*, but *malesh* implies more despondency and less defiance (it invokes no kindly god), as if any expression of optimism might ricochet on the speaker. Like *magari*, *malesh* is also trying to keep jealous fate from noticing and taking revenge and is often uttered to avert disaster. Its meanings shift between a casual shrugging off – as in 'never mind', 'it can't be helped' and 'no worries' – an expression of sympathy, 'I'm sorry to hear that', and a deeper sigh over the vagaries of fate. It can also convey an apology. My mother used to say that *malesh* caught the Egyptians' strong sense of fatality, that nothing could be done to change anything – *malesh*, 'that's how it goes', 'there we are', 'don't kick against the pricks', 'dream on'.

Yet its resignation can be used to comfort someone, shading from 'let's hope' towards 'never mind' and 'there there'. Like *magari*, it can be another way of crossing fingers that nothing worse can happen. Such terms are shifting and they're rich in implicatures, as when a speaker attributes an eventuality or behaviour to someone in the hope that this will bring about the desired outcome. They're filled with far more power and magic than mere sighs or cries or empty interjections such as 'like, you know'. *Malesh*, like *magari*, belongs to the subjunctive mood, to wishful thinking, to fatalism in retrospect and superstitious hopefulness for the future. Both words are left over from a time of pervasive apocalypticism that used speech acts to withstand danger, like guardian monsters at the entrance to a home.

Malesh is one word of Arabic that I never forgot. There are a few others: *habibti* – darling, sweetie; and *mish-mish* – which means apricot but is often used for a pussy cat. Several words have migrated and partly settled in English, like meze and lokum, pasha and khedive, hookah and narghile, tarbush and fez, babouches, galabiyya, houris and hashish, divan and sofa, trailing a feeling of a world where human beings lie back and let life and its complexities flow over them. Sofa: of course, this had to be borrowed; of course, there had never been sofas before the West went east. Pews and settles, couches and benches, yes, straight-backed and hard, but daybeds and sofas, divans and ottomans awaited discovery. They had to be imported (and they became the sites of pornographic imaginings, invoked by titles of eighteenth-century *littérature galante*, and its orientalising mockery).

When I was a child in Cairo, and learning from the grown-ups around me, I'd say if I broke a toy or dropped honey from a cake down my front, and I remembered the word – and went on using it with my mother – when the rest of my knowledge of the language had fallen away.

Early memory i

Hoopoes

*My young Italian mother went out — or rather, my father and
mother went out — every night in Cairo, around 8.30 p.m., to go
to a party, and she wore lovely rustling skirts of tulle and taffeta
with bodices she embroidered and beaded herself; she tinkled and
rang with her bracelets and jewels when she clasped me close to say
goodnight, and she smelt delicious. She was 24 when we arrived in
Egypt, from a bleak, rationed England and before that from Italy
where there had been shortages for years alongside a vicious black
market, and she and her sisters used to make their much-admired
outfits from old tablecloths and curtains (or perhaps I have mixed
her up with Scarlett O'Hara, who figured vividly in my mother's
mythology). But there were no shortages in Cairo for us, the society
milling about the foreign embassies and local high society and on
the fringes of the court. King Faruq was young and fat and rich
and gambled wildly and had lots of foreign girlfriends and drank
only orangeade and liked to play feeble conjuring tricks on guests
who couldn't object when he lifted their wallets or their watches
and smiled knowingly. Daddy made contemptuous remarks about
him: he was a poltroon, and his loyalties flickered — he had to be
kept in line. That was what was said, then.*

In the mornings on the front balcony, Mummy sat hemming her clothes by hand, stitching buttonholes and adding other fine details to her cocktail frocks as well as making my clothes and smocking my dresses – every fastening (hooks and eyes, press studs, zips) all sewn as if someone would be inspecting them closely and demand a certain standard. She even made her own underclothes in those days. Her petticoats with lace trims and satin straps were suffused with her warmth and smell that I searched for in the night when I had a bad dream.

The dresses which she was making for soirées and concerts and supper parties swirled full layered skirts of taffeta and silk from her tiny waist, made up from bolts of damask figured with roses on gold satin, of embroidered brocade in a colour with no name (magenta/chestnut/vieux rose); she made frocks of flowery prints with broderie anglaise and ribbon trimmings and tulle petticoats, according to the latest fashions Paris had introduced to proclaim the end of wartime shortages. In Europe, very few could manage such extravagance.

She was always aghast at my slapdash workmanship – as a teenager, I'd run a party outfit through the sewing machine at the very last minute on the largest possible (and therefore fastest) stitch settings and not bother with anything that wasn't immediately visible. Today, I still use the small pair of scissors she used to nip the threads on the inside of a seam she had knotted and secured and trim the fabric to the edge she had overstitched to prevent fraying on the inside (she was shocked the nuns at my school advocated using pinking shears).

While her head was bent down over her stitching, hoopoes sometimes flew down around her to feed on the crumbs from her lunch. With flowery corsages and beaded bodices, the clothes she was making floated and fluttered like the birds at their flirty display, spreading their dappled wings and raising their tail feathers and sharp crests as they flew down to share our breakfast.

12

A Record Collection

An album of Hildegarde's hits, His Master's Voice, 1922–38: two volumes, bound in red morocco (imitation); inside, stacked side by side, discs of show tunes and dance numbers, both sturdy and fragile in their blue paper sleeves and shellacked, brittle, patent leather blackness. The trademark dog's a bit stocky, possibly some kind of terrier – a Jack Russell? – though I don't know about dog breeds and dogs' looks seem also to have changed since the 1930s – the equivalent of hemlines rising and falling happens in canine aesthetics, too. The dog's ears aren't especially pricked, but rather lie flattened to his head, but the angle of this head, the alertness of his straight posture, together with his open eye and inquisitive nose pointing into the mouth of the horn of the gramophone – already antiquated by the time these albums were pressed – add up to an appearance of total listening: he is tuning in to what he is hearing with every one of his senses, not only his ears, even perhaps assessing how edible the music issuing from the machine might prove to be. (The two bulky albums have a rather biscuity aroma, from many teatimes when Ilia would toast crumpets in honour of tradition.)

Esmond first saw Hildegarde perform in 1928 at the Adelphi supper club and became her adoring fan. Each album contains twelve discs, heavy as plumb-line lead, sheathed in ultramarine endpapers with matching sleeves, each with a round browny-red or dark blue label, giving the song title and listing the names of the performers: 'Listen to the German Band' was one of Hildegarde's greatest hits of the Thirties. Its lyrics mock German militarism, and found favour with H.G. Wells, as Hildegarde would remember on *The Dick Cavett Show* half a century and another world war later.

The records are sheathed inside the albums in sleeves which the bookbinders for HMV fluted and pleated so that the thick vinyl discs have enough room to sit side by side without cracking; they added a flap on the outer edge to tuck the records in. The chemical dye in the paper has faded as, even inside the small mahogany cabinet, enough light managed to reach and leach colour until it turned a variety of shades of blue, suggesting something emergent, not yet quite set firm. These shifting blues seep into the tunes that Hildegarde sings on the records as she accompanies herself on the piano, wearing gloves as she always did, sometimes with a big band backing her – the first of these was called the Baby Grands, and later there were many other numbers, sung with Carroll Gibbons and His Boy Friends (ah, guileless times), and lots 'With Mantovani and his *tipica orchestra*'.

Looking at the dog, I was the dog; I became one of the pets of the singer, that Incomparable Hildegarde (she would arrive at Dover with an animal or two, and protest in hot indignation that she had to place them in quarantine for months). Like the Inuit fisherman who, in Robert Flaherty's film *Nanook of the North* (1922), picks up the record that has been playing on the turntable and bites on it to test it for properties that it might share with other things that live and move and speak, the dog in me wanted to go beyond listening and pass through the audible and the tangible into what has evaporated and taste it, eat it . . . commune with the person whose voice was coming out of the shiny black planet in orbit on the gramophone.

∼∼∼

One evening, when my mother came into the nursery to say goodnight, she was all dressed up in the emerald cocktail frock with the full ray-pleated skirt, gathered into a slender, satin bodice with padding to fill out her small breasts, and fluted according to the latest technology. She couldn't hug me without mussing herself up, but as she bent over my bed to blow me a kiss, the delicious scent she wore wrapped me as closely as her arms would have done. Her bracelets chinked and clinked; from one hung the souvenir charms from cities my father had taken her to – the Colosseum in Rome and (the most recent, for her 25th birthday) the Great Pyramid of Giza, which he had bought in the gold market of the central suq – while from the other dangled heraldic seals set with gemstones: this sound remains my first memory of her being near.

That evening in 1948, Sir Robert Greg, a longtime influential figure in the city, had invited the couple to join his party at the New Year gala at the Opera House. It was their first Christmas season and for days before, Esmond was tense with excitement; Ilia too. Of all the contacts he had made, his friendship with Sir Robert made him glow with more happiness and pride than any other, and this surprising and exclusive summons surpassed all Esmond's achievements in making his way in Egypt. Greg had first come to the country before the First World War, working in what was called 'the British Agency', the dominant arm of the Occupation; when promotion took him elsewhere, he'd longed to return, finally securing, in 1929, the unique and powerful post of 'British Commissioner for the Egyptian Debt'. He administered his heavy duties exactingly, but still left himself a great deal of time to pursue his chief passion, collecting antiquities. He had a beautiful garden villa on Sharia Wisa Wasif, in Giza to the west, and he'd filled it with Egyptian treasures, carpets, lamps and furniture. My father used to chuckle with appreciation that Sir Robert's figurines – a splendid array of small bronzes and the gorgeous ancient turquoise-glazed faience statuettes – gleamed subtly, by contrast with their dusty counterparts in the Cairo Museum. The Greg legacy finally arrived at the Fitzwilliam in Cambridge in 1964 (after some difficulties following the Suez crisis), and Esmond would remember, 'Sir Robert always said, "Look how my things gleam! That is because I dust them myself every day – with a goose wing."'

The following morning at breakfast, after the concert and a late night party at Shepheard's Hotel, my tired but jubilant parents were full of the evening's entertainment and their unexpected inclusion in Cairo's *gratin*: King Faruq had been there at the Opera House, plumper than ever, filling the royal box, and *le tout Caire* were seated on the velvet armchairs in the stalls below, the men coiffed in fezes, the women in sparkling rocks, and for the first time, Ilia and Esmond had heard live and in person the *diva assoluta* of the Middle East, Umm Kulthum, when she made a surprise appearance, to exultant applause. The Voice of Egypt, the adored performer of classical Arabic poetry, of wild yearning, homesickness and loss of love, sang to a phalanx of string-players and lifted far above their heavy sawing of their instruments, as with dizzy and inventive ornamentation and long sustained vocal cadenzas she inspired sighs and acclaim from the audience.

'She is rather well-covered,' said Ilia (it was her word for fat), 'but then singers need to be, it helps their voices to resonate.'

'Yes, *plantureuse*, indeed. Yet Hildegarde was as slim as . . . you, old girl.' Her husband had taken to calling her old girl, which she did not yet resent, though she would, later. 'And she had a lovely voice and the technique to match.'

Ilia, who had been so jealous and possessive during their courtship, now liked to hear about Hildegarde, a girlfriend of her husband's from before the war. She was smiling, purringly, 'I wonder if they know each other? Could it be that Umm Kulthum has picked up some tricks from Hildegarde? It seems such a coincidence, the way Umm waved her beautiful embroidered hanky as she was singing.'

It was always surprising to me that my mother seemed to approve.

'It's just one of those things . . . a fashion. You're the one for fashion!'

'Magazines keep me up to date.'

'There you are . . . Hildegarde is featured in all the magazines! For heaven's sake, she was on the cover of *Life* in 1939. That's exactly when we were chums. I'd lay a hundred to one Umm Kulthum noticed her rival in the supper clubs and stole an idea or two!'

'But she doesn't wear gloves, not like Hildegarde. They're her trademark – long, elegant cerise gloves,' Ilia gestured up to her elbows and higher, 'suede, velvet, luxury gloves.'

'She wasn't, not last night, but you never know.'

'The Incomparable Hildegarde' trailed clouds of sultry glamour from Berlin and Paris, of the Blue Angel, Mistinguett and Arletty, foreshadowing more recent divas – Dalida, Madonna – and she liked to lay claim to this quasi-royal first-name intimacy as a novelty she had introduced.

During the bleak aftermath of war, when victory had not brought an end to the struggles to keep up appearances in the beau monde of Cairo, it was rallying for Ilia to think that inside anxious, well-covered Esmond there was a young man about town, unlikely as it now seemed. A blade, a swell, a Bertie Wooster – 'There's a fine fellow', and 'He's a good chap, I say, what?' Ilia looked at the English soldier she had married a few years before, and she could clothe him in a younger self, a more exciting, raffish young man, freckled and golden-haired, sitting at a linen-covered supper table where the champagne bucket was dissolving in puddles, listening tipsily and enthralled to the singer's whispered accented witty lyrics, as the singer accompanied herself on the piano sheathed in her silks with her sleek gloves over the elbow and the rings on the outside, exchanged smiles with the red-haired young man in the garnet-studded dress shirt and initialled cufflinks who had come every night that week when she was visiting London, who, in 1928, she thought must be the fan who, knowing she wore only white gowns and liked only white flowers, had sent a white rose round to the stage door the night before.

Inquiring into a parent's sex life, especially before he had even met your mother and your existence was not even imagined, feels vertiginous and voyeuristic as well as a bit sordid, but I have long been curious about the family story that my father had a long love affair with a nightclub singer, 'Chanteuse Internationale, Hildegarde'.

The voice is melodious, light and silvery, the delivery whimsical; she can sound as if she's on the verge of pealing laughter even as she yearns and croons. She queened it in the supper clubs, doing numbers such as 'I'm in the Mood for Love', 'Cheek to Cheek', 'Gloomy Sunday', 'The Touch of Your Lips'. It was the apogee of the big show tune, of Irving Berlin and Cole Porter, and many less remembered composers and lyricists for the stage and screen. Her trademark – her USP – was jumbling languages: she was fluent across borders, at home here, there, anywhere. She mixed up English and German with a bit of French and Spanish: 'Darling, Je Vous Aime Beaucoup' was her signature song. Even when the lyrics were in English, she sang in a slight accent and sounded vaguely French or German.

The gramophone itself was rather a distance away, across the hall and the sitting room on the covered verandah over-looking the Nile where Ilia and Esmond would sit together and listen to music – to numbers from the films of Ginger Rogers and Fred Astaire, to Sinatra and Ella and Satchmo – both of them singing along, Esmond strumming with his fingers, cheerfully out of tune, Ilia doing a fair imitation of crooning, with added vibrato. Sometimes Esmond would stand and sway, lifting himself on the balls of his feet and swinging his hips, stepping out as he hummed under his breath. It was an incongruous sight, not only for being so very out of character for the man we knew, but also because something about his shape made the movements comical. By the 1950s, the trousers of his suits were cut with a high waist so that they hung straight down over his expanse of belly – an art that tailors for the retail trade today haven't mastered, leaving tummies cruelly bounded and defined by belts done up below the bulge (in the case of men) or above (in the case of women).

He wouldn't initiate a session of listening to his old flame. But when one of us – usually me – carefully carried a shellac disc across the polished floor of the hall into the carpeted sanctuary where they spent most of their time to settle the record on the stalk of the turntable, and the notes from her piano would announce the tune, he knew all the words and sang along with her 'Darling, je vous aime beaucoup / Je ne sais pas what to do . . .' She sang as a man wooing a girl whose language he doesn't know: my sister and I recognised the situation, as we knew our parents couldn't really communicate when they first met.

'You know I appreciate your beautiful friendship. Fondly, Hildegarde', c. 1930.

Inside the flap of volume 1 of the album, next to the careful inventory of songs written out in my father's handwriting, an envelope was filled with photographs: two sepia studio portraits, both inscribed in black ink with a flourish. One of them says:

To dear Esmond:
A fine, charming
person – May you always be
happy, and have all the good things

your heart desires.
You know I appreciate your
beautiful friendship.
Fondly
Hildegarde

The singer looks very young in these studio shots: she poses wearing a twisted hair band of black and white seed pearls; although the ornament is luxurious, the way it holds her hair away from her clear face with its bright eyes gives her a wholesome look – but I saw her in pale washes of Rhenish green and gold, a Lorelei, twisting and vaulting in the rapids of that surging river, sinewy as a modern tennis star, or Esther Williams in the movies. For one close-up, the photographer has lit points in her eyes, using the vivid feint the artists of the Fayum cartonnage mummies in Upper Egypt introduced over 2,000 years ago to give life to their images of the dead; her lashes are spiky, separate – possibly added? – fringing her eyes with sea urchin spines; her smile, lipsticked so richly and darkly that her lips cannot be seen apart, hangs on her face like a painted crescent moon in negative, like Dali's sofa of Mae West's smile; her neat small left ear is showing; no jewellery. The photographer has airbrushed her so that a soft misty radiance swirls around the contours of her face and dissolves them into the light flowing in from the left, where her eyes are fixed. This is a face that doesn't turn cold and lifeless however long I look at her; she is mischievous-looking, alert, and very likeable. Like spangles of light dancing off the swirling Rhine, you could even say she was *twinkling*. I imagined her drinking sparkling water from the river's cascades and rinsing her long hair in it and nothing but it, keeping her blondeness, her fair eyes, her skin nacreous, and her hair silvery-green.

In a different shot, head and shoulders down to below her

waist, her dress is visible: a satin sheath with the sheen of mercury against the blurry studio drapes behind defines the litheness of her body and shows off her slim young roundedness (and she was *not* busty, neither then nor later). She has her hands firmly on her narrow hips and her expression is more faraway and dreamier than in the close-up, with the effect that her self-display doesn't become a challenging come-on like so many film-star publicity shots. There is a big satin-covered button at the waist, and the only discordancy in this otherwise serene image of a young woman turning an expectant face towards her future is the dressmaker's dart that cuts a diagonal across her ribs from the button towards her right breast like a scar.

Hildegarde always dressed in gowns from the great houses, and after the war, when she returned to the entertainment circuit of the surviving clubs, she would complain of the spiralling costs of her wardrobe. This clinging, luminous number – that diagonal dart – shows the bias-cut bravura of the Poiret and Schiaparelli school of Paris haute couture of the 1920s. In another photo, a little cut-out pin-up, the singer's wearing a draped dress of this kind: she was so slender that the fabric is gathered up into a rosette of pleats over her tummy. This pin-up shows the early effects of her manager's impresario-ship: she has been made over, with slick gloss eyeshadow; glycerine highlights no longer put stars in her eyes, but on her eyelids, on one wet pearly tooth, and her bottom lip. She is looking out, not quite focused, with the inviting gaze of the film siren close-up but still pushing her face towards us as if waiting to be kissed. More airbrushing on her face and arms, and a very rich lace hanky held with both hands to her right cheek. Her hair fluffs out, haloed.

The dresses she wore were gowns of satin or silk, bridal, lunar, nothing plunging or curvy; the gloves are different in each photograph – some light, some dark. This decorum appealed to Ilia, too; she took this as a sign that Esmond had good taste. Hildegarde was no trollop – and Ilia, as she was adjusting to the English world Esmond was born into, valued the decorum of the star's unassuming décolletage, and her thinness, that lack of obvious beckoning flesh. In Ilia, this was a genuine consequence of scarcity. Besides, nobody in southern Italy in the 1930s and 40s was plump. On Hildegarde, by contrast, the lean look was healthy. She could be a student – as she was when she first started playing the supper clubs.

Across one of the photographs she has written in purple ink:

> To Esmond:
> Knowing you has been so
> sweet – and always I wish
> you happiness.
> Fondly
> Hildegarde

Another, showing her in a much worldlier mood, no longer such an ingénue, is inscribed in a movie-star scrawl and again, in purple ink. 'To dear sweet Esmond I shall always remember.'

Do these messages follow formulae that were just standard for a nightclub singer to an ardent stage-door-Johnny? Or is there more to them? She seems to have written to him from New York, on an invitation to the Café-Lounge at the Savoy-Plaza: 'Dear Esmond – How I wish you could come "and see me sometime" – Love, Hilde.'

The gramophone has a side compartment where the more recent acquisitions were shelved, whereas the purpose-built record cabinet was a family treasure chest, and opening its doors with the little key and taking out its contents was not exactly forbidden, but aroused a similar order of excitement to trying on Ilia's clothes when she would let us play at dressing up in them, or putting on her jewellery and stepping into her shoes and even her underwear. The cabinet in the hall had an aura, like Ilia's jewellery case, where she kept her most precious things, which she hardly ever wore. It opened paths into the past, when Esmond was young and fairly slim and still had freckles, and red hair everywhere.

In the Renaissance, painters sometimes used to encase a portrait in a box with a shutter, partly for protection, but also to add surprise and intensity to the revelation of the person inside: when it was unwrapped, it would seem the person had suddenly appeared (daguerreotypes likewise hid the beloved image in a locket which had to be unclasped to reveal the portrait inside). The covering or lid of these early portraits was called a 'persona', the word which was chosen by Thomas Aquinas when he was translating Boethius from Greek and looking for a way to render 'hypostasis', the term Boethius uses for the Trinity being manifest in three . . . *forms*. He chose *persona* (Latin for mask) for this conundrum, producing the momentous consequence that this Catholic doctrine holds that there are three *persons* in the godhead.

Trying to think back to what happened before I knew how to pay attention to adults, the scene seems thronged with such personae, or rather, Ilia splits and multiplies, as do Esmond and Hildegarde.

Our parents are perhaps the people we have the opportunities to know best, but these opportunities are missed – I never even noticed, really, times when I could have seized such Chance by his dangling cowlick and held on till I had, for example, their feelings for Hildegarde in my grasp.

Proust famously has Swann reflect that he had given his life for a woman – Odette – who was 'not his type'. Swann saw this, and he too dreamed of a time when Odette might be different – in their future. His *amour propre* didn't altogether depend on

Odette's *persona*, because he had his own, high-status, worldly, rich and various personae. But Ilia, like so many women then, so many girls of slender means, of little education and no social connections, had to adapt. And she took a different path – like Nature in her laboratory with the colours of the rainbow and the wings of butterflies, Ilia was a clever and beautiful mimic, and I suspect – no, I know – that Esmond wasn't her type either.

As Esmond's girth broadened, the rest of his hair fell out, his jowls thickened and . . . well . . . let's leave this sad theme. For a time, the dashing liaison was the crucial assistant in the necessary illusion she wove to protect her marriage. The type of man my mother was attracted to – and there would be several who would correspond, later on – was in many melancholy ways an inversion of Esmond – almost precisely, as when a funhouse mirror beams back the image of a dwarf when the subject is a lanky giant; the contrast would be funny if it weren't so wistful. In 1939 *Gone With the Wind* was one of the last Hollywood films to be screened in Italy before American film companies withdrew from the enemy country, not to return until after the war was over. The dearth added immeasurably, in their absence, to the brightness – the starry effulgence – of Leslie Howard, who was always lit by the cameraman on *Gone With the Wind* with full moons lambent in his melancholy eyes. Leslie Howard – of elegant height, with richly waving blond hair, full everted lips, and a long slender neck that meant he always seemed to be dipping his head to pay fuller attention . . . to Melanie, or to Scarlett, submitting heroically to his role as the long-suffering, self-sacrificing Southern gentleman Ashley Wilkes – became for Ilia the lodestar of male perfections; she had many words for the qualities she liked. Where others saw a drip or a cissy, she admitted, she felt a strong attraction. She came to long for the gentle in 'gentleman' to mean something other than born to gentility.

Women on the other hand she would condemn for being 'feeble'. 'Prudes', we know, described the worst of them, whereas in men, shyness, sensitivity, modesty and reticence were prized.

Ilia liked to talk about Hildegarde far more than Esmond did – although he didn't stop her doing so. This story of the past was more important to Ilia than it was to him. And she made a point of passing it on, so that we his daughters would obey and respect our father, who had had an enchanted existence before she met him, before we arrived, before he became . . . the man we knew.

A friend recently suggested that Ilia recalling Esmond's love affairs was a way of justifying her own later amours, but this idea, which seemed to me shocking – indeed I was surprised by the intensity of my resistance to such an explanation – still doesn't convince me. Because the affair happened before my father met my mother, none of us felt the anger that a father's unfaithfulness provokes in daughters. The singer had prepared the way. My ignorance about her surely didn't arise from lack of interest but from the tacit prohibition against examining fathers and their sex lives at all. It's just about tolerable to accept that a father had to do it so that you could come into being, but after that, and with someone else besides your mother, the thought is appalling. Certainly, Ilia never presented the story with anger or resentment – let alone retrospective jealousy. And because our mother was tickled by his affair with a nightclub singer my sister and I caught her amused approval and we didn't look closer. But rather than dwell – or inquire more – I turned away from the scene. Now, if I make myself think about what the name 'Hildegarde' meant, another cliché superimposes itself on the Germanic Lorelei, of a blowsy good-time low-lifer out of Toulouse-Lautrec (La Goulue with her falling garters and quiff) holding court in a bar out of George Grosz, failing to disguise under the slap the after-effects of a long and rackety career, a strong, raddled woman, older, much older, than my father.

Any closer inspection would have felt obscene: envisaging Daddy in bed with Mummy was already nearly unthinkable but imagining him in bed with someone else demanded something more, and I wouldn't – couldn't – go that far.

Somehow, Esmond never put paid to our fantasies of the Rhine maiden, the enemy alien who'd been his friend before the war, the sophisticated foreign mistress with whom he'd enjoyed spells of heedless, well-heeled depravity in his salad days. Did Ilia know that the singer was in fact American, the daughter of German immigrants, a Catholic girl from a small Midwestern town (Adell, Wisconsin), part of one of those large farming communities in the Midwest where her family had settled in the mid-nineteenth century? If she did know, she let the fantasies flourish. A predecessor speaking broken English suited her better, I sense, than an American at home in the language which Ilia had begun to master. A Hildegarde of the dives and bars of Berlin was also so much more exciting than a graduate of Marquette Academy, Wisconsin.

It's not often probed, the coexistence of *nostos* with a hunger for the exotic that pervaded the colonial world which my father orbited in his post-war Cairene venture. He had admiration for the mother country left behind, evident in all that silver for the table and prints on the walls, but this home-from-home re-enactment continued as a form of insurance, a ritual that formed a counterweight to the passion for the foreign, the not-from-home and the nothing-like-home. The rings circling out from the centre to the periphery don't lose force: British ways of doing things loomed larger in Egypt in principle and in assertions of principle, even as the incoming bankers and dealers and traders – and a bookseller like my father – relished living in Egypt for what they enjoyed of Egypt, and not for what they imitated from a phantom Britain of the mind. But the antithesis that becomes established between adapting to the local ways and imagining undimmed loyalty to British values, also resembles those resonances in engineering when a bridge begins to weave and then judder under the tread of a certain number of feet, as happened with the Millennium Bridge between St Paul's and Tate Modern which began, when it was first opened to the public, to swing and sway to danger point. The analysis of the mysterious problem later showed that when pedestrians felt the bridge tack one way, they compensated by instinct and adapted to its motion in counterpoint, and this ballast only made matters worse. The same happens with colonialism . . . and today, when voters who have retired to Spain want the nation to leave Europe. Like so many other Brits, Esmond would hurl himself into contrary, furious patriotic self-righteousness, the more he felt Egypt swing in the direction of national autonomy, even though he had chosen life in Cairo for so many reasons, but above all so that his young, Italian wife would feel at home.

If you are exotic – as Ilia was in relation to Esmond's family, and customs and tradition, which she was of course learning fast – there is comfort in others' mistakes, and the song 'Darling, Je Vous Aime Beaucoup' conveyed a lot of sympathy with the state of being a foreigner trying to make her way in an unaccustomed tongue.

I had romanced Hildegarde into a Berliner, a Dietrich-like siren, a dominatrix to my greenhorn father. But another discovery followed, and this one took Ilia by surprise because it didn't fit the story as she had understood it – not exactly.

~~~

It was the winter Hildegarde turned seventeen, when Anna
Sosenko opened the door to their latest lodger from the music
school in the town. The Sosenkos were originally from Krakow,
from the small community that obeys Rome but follows a
Greek rite (the same sect that Andy Warhol, in Pittsburgh,
was born into and followed all his life), and Anna's mother
taught violin and her father played oboe in the Milwaukee
symphony; on Saturday nights, if there wasn't an official
concert, they gathered neighbours to sing and play round the
upright in their sprawling front room. There would be some
interruptions, in winter for *boreks* hot from the oven and apple
brandy and in summer, for full dark cherries and plum
schnapps.

Anna saw the new arrival's small white face peeking out
apprehensively under the pulled-down brim of a hat which
she touchingly hoped was stylish; Anna herself was in harem
trousers with a high waistband and a turban around her head,
styles which Hildegarde had never seen before except in a
fashion magazine. Anna was a springy, fiery young woman but
the outfit made her look like one of the Forty Thieves in Ali
Baba, as she was a lot shorter than her new friend, and a great
deal rounder. The two girls were two years apart, and though
Hildegarde was the elder, she would discover far more about
everything from Anna, who was infinitely expert. That first
day of their alliance – and it was to prove a lifelong alliance,
only briefly interrupted, in the 1950s, by some quarrel over
business – the younger girl drew the tall blonde music-
scholarship awardee from the country into the warmth of the
narrow hall crammed with things – with a loaded coat-rack
and an overflowing bookcase and a chiffonier heaped with glass
and crockery – and plucked at her to follow her down the
narrow dark passage, past the family living room where the
piano stood, and the master bedroom, to the back of the

apartment where she showed Hildegarde her room. She would be next door to her, Anna said, while Grushka, whiskery and a bit toothless, who had come with them from Poland ages ago, slept next door down a flight of stairs on the mezzanine; everyone had to share the bathroom. Anna frowned: 'Grushka will do everything for you, too – your laundry – mend your clothes – pretend you were here when you weren't if my parents ask. One day, I am going to have a bathroom of my own.'

Hildegarde had found the room to let through the cinema where she was accompanying silent films; one of the usherettes was a cousin and she knew that the Sosenkos regularly took in one of the students who had come from outside the city. But this time, Anna said, was the very first time the student wasn't some deadly dull young man, old before his time, who was so uncouth he'd eat the soup by sucking his fingers. The new lodger wondered if her table manners would do, as the younger girl hauled her suitcase up on to the bed, gestured at it, demanding she begin to unpack.

The temperature around Anna was somehow heated, explosive, as if every incident tossed her to extremes of amusement or of boredom.

When Hildegarde showed reluctance to begin unpacking, for she was sure her scant, provincial things would provoke her sudden companion to yawning or, worse, mockery, Anna instantly agreed. 'Listen,' she said, 'I'll play something and you can too – everyone is out, but Mamulka' – though her mother turned out to be a gaunt, tall crane of a woman – 'will be back soon and I can see that you are very shy. But not of me!'

Anna sat down at the piano, leafed through some sheet music on the stand and launched into a piece of Fauré, soon closing her eyes and making, as Hildegarde couldn't help noticing, cascades of mistakes as her expression remained rapt in bliss.

'Now you! Your turn.'

Hildegarde was trying to brush her away; trying to sputter that she wasn't prepared, that none of the music on the piano was familiar, that she was too tired from her arrival in the city.

But Anna looked so utterly cast down that her new friend relented and sat herself on the piano stool and twiddled it till it was lower – she was much rangier than Anna and would grow even taller that year, while Anna's height stuck, and she only got wider. And once Hildegarde had launched into a piece she knew, she felt the music reorganise her inner turmoil; the light and flashing energy of the Chopin impromptu she had chosen ignited her own reserves, and as she played, it filled her muddied and disjointed spirits with their lovely translucency and shape, and all her feelings about her leaving Adell, her tiny birthplace, to study in the state capital where she knew nobody, began to crystallise around a bright excitement. When she stopped, she breathed out as if she had been running up a long flight of stairs, and found Anna sitting tightly near her, watching her intently, the look on her face no longer mobile with passing impatient reactions, but absorbed in a steady questioning, as if a deeper idea had come to her.

Hildegarde remained suspicious of Anna for several days and nights, feeling that her landlady's daughter's eagerness must be a pretence and she must be, with her quickness and dynamism, someone easily bored, who was just toying with her, a girl from the country, and would be ready to cast her off – like the succession of boring young men who had been lodgers before. Nevertheless, she found herself looking forward to finding her there when she came back from the Conservatoire or the cinema, and let herself be drawn into the ways of playing – and not only music – that Anna made up.

Anna would knock on her door soon after she arrived back,

if she had not already sprung out into the hall or the passage to pluck at her, and the understanding, since the first day and Hildegarde's reluctance to unpack, stood between them, unsaid, that she visit Anna in her bedroom, never the other way around.

There, she kept her secret hoard – of photographs and magazines, sheet music of popular songs, a vanity case with two lipsticks in it, one bright pink the other plum purple, and an old pot of rouge she had borrowed from Mamulka, a pair of beaded slippers also extracted, also unbeknownst to her mother, and a single silk stocking embroidered on the ankle with a pale blue curlicue; she had two odd gloves, one above the elbow and a deep soft black suede, and the other white satin, a little grubby round the pearl buttons that fastened it, for it had been worn before its pair was lost; she had a feather or two, one dappled brown, another from a parrot's tail and iridescent emerald; some jewels that were not jewels but buttons which she traded with her schoolmates against fruit and chocolates she took to class; but Anna knew how to thread the buttons on ribbons to make necklaces.

She wore none of this herself. Instead she liked to dress up her beautiful friend, and she'd purr around her and tut-tut as she adjusted an effect.

Anna's prized possession was one of her father's cameras, which he had let her have officially, unlike the items she'd squirrelled away from her mother's cupboards, and when she'd dressed Hildegarde up to her satisfaction, she'd take photographs of her, the first of the shots that would eventually inspire kings, or so it was rumoured, to pass large sums to head waiters to secure a place in the front row at one of her soirées in the Savoy or the Café de Paris, when Anna would be backstage, waiting and watching, checking the effect.

By that time, Anna had filled out: a little tub of a woman

with a fierce voice, roughened by the small cigars she smoked. She did not look as if she had grown up beside Hildegarde in the same world and that they had come through the years together, inseparable, for they seemed to be living at different hours of the day, in different areas of the social scene, the singer in her columnar satin gowns sheathing a body that was long and slim and flat and serpentine, tantalisingly wriggling as she sat at her piano playing with gloves on, a mannerism which had begun in one of their games.

Grushka had been ordered to remain on hand when the lodgers had been male; now that the two girls had become such friends, Anna's parents were no longer worried.

Soon after Hildegarde took a room at the Sosenkos', Anna, who was always the more ambitious one, saw how they could combine their musical interests. As she started writing songs for the piano student from the country to perform, she began scouring the music entertainment magazines, to turn her into a star in Europe on the club circuit, starting in Paris, and continuing to London, Berlin, et al. Anna steered her towards the limelight, and cast her as a siren, though she really wasn't a Lorelei and the star treatment can't altogether conceal her healthiness and her humour, her twinkling smile, her practical sense: the poses are a game she's willing to play, but you can't help feel she would rather be out in the fresh air.

The full-length gloves, the handkerchief flourishes became the mark of the cabaret star's persona in performance; it declared that she was elegant and expensive and refined; she was emphatically a lady, not a vamp. A linen manufacturer even franchised her name; they chose to imitate her flowing handwriting on sets of sheets and towels, embroidering on them the message, 'With my loving blessings, Hildegarde'.

So, from the first moment, as they say, that Anna and

Hildegarde met, their future was in view: their lives became intertwined, the younger girl the impresario, the manager, the companion, the director of the singer's career – and the composer of her most famous song.

It was Anna who wrote, when they were both in their twenties, 'Darling, je vous aime beaucoup / Je ne sais pas what to do . . . Ah, chérie / My love for you is très très fort . . .' Hildegarde used to sing a preamble, explaining how a boy met a French girl but couldn't communicate his love, and Anna would tell interviewers how they'd been in Le Touquet playing the casino and had visited the First World War cemetery there, which had given her the idea. They were times of cover-up and persecution but of innocence, too: nobody questioned the story, or noticed that in this love song, a young woman, taking on the role of a love-smitten young man, is singing to a young woman who is 'très jolie'.

~~~

The *Guardian* published an obituary, which I found among the papers my mother had kept. It turned out that Hildegarde was born only a year before my father, but outlived him by over twenty years, dying in 2005 at the age of 99 – Anna predeceased her, aged 90. In a shaky hand, my mother has marked two passages: 'By the mid-1930s, [Hildegarde] was a star in London.' And then later, 'In mid-decade [of the 1950s], she broke up with Sosenko, which she called the "inevitable result of 20 years' close collaboration".'

It was the nature of the friendship that was news to my mother, not the manner of its disruption.

In this way, looking through my mother's papers, I realised that my father's fabulous decadent nightclub singer lover was a family romance: she wasn't German, nor an experienced older woman. In interviews she said she'd had many loves but nothing had ever worked out: it doesn't appear that she discovered later in life that she was gay, but had always been so. Wikipedia includes Anna, but not Hildegarde, in their list of lesbian musicians.

The obituary goes on to relate how Anna and she were reconciled and how Hildegarde converted to Anna's Polish Catholic sect. And then, before the days of civil partnerships, both women took vows as tertiaries in the order of the Carmelites: Hildegarde asked to be buried in the habit of a Carmelite nun.

~~~

None of this means, of course, that the young Esmond didn't have a love affair with the glamorous singer. My mother's diary reports that he was very tender with her on their wedding night and seemed to know what he was doing (it is very strange to read such things, even at such a distance in time). But Hildegarde being so faithfully attached to one woman makes a difference to the story – she wasn't simply bisexual over a lifetime, it seems that she and her long companion, partner, lover were also religious, maybe to a degree that excluded anything close to playing the field.

I began to wonder if the appeal of the story for Ilia didn't arise from the glamour that radiated from it, retrospectively romancing the middle-aged man she had married, but instead was founded in a deeper sense she had of Esmond's inclinations, the compass of his desires and his true loves. Proust describes the torments of jealousy that his narrator suffers at the thought of the young girls in flower and their tribadic adventures – he sees them here, there, everywhere, he tortures himself imagining Albertine's sapphic pleasures and pursuing the facts of them, facts which keep shifting from fantasies to realities and back again. This wasn't what happened to Ilia, but it is the case that Esmond was quick to outbursts of miserable, raging jealousy at her friendships with women, but never with her affairs with men, men whom he often liked and admired. And the deepest and longest friendships Esmond made were with his friends – his chums. Like so many men of his schooling, his class, his club and his politics, he stayed bonded to those young men as they grew older with him. A girl could be a chum – and in his account, Hildegarde indeed was – and several of them, I now realise, weren't interested in men either, except as chums.

In the course of Sir Robert Greg's party, Esmond indicated, insofar as a gentleman may do so, that he was an habitué at such entertainments; as a result, he felt his cachet in Cairene circles palpably rise.

The next morning, driving to the office, he was in a very good mood; the order book would start filling now, he knew.

Early memory ii

Lice

I'd caught lice, and Mummy said they'd hopped from the curls of my playmate, who lived next door; a little older than me, she was entire perfection in my eyes. Something felt sharp about this verdict, and it wasn't just the razor, which frightened me. Pussy and I — I can't remember what her real name was — used to sit together outside the kitchen door on the landing of the fire escape that twisted between our two apartments, and there we would squat to play teatime together, with the little china cups and saucers and the miniature brass cafetière that Nanny also gave me to play tea parties with. We'd take tea through our dolls, who spoke together in Arabic.

They were shaving my hair off, close to my skull, and I was distressed. 'Keep very still, darling,' Mummy coaxed, but she was handling the instrument anxiously while Nanny held me to her, crouching at my height on the chair where I was sat down for the operation. She had a basin of soapy water on the floor beside her, into which she dipped the razor every now and then. Afterwards my head felt fragile and cold, like an exposed china cup. I also knew that it made me ugly, because Mummy liked to doll me up, to use one of her phrases, with a ribbon in my hair making a topknot. She made me dresses with puffed sleeves with trimmed

edges *and flowers on the rounded panels of the collars; she tucked
and smocked them across the bodice. In the photographs the clothes
are luxurious and lovely, but I do not think they suited me then. I
was a solid child, sturdy and square, 'a bit of a tomboy' Daddy
used to say, chaffingly. But my mother was upset when she shaved
my head because it distanced me even farther from the pretty and
dainty little daughter she would have liked.*

*A photo of me with this shamed-collaborator look is dated on
the back in Daddy's writing, October 1948, that is, just before I
turned two. Perhaps I often caught lice and the scene I remember so
vividly happened later, but if not, this must be my earliest memory
of all.*

*I know I liked Pussy very much and loved having her for my
friend, but after this fragment of memory, with its sad load of
assumptions, there is nothing more of her that I can recall.*

Ilia with Marina, aged two: 'my head felt fragile and cold, like an
exposed china cup.'

13

An Egyptian Cigarette Tin

A girl looking sidelong smiles from the lid, her black hair escaping in curls from a red scarf wound round her temples and rising to a suggestion of a cone at the back of her head; the bandeau escapes near her ear to form a loop as if it were a large gipsy earring. Another piece of fabric, pale and lighter looking like muslin or silk, falls from the folds of the red scarf – she's both veiled and unveiled at once, as she breathes out smoke from small bee-stung red lips the same tint – the same paint – as the scarf in her raven hair, the smoke issuing from her mouth like a soul, like ectoplasm, like Mallarmé's cigar-soul . . . where copper in the metal has oxidised over the years, her skin has turned green. The rest of her dress, her shoulders and breast, are completely covered, in a kind of fichu with a suggestion of many beads, but the artist here has not given his task full attention. She's in an oval, peeping out through a window cut in the lid as if from a balcony; the frame is scalloped, as is the rectangular lid of the entire box, which is painted a saturated, highly satisfying ultramarine. Along the front side of the box, the inscription says, '100 Cigarettes Miracle mélange hors concours'. On both sides of the tin, a cigarette floats suspended in an art nouveau cartouche framing this same intense blue; the picture of the cigarette shows the stamp on the paper near the unfiltered tip in lovely art deco very thin pale blue letters, like the neon sign of a cinema of the epoch:

MIRACLE
DIMITRINO
CAIRO

On the underside of the tin, a painted picture of the factory of Dimitrino & Co. appears in the style of a children's encyclopedia illustration, much more factual and deadpan than the Carmen-like hoyden on the front: a scarlet twin-pointed pennant streams from the archway over the front entrance above a fascia giving the company's name and the date, 1896; each of its sixteen green shuttered windows on the top storey are rendered exactly alike; in front, a calèche, drawn by a lively pony, is bringing two visitors in European dress, while a camel with bulging panniers, its rider swathed in a desert cloak, is also approaching. (The rider has a gingerish beard, so perhaps he's the European and the visitors in the calèche are the locals.) The figures are very small in relation to the building, and the sandy – untarmacked – street in front of it stretches widely, an almost empty expanse. Palm trees curve in the breeze. The impression given combines pleasure and prosperity, luxurious quiet and exclusivity, tradition and modernity, self-confidence.

On the inside cover Dimitrino & Co. have abandoned English and communicate to their exclusive clientele in French, the language of diplomatic communiqués and corridors and *escaliers*, of *le gratin*, *le beau monde*, *le haut ton*, the lingua franca of the international luxury trade, the idiom of the Levant among Greeks and Italians and other peoples manufacturing to the standards of the hedonistic Cairenes . . . Dimitrino's are the patented suppliers ('*Fournisseurs Brevetés*') and the constellation of their imperial and royal charters, conveyed by enamelled heraldic devices, floats in the gilded ground of the cigarette tin: these ciggies are the favoured smokes of '*le Grand Duc Boris Vladimirovich de Russie {et} Prince Henri de Prusse*', and are officially approved by '*la Régie Tchecoslovaque, la Régie I{mpériale} et R{oyale} Autrichienne, la Régie R{oyale} Hongroise*', and so on through the courts of Europe – and Japan. They proclaim the awards, diplomas and medals the firm has won, which are all emblazoned on the tin under the central flamboyant trademark, an imperial eagle with wings spread.

~~~

Esmond smoked these cigarettes prodigally, forgetting that one was fastened to his lip where it would hang quite safely once the delicate paper of the untipped end was moistened, and he'd let the ash form without noticing and it would begin to curve downwards, sometimes juddering a little as he talked or moved about the room unconcerned, until it would fall and he'd sometimes notice and say 'Damn', but he didn't mind. Nobody seemed to mind smoking then – the scent of the cigarettes delicious, the gestures involved elegant, the paraphernalia fascinating and sophisticated – while the cigarette boxes, to which the cigarettes were transferred, were monogrammed, cedar-lined and silver.

My mother never smoked, but guests did, often preferring the Virginia tobacco brands that were also offered by Mohammed, the *suffragi* in our Soliman House apartment, after he'd taken round the tumblers of gin and tonic and bitters, or other mix of choice – whisky and soda, or whisky and water or Coca-Cola.

The mornings after, Mohammed, with the help of Abdel, who was the other member of staff and inseparable from Mohammed, would attack the residues of the night before, taking the Persian rugs out on to the back of the building to shake them so vigorously that Esmond worried they'd wear out the pile and damage the sheen of their warp. But on reaching Cairo in 1947 Ilia was glad to find that in Egypt the danger of dust and dirt was understood.

Esmond knew about carpets, and he kept adding to the few he'd shipped to Egypt. In the suq downtown he picked out a couple of Egyptian rugs made in the Persian style of Shiraz and Bokhara, but also less luxurious kilim druggets and shaggy *gabbehs* woven in Turkey and Upper Egypt; the best spread out a deep lapis lazuli field with a central medallion of greens and crimson, and it was fine and smooth and soft.

In the rooms kept dark and shuttered all day and only illuminated when friends came to dinner, the floors were covered by these rugs laid end to end; some were softer and silkier for playing on, but for knucklebones, marbles or jacks, the pile was too deep. It wasn't easy to find a smooth surface for these games except in the kitchen; if they weren't cooking or cleaning, Abdel and Mohammed would sometimes agree to play with me on the kitchen table but then the counters would shoot off and get lost in the stacks of bowls and pots, and sometimes even fly out through the door on to the fire escape which was always kept open to make a through-breeze, and then the marble or jack might fall through the wrought-iron landing of the zigzagging stair where I played with Pussy.

The *madrab* Abdel wielded, the first weapon of attack on fallen cigarette ash, mites and ticks, was strong and supple, made of rattan that Ilia saw standing in the market in tall stooks, from which the basket-weavers singled out this reed or that reed and then, sitting cross-legged on the earth or perched on a stool, wove them with hands flying quick as startled starlings. A matter of seconds in the basket-maker's fingers, and there it was – sturdy and useful and, Ilia thought, a thing of beauty, hand-wrought into a flat knot like the efflorescence of the medallion at the blue centre of that favourite Shiraz.

It would be usurped when the salesmen from foreign companies arrived to trade in metal goods, in Hoover and other makes; and once the by-products of oil began proliferating, they'd bring a million garish plastic brooms and dustpans and bowls to the global supermarket; a plaited *madrab* such as Abdel flourished with such insouciant eagerness was to be advertised in the not-so-distant future on eBay and fetch real money, to bring back a memory of a time of natural materials and organic rhythms.

When Abdel returned from the balcony, the cleansed and aired rug rolled under one arm, the *madrab* tilted over his shoulder, striding loose-limbed on his bare feet back into the flat, he looked like a boy playing soldiers with a broom for a rifle. And he'd swing up another rug from the floor and carry it off to the balcony again to throw it over the balustrade, and the little dust and some sand that had infiltrated the weave since the last session would scatter over the lawns and fuse with the heat pulsing over the polo field and the racetrack of the Gezira Sporting Club below, and some of it would fall on the path that Nanny and I took every day to play there on the swings or in the swimming pool.

During the week, Esmond would leave for the office early and come back for lunch and a siesta and return into town at 4.30 p.m., the hour when visitors would come calling on Ilia. Mohammed would glide across the cool polished floor in his soft slippers, his slight shadow cutting through the stripes of the shuttered twilight of our interior world. He'd open the door to the guests, and she'd offer them tea or soft drinks on the western terrace at the back of the flat, from which she could see Gezira Sporting Club where I would be playing. She'd covered the loungers and the swing sofa and the other rattan chairs and cushions with chintzes she'd bought at Cicurel's department store the first time Esmond had let her borrow the office car, with Nasrallah at the wheel. The bolts of cloth in the store made her cry out in wonder, not only at the dyes and textures, the variety and splendour of them all, but at the mere fact of them being there at all, and within her grasp.

The variety and splendour of Cicurel's department store: the Harrods of Cairo.

Ilia had once been to Naples with her father on a family outing when she was a little girl and she remembered going to the famous Galleria there, with its soaring glass vaults and little boutiques below sparkling like jewel boxes. They hadn't bought anything, but it didn't matter, the gleaming treasure house was the point.

Once, in Cicurel's, the shop assistant turned out to be an Italian, who'd lived a long time in Egypt, so they'd exchanged some excited words, but as the assistant came from Bolzano in the north, they found little more in common to talk about.

Ilia had then concentrated on choosing fabrics for the curtains and the covers of the new rattan furniture on the verandah. The Italian encouraged her towards a splashy, exuberant chintz, mazy with flowers of debatable species, certainly none Ilia herself knew from the oleanders and hibiscus of her own region.

'Ah, the English herbaceous border has arrived! You clever girl!' Esmond exclaimed, and laughed his great gusting laughter as he stretched himself out on an easy chair. 'You are quite a seamstress, my clever little girl,' he said. 'What could one call this gift? Not green fingers, but what? Let me see? Silver fingers? Like needles and thimbles and scissors – yes, silver fingers.'

When a visitor came to call, Abdel would wheel in the trolley Mother Rat had presented to them as part of their wedding list, its double shelves and extensible trays laid with linen mats of drawn threadwork and the silver teapot with its matching hot-water jug, creamer, sugar bowl, tongs, smaller bowl to hold the strainer and the muffineer filled, in the absence of scones, with sweetmeats from the suq. As Esmond and his mother had also shown her how to do, she would offer her guests something to eat. In another bowl, made of glass, there would be jam with its own curiously flattened spoon; it was made of figs or apricots or peaches or mangoes. That first year in Egypt, she would learn that marmalade was never to be offered at teatime. In Egypt, where the fruits ripened all year round, the glow and scent of oranges connected her to her grandparents' farm. 'The best marmalade,' said Esmond as he watched the cauldron where the pulp and rind were stickily seething and now and then spurting a scalding jet of treacle, 'really requires bitter oranges – Seville oranges – but here's the thing, these ones from the Delta don't have the necessary bite.'

Cairo was a destination and a desirable posting, and many

visitors turned up, family and others, looking for adventure or reinvigoration, bringing with them gossip and yet more invitations. Esmond's sister Betts, now known as Betsy, had married Harold Henderson, an officer in the Royal Navy, and he had arrived to take up the post of naval attaché in the Embassy. 'Top spy,' said Mungo, his son and my first cousin, who'd come out by seaplane to spend the Christmas holidays in Cairo and swim and play tennis at Gezira, and sail on the Nile and have a game of cricket. He was 17 or so, with a *tendresse* for his young Italian aunt.

Towards the end of his life, Mungo remembered, with a sense of guilt, what a fabulous, heedless time he'd had in Egypt. He remained close to Ilia – and protective of her. Once when I became impatient with my mother – she was trying to find her glasses to read some small print, and I said testily that I could read it for her – Mungo ticked me off roundly.

In Cairo many women came to call too, and if they were part of the society of which Esmond approved, he would glow

In the early evening, when Esmond came back from work, he'd often bring a friend he'd met in town. He'd stop in the hall and loosen his tie and undo his collar, and she'd hear him encouraging his guest to do likewise.

'Don't stand on ceremony, here, old boy! Ilia won't mind.'

He wouldn't yet announce himself, happy watching her when she was sufficient to herself, keeping her own company. She might be sitting on the sofa on the verandah in the front of the flat, her head bent to some task. Or sitting up straight on one of the wicker chairs at the glass and wicker table, sewing. Fabric would stream over her knees from the table as she hemmed a dress, silks and taffetas, organdie and tulle: she could make dresses from the latest styles shown in the pattern books that Cicurel's brought from Paris, and from the magazines they also stocked, downstairs, in the news-stand outside the main revolving doors. When she went out in Cairo, admirers asked her who her dressmaker was. Ilia would answer, 'It's a secret.' When she put in a zip on the side of a bodice, her photograph appeared the following week in the social gazette: 'No one could understand how I put it on or took it off – the fastening was invisible, and I wouldn't tell them. Mystery is a great weapon.'

Or she'd be reading or making lists of words and idioms and phrases or jotting reminders to herself about other matters. Sometimes she had a record on the gramophone, and would be standing to listen, waiting to put on another, her eyes closed, sometimes singing to a despairing Mario Lanza: '*Vesti la giubba, la faccia infarina . . .*'

My mother, if she'd settled herself on the sofa in the drawing room, would then rise to greet her husband, springing forward, her light shawl left drifting on the chintz soft covers and cushions. When she came to a standstill – she alighted, it seemed to me – I'd catch hold of a bunch of fabric from her dress and steady myself to look from behind her at whoever it was who had come with Daddy that evening.

Calling out, 'Darling girl, I'm home, it's a bloody dustbowl in town,' he'd stride into the drawing room, rubbing his hands.

'Had a good day, old thing?' he'd ask. Then he'd catch a flurry of my cries and yelps as I careered around the balcony, now a pony going giddy-up giddy-up, then a rabbit leaping hoppity-hop, clamouring for or protesting against something or other. But as soon as I heard him in the hall I'd whirl down the corridor to hurl myself at him, knocking the breath out of him as I flung myself at him to climb up his body to his shoulders, flooring him – not for real but in the spirit – with the flaming fireball of a child's ardour. Almost before he'd put down his briefcase, I'd make him catch me up and walk me up his body and swivel to sit on his shoulders. He laughed, and when I sailed up his torso and took my seat in triumph on his shoulders, his laugh was then pure delight – he was in many ways a stiff and clumsy man physically, who never communicated anything voluptuous (and my mother suffered from this), but my earliest memories of him are physical in a light and happy way.

At the sound of my hurtling towards Daddy, Ilia would lift her head and set aside what she was doing and come towards him, and say, 'How was the office today?'

He'd answer her, saying, for example, 'Chap called Dimitrino came by – a decent fellow – from the family whose outfit makes the cigarettes I like so much. He remembers you, darling *piccolina*, and made a point of saying, several times, that he would like me to give his respects to *la charmante* Madame Emilia – he has that Levantine habit of calling one "Monsieur Plum", "Madame Mariam", and so on. He's a writer but he has block. Everyone says so. Wrote terrific things before the war but since then . . . well, he's blocked. But he's dead keen on my finding him books about birds, migration patterns over the Delta, winter and summer plumage, that sort of thing. We got to talking about . . . Moustached Warblers! Blue-cheeked Bee-eaters! And flamingos! I think he knows more than anyone about flamingos. But a little flamingo flamingoes a long way.' Then he'd laugh his big gusty laugh, which always sounded incongruous when she echoed him, as if she were using a megaphone to produce the boom from her narrow ribcage or biting on an invisible reed like the Punch & Judy man with a swazzle clenched between his teeth.

Esmond would then pour himself a sherry from the decanter kept for him in the drinks cupboard and light a cigarette and call for more ice and mix himself a different drink and something for his friend. Or, if he weren't accompanied, he'd move out on to the terrace, and flop down on the chintz cushions of the swing sofa or one of the loungers and remind her of the evening's engagements ahead: 'We're due at Robert's at

8.30, you know. I've told Amin we'll need him for the evening – I told Jamie we'll swing by Shepheard's to pick him up. He seems to be taking to the job, by the way. A born bookman! We'll give Amin a day off next week to make it up to him.'

She would say nothing. Then she'd brighten: 'I'll wear my new taffeta skirt with the black braid trim. I just finished it – I think Robert is such a *cognoscente*, he'll appreciate it.'

'"Connoisseur" in English, dear girl. Beware the *faux amis*! Nothing translates directly, what? And we'd better have a bite to eat before setting out – you know how it is, never much grub at these soirées.'

The young friend who was going with them that evening at Robert Greg's was James Chantry, who'd come out to Cairo to find his way, as his father, another chum of Esmond's, had explained in a letter of introduction he'd presented to Esmond over a drink at the Turf Club. Jamie, as he was known, was at a bit of a loose end – things were still very tight in London when it came to jobs and so forth. Could Plum take him under his wing for a while, to put some vim back into him? A spell of apprenticeship in Cairo, learning an honest trade like bookselling, would set him on the straight and narrow.

What Jamie had done wasn't explained; but he had come down – or perhaps been sent down (or run away) – from Oxford.

Esmond liked his wife to be admired and seeing her through Jamie's eyes as they arrived together, he saw she made a picture that could not but be entrancing to his protégé.

Jamie Chantry became a regular visitor, indeed inseparable from Esmond, and eventually he moved into the spare room. 'Such a waste of money for him to keep a room at Shepheard's. So I said, "Come to stay with us, dear boy. You'll be excellent company for Ilia."'

Jamie was the first of many habitués who gave Ilia an insight into her own gifts, and by contrast, revealed to her that her husband understood very little about feelings, towards her or anyone else. Jamie was a year or so younger than her; he had the face of a Botticelli angel, except for an oddly long neck and prominent Adam's apple; he was learning Farsi and Arabic with huge enthusiasm from personal tutors he hired, and eagerly planning expeditions not just to the pyramids but much farther, to Sinai, to Luxor. He wanted her to persuade Plum, as he called Esmond, to come, and wanted her to as well. But he didn't understand anything about her, she pointed out to him, kindly. 'I can't leave Marina behind to go wandering in the desert.'

He blushed – he was a young man who blushed – and tugged at his floppy hair, 'Oh I have been crass, as usual.'

She was touched.

She didn't call them habitués. They were her 'beaux', recalling Scarlett O'Hara's triumphs and disasters in *Gone With the Wind*; or her 'admirers' (Esmond), or her 'swains' (often the young men described themselves as such, half in earnest, half in jest); they were *cavalieri serventi* (Ilia, sometimes, with a little dash of pity), they were *soupirants*.

I will never know how many soupired to effect.

She soon understood what Jamie's trouble was, what the unnamed problems at home had been, what he had fled. She kept it to herself, as Esmond made cruel fun of 'pansies'. But through lighting up her sympathy, Jamie prompted her to discover in herself her inner fund of perceptiveness – as mother and geisha combined.

One afternoon, he came back early on his own, dishevelled and flushed and ran in from the front room, past Mohammed, over to her where she was sitting, sewing, on the sofa.

'You have to help me,' he said, and he knelt down in front of her and clutched her clumsily round her knees. 'I'm in love with you, I can't sleep, I can't do anything, not a word of Arabic goes in because I keep imagining you naked, and you're so beautiful I keep wanting to . . .' His eyes were gaping wide and his Adam's apple going up and down. 'But I've never done it with a . . .'

I know she didn't laugh, but accepted his wild words, undoing his arms from her legs and picking dressmaker's pins out of his hair. 'With a girl . . . that is it, isn't it?'

This scene was perhaps the first of its kind in her life, but she became used to such, to being asked to perform miracle cures of Englishmen's besetting woes – and women's, too. Her protégés and strays lived in and out of my childhood and my sister's, and later, when she joined the Samaritans, became her 'cases' whom she cared for often beyond the confines of the organisation. In spite of her outward vivacity, she had an insider's knowledge of their state.

In the case of Jamie Chantry, they stayed friends till he died, a few years before she did. By then he had been cheerfully installed for decades with the lover from his Oxford days, the very one he'd been ordered by his family never to see again.

Through the weeks and months of those early years in Cairo, my father would come home from the office and ask, 'Had a good day, old thing?' as he kissed my mother on the cheek. Then to me, he'd add, 'And what about you, little woman?' and swing me up in the air once, twice, three times even, and then set me down again and make straight for the drinks tray, shouting to Mohammed to bring a bucket of ice.

Early memory iii

Being painted

In the cool, darkened dining room where I never went, a lady was waiting for me, I was told, and she was going to paint me. This filled me with terror. I refused, crying and fighting back against Nanny when she began bundling me towards the door that opened into the room where this assailant was waiting for me with her implements. Mummy had to be fetched to calm me down, but as she kept saying, gently, 'She's only going to paint you – nothing is going to hurt – she's not going to do anything to you, just paint you,' I remained wretched with apprehension. Even as I quietened and let them both take me to the stool that was positioned ominously in front of the equipment, I was determined not to be painted. A tough-looking old woman, as I saw her, was standing beside the stool with her brushes at the ready, waiting for the blue bow my mother had tied round my scanty tuft of hair to be plumped and straightened to the desired effect.

I glared at the artist, certain that she was only pretending to stay on her side of the gap between us, and might at any moment spring forward and capture me and start applying paint all over me and turn me into a statue like the slaves in their pantaloons and boleros who held up the lamps on either side of the mantelpiece in the drawing room. I didn't understand that painting me meant putting me in a painting, like my friend the little girl in the picture.

14

The Little Girl in the Picture

Swathed from head to foot in bulky robes, gold-embroidered on pale crimson over a blue tunic, with her hands neatly clasped together, the little girl in the picture became my secret sister, my other self, the pretty, female child that I was – inside – in spite of my stout and clumsy outside and, at times even, my ugly convict skull. The towering scale of her enveloping coif, a wimple-like structure of translucent organza, trailing behind her like a cloak, and her imperturbable look filled me with longing. I was a changeling; I knew it and in my heart of hearts I knew that my mother knew it too. Not the right shape or temperament to belong to her – and I wanted to be changed once again. And become someone like the girl in the picture, a beautiful exotic Mameluk princess, standing on her own like a little adult, an expensive doll just unwrapped from a tissue-paper cocoon in a luxurious box.

Even the shadow she casts behind her, I see now, intensifies the excitement of this tiny person alone in her own portrait, not on anyone's knee, or surrounded by siblings but on her own. How old is she, three, four?

All my life I thought of this child as Egyptian. But looking carefully now for the writing of this book, I see an insipid face, baby pink with wide-apart pale blue eyes, slightly tense in expression, in which one might read forbearance of the kind Victorian women were trained to show. She gazes out of the elaborate veiling and embroidered panels of her costume like a plump English handmaiden trying to play the innkeeper's wife who turns away Joseph and Mary in a school nativity play. Her role as a fantastic dream creature of independent imagination, different from the ladylike prescriptions of my upbringing, tilts into something quite other. Is that quality I took to be heroic self-possession a far more conventional maidenly demureness, even complacency? Is there something smug and placid in those folded hands over her waist?

I also notice that what I had thought was a watercolour is in fact a lithograph from a chalk drawing with wash. Along

A beautiful exotic Mameluk princess: David Wilkie, *Daughter of Admiral Walker*, Constantinople, 1840.

the bottom runs an inscription in a delicate copperplate hand: 'The daughter of Admiral Walker', followed by a signature 'David Wilkie f[eci]t 1840'.

Admiral Walker features in another picture that used to hang beside the little girl in my childhood home: a fantastical fellow in a tarbush with a feather, erect in a dress uniform with prominent epaulettes, medals at his throat and a scimitar hanging from his sword belt. I hadn't connected him with the little girl, but the picture is inscribed 'Constantinople 1840' and it turns out to be not a portrait of an Ottoman officer – not exactly – but of the child's father. The little girl who had beckoned to me so strongly all of a sudden turned into an English child in fancy dress.

~~~

Fancy dress was a craze in Victorian times – the Queen and Prince Albert held a *bal costumé* at Windsor in 1842, the same time as Wilkie was portraying the Walkers; the party took place soon after Victoria and Albert were married: the couple appeared as Edward III and his consort, Philippa of Hainault, and were painted in full medieval splendour by Edwin Landseer. A glance at British portraits will reveal one landowner after another taking part in cosplay, posing as peasants, goddesses, heroes and heroines from Shakespeare, Alexander Pope, balladry and folklore. Later, society photographers – Madame Yevonde, Cecil Beaton, Angus McBean – encouraged fantasy play-acting in their subjects (McBean began as a maskmaker). The fashion spread – scratched photographs drifting on the bookstalls in Cairo show tableaux vivants with family members dressed up as houris, camel-drivers, hookah-smoking vagrants, or simply as the people they might have been if they had not moved into the city and adopted its sophistications. The servants of empire, scattered over the world, loved dressing up – often masquerading as the locals: Christmas cards sent from posts abroad in the empire assemble the colonies' officials and their families in fancy dress – and many often cross-dressed. Pageants all over the pink map in the nineteenth and early twentieth centuries, caught in photographs sent to loved ones back home, include second secretaries and civil servants, army officers and other dignitaries and representatives of British authority abroad guising as exotic strangers – Aladdin, Lady Precious Stream, or the Black King at Christ's nativity, among other Orientals. When Mr Rochester disguises himself as a gipsy woman and tells Jane's fortune, the sequence of inversions and impersonations in the scene are dizzying: insider playing outsider, master subordinate, male female. It's the prerogative of his mastery to play whatever part he likes. King Faruq went as a desert Arab to his own ball in 1943 with Queen Farida in long blonde plaits as a Hungarian maiden. But as with labelling and jokes, so with costumes: it matters who is calling the names, who is putting on the pretence. The Canadian prime minister Justin Trudeau's blackface impersonation as Aladdin has a long history but caused him serious trouble in 2019, while a couple of years earlier, sombreros were disallowed at Halloween parties: 'My culture is not your costume', went the slogan.

Yet, in the traditions of the Caribbean carnival, dancers and masqueraders repay the travesties in kind, with stock characters of bosses featuring in scenes of High Mas and Ole Mas: Dame Lorraine, Queen Patroness and Jab Jabs, wielding whips like plantation overseers.

My father gave me a sari for my birthday one year; he bought it in Liberty's. It was sprigged with tiny flowers in pale pink on a lighter shade of primrose and I wore it for best. For Ilia, he also bought a Chinese dragon robe which she sometimes put on for charity balls, though she preferred outfits

with more fluidity and female shape. We also had a dressing-
up trunk and my favourite disguise consisted of Turkish
trousers below my belly button and a swathe of cloth over my
mouth and nose – what I then called a yashmak – I would
then wiggle my hips while making eyes over it like an irresistible sloe-eyed dancing girl from the posters I saw in the
streets in Cairo. Veils were glamorous in that epoch – a tease,
a lure, the equivalent of a slashed skirt to the thigh, and
elegant women, like Ilia, also veiled their faces with spotted
nets fluttering from their hats.

If Englishmen and women abroad weren't play-acting, they
were often dressing up in earnest, furled in splendid brocades
and velvets and festooned in braid, galloons, decorations,
orders, medals and jewels. The same might well be said of the
French or Austro-Hungarian courts, but, as the historian David
Cannadine has discussed in *Ornamentalism*, the servants and
rulers of the British Empire were enraptured by the spectacle,
the splash and sparkle they encountered among the cultures
they conquered or wished to hold sway over – the diamonds
of the rajahs and the silks, feathers, damasks and gems of the
Ottomans, and also the bright hues and flowing shapes of the
dress of lesser ranks. Cannadine's title gives an ironical nod
to *Orientalism*, Edward Said's far more famous book, and while
making light of Said's arguments, he borrows from them to
add to the force of his own: fancy dress as a frivolous performance of culture, saturated in the perfume of seduction
emanating from the peoples they had subjugated, or were
attempting to, militarily and commercially. Viceroys and High
Commissioners were not to be outdone by local maharajahs
or tribal chieftains in their panoply and splendour, and British
court dress and military uniforms sprouted feathers and furs,
and gleamed with gold and jewels, hats, helmets, bandoliers
and sashes. And yet, even while no less a figure of grand

respectability than Lord Mountbatten arrayed himself in gems and feathers, the whiff of something faintly ridiculous clings about these bedizened figures of power, with their plumes and jewels, braid and enamel and gold. When John Singer Sargent's tremendous 1904 portrait of the colonial administrator Sir Frank Swettenham (1850–1946) inspired Rebecca West to comment that 'he looked as if he wasn't quite a gentleman', was she showing her sensitivity to his flamboyance? To the unfurling, regal brocade drapery behind him (from his collection of Malayan fabrics), the swagger of his hand on his swivelling hip, the sheen of his white uniform and the grandiose hauteur of his whole mien?

One of the ways that social life in England has changed altogether is that you now have to be Scottish to put on a kilt, come from the subcontinent to wear a sari, and so on. Masquerade – especially when it implies ethnicity – is no longer acceptable, though it has long been one of the many unwritten, and indeed unexamined, customs of the country. David Cameron, then prime minister, had to apologise for posing with some Morris dancers near his constituency – a troupe which continues to black up – claiming it began as a traditional disguise when the dance was illegal.

But did my imaginary little friend, Admiral Walker's daughter, know she was in costume? Or did she, at that early age, living in Constantinople, feel herself to be the Ottoman child I took her for? Did she long to be one, as I did?

Those days when I was growing up in Cairo, I could happily dream-play at being a local girl.

~~~

The artist David Wilkie was 'a raw, tall, pale, queer Scotsman', wrote one contemporary on his arrival at the RA in London in 1805. Six years later, the artist was elected a fellow. Success followed success but no peace of mind. He became, rather unexpectedly, a great favourite of the establishment: both the regent – later George IV – and William IV were enthusiastic patrons (the latter knighted him in 1836). The Duke of Wellington commissioned the celebrated scene *The Chelsea Pensioners Reading the Waterloo Dispatch*, in which the artist doesn't hold back from expressing the heavy costs to the ordinary man – and woman – of the nation's victories. His work would be Hogarthian if it were not for the intensity of his sympathy with his subjects. Contemporaries mentioned Lawrence, Rembrandt, Rubens.

A troubled and singular man, he lived with his mother and went to pieces when in the space of a few months, he lost her, his two brothers and his sister's young man, too. (Something of his inner anguish can be seen in a fine self-portrait of 1840.) A doctor prescribed going abroad, and in 1825, he left for Italy and France, and discovered a taste for more distant travel. In 1840, he set out for Constantinople and the Holy Land. Henceforward, like the admiral whose portrait he made in the Ottoman capital, Wilkie was never again to spend much time in the British Isles.

During his sojourn in the Ottoman Empire, Wilkie drew many vivid, skilful studies of local people: *The Dragoman of Mr Moore English Consul at Beyrout*, and the family of Sotiri, Dragoman to Mr Colquhoun, Constantinople, which includes another small child in rich local dress, holding like a page a gorgeous crystal shisha pipe. His study of Rembrandt's prints is evident in all his work, and, like the Dutchman, who kept a trunk full of dressing-up clothes in his studio, and liked to wear dramatic headgear or drape an encrusted scintillating tapestry on a model, Wilkie was powerfully attracted to the distinctive costumes of the people he encountered: Ottoman society differentiated people by their dress – status, occupation, religion and ethnicity were all encoded in headgear and accessories. This meant that costumes could therefore also act as a disguise, necessary for playing a certain role.

A family in Istanbul: David Wilkie, *Sotiri, Dragoman to Mr Colquhoun*.

His travels in 1840 when Wilkie met Walker and his family were to be his last. He began the long journey home, took the overland route down the Danube, spent a few months painting in Syria and Palestine, and stayed five weeks in Jerusalem, where he made many chalk drawings in the orientalist style of the period, recording the pursuits and clothes and trades he observed around him. He sailed from Egypt, where he painted his last official portrait, of the ruler

Muhammad Ali. But he died soon after he sailed from Egypt for home and was buried at sea off Gibraltar.

The debonair Turk in his tarbush in the portrait turned out to be a Victorian adventurer, a Hornblower, a Scarlet Pimpernel, a hero from that favourite reading matter of mine as a child; his story was to lead me into the labyrinthine coils of British and Ottoman imperial diplomacy.

A debonair Turk in his tarbush and medals: David Wilkie, *Admiral Sir Baldwin Wake Walker*, 1840.

The full name is Baldwin Wake Walker; having entered the Royal Navy in 1812 when he was 10, he was then posted to the Caribbean, where he rose to become a lieutenant by the age of 18. He was destined thereafter to spend far more time travelling and fighting in the British seaborne empire and beyond – in the Caribbean and South America, the Middle East and southern Africa – than he would ever spend on land at home in England. In 1838 he became, with the full approval of his masters at the Admiralty, a commander of the Ottoman navy, and was thereafter known as Walker Bey and later, as Yavir Pasha. In 1840, the year of the portrait, the sultan – Mahmoud II – died, causing widespread alarm that the Russians would seize the chance to move on Constantinople. Rather than stand against them, Admiral Walker unpredictably decided to sail the Turkish fleet to Alexandria and hand it over into the control of Egypt's ruler, the highly ambitious Muhammad Ali, who held power for thirty-five years. Delighted with the ships so suddenly given over to his care, Ali refused to relinquish them; Walker then dreamed up a scheme to kidnap him from his palace and carry him off a prisoner to the Sublime Porte.

This plan, which strikes a reader now as more like a comic-strip heroic exploit out of *Tintin* rather than the serious tactics of a major power, was forestalled by the British naval commander in Egypt who packed Walker back on his own to Constantinople in a steamer – the kind of modern vessel which the admiral opposed till the day of his death several decades later. Undeterred, by that summer, perhaps a short while before the portrait of his daughter was painted, Walker Bey was again at war, fighting alongside the Turks in sorties against the French in Syria. The *Oxford Dictionary of National Biography* entry commends him: 'In September and November he co-operated with Turkey's allies in the reduction of Beirut, Sidon, and Acre, showing great gallantry, both in organising naval operations and in landing and leading detachments of Turkish troops to seize the towns in the name of the sultan.' Such is the language of unexamined military glory.

Admiral Walker's naval career continued to flourish, taking him to battlefields new against new enemies. He was knighted by Queen Victoria for his exploits at sea, awarded the Iron Crown of Austria (second class), the orders of St Anne of Russia and of the Red Eagle of Prussia, and was made a hereditary pasha of the Turkish Empire. These honours were added to several he had received earlier in his career, including the Redeemer of Greece, and the cross of the Légion d'Honneur. He seems to be wearing at least two of these in Wilkie's portrait.

He had five sons and four daughters, and I can't tell which of his little girls posed for the picture. I've traced one, Evelyn Laura, who'd be around the right age: 28 in 1864 when she married a sailor: Captain Hugh Burgoyne. In his mutton chops and beard he doesn't look like the husband I would have wished on her, but he's cut to the same jib as her father, and was awarded the VC, then in its earliest years. Six years after they were married, his ship the HMS *Captain* sank and he was lost at sea.

The debonair Admiral Pasha in Wilkie's portrait attracted my father because he was a keen follower of British naval history and a popular crew member on friends' boats at Cowes and Bembridge. He especially loved going out with his uncle Basil Lubbock, author of *The Last of the Windjammers* (1927); Basil sailed a Solent Sunbeam, a swooping racing yacht he'd helped design. In Egypt, Esmond used to go out on the Nile, and I remember him taking me with him once or twice; we also used to watch the boats on the river below us from our front balcony: the feluccas floating by, their reddish-brown lateen sails making lovely curves on the slant rig's stiff hypotenuse as they swelled in the wind. One of Esmond's party tricks was making drawings of every type of vessel that carried sail – from a dhow to a man-of-war – each bit of the rigging neatly labelled. The words fascinated me, the mizzen, the topgallant, the spinnaker. But it is also the case that I remember crocodiles with dreadful overbites sunk in the sludgy mud on the banks, and hippos basking in the papyrus reeds.

Is it possible that I really remember crocodiles? And hippos?

Heavy and slumberous and whiskered, lying half submerged in the shallows of the Nile in the silver mud and the broken reeds? Was it really the Nile, with this muddy bank, where my father took me to look at the hippos? He was pleased there were so many of them, and we waited for them to move, to open a rolling, pouchy eye and swivel it at us, heave one of their great smelly sighs. They floated like huge inflatable leather poufs, the local kind, buttoned down in the middle so that the stuffed bulk swelled up on either side: the hippos wallowing looked like that, sofa-like. The insides of their jaws, when they obliged me with a fantastic deep yawn, contained millennia of world-weariness. Their gums were also cushiony, but very pink and girdled with teeth like the battlements of a medieval castle.

In 1846, towards the close of Muhammad Ali's long reign, another imperial and adventurer and aristocrat, Charles Augustus Murray, arrived in Cairo to take up the post of British Consul General, which he would hold with great success till 1853. He soon established ties with the ruler, and through this alliance, managed to arrange the construction of the railway line linking Cairo to Alexandria. But his more famous exploit by far was transhipping the first hippopotamus back to England and the London Zoo. For this achievement, he became known as 'Hippopotamus' Murray.

Murray's long life is almost unbelievably packed with adventures out of those swashbuckling yarns I devoured, while his ornamental, even orchidaceous sense of style continues the love affair of the British colonial with exotic rogues.

Born in 1806 into a web of powerful and rich aristocratic connections, he was a classical scholar, famous for taking a bet as an undergraduate that he could ride from Oxford to London and be back in time for dinner. He collected languages (it is said he read and spoke fifteen), was a fellow of All Souls, and much praised, in an era of unselfconscious homoeroticism, for

his 'charming' looks. But he was a younger son and had to find
a role. He chose diplomacy, embarking on a long and tumultuous
life. In the United States, he successfully courted an heiress,
Elise Wadsworth, but her father suspected Murray for a fortune-
hunter and forbade the marriage. Murray then spent time
travelling with Pawnee Indians, and wrote a two-volume novel,
The Prairie-Bird (1844), dramatising the romantic adventures
of his dashing hero/alter ego, living with Indian braves (some
of them virtuous, others vicious), and glorying in their noble
savagery, their pacts of brotherhood to the death, and the wild
spirit of their magnificent stallions. The book isn't exactly read-
able but the ethos Murray conjures up offers an interesting
historical context for imperial masquerade and the spirit of the
Boy Scout movement, which developed earlier than Kipling
and Baden-Powell. Murray's fantasies also anticipate home-
grown romances of the Plains, such as the fiction of Zane Grey,
the Ohio-born dentist who wrote *Riders of the Purple Sage* (1912).

Murray continued his suit to Miss Wadsworth, and they
married in 1850, her father having died in 1844. A year later,
she died in childbirth. After these travels in America, Murray
was posted to the Middle and Near East. But there was some
trouble over a highly placed woman in the shah's court, a
contributing factor in the first Anglo-Persian War, and Murray
moved on.

William Beckford, the writer, aesthete and orientalist, heir
to fabulous wealth from Jamaica sugar plantations, was Murray's
great-grandfather, and Murray had fond memories of meeting
him in his youth; it is one of Beckford's last protégés, the artist
Willes Maddox, who painted a portrait for which Murray posed
in a very studied *mise-en-scène*: he's seated on silk cushions,
dangling a tasselled cane – or is it a hookah, known in Egypt
as a *narguile*? – and wearing a luxurious striped silk *robe de
chambre*, a loosely knotted cravat with a large jewel in the pin,

and extending his right hand, the index finger carefully crooked in a gesture like a baroque court dancing master beginning to make a flourish. Murray's studied self-presentation remembers, in a performance of aesthetic imperialism, his forebear William Beckford's notorious nostalgia and theatricality.

An English gentleman in the Orient. After Willes Maddox, *Charles Augustus Murray*, Cairo, 1852.

The sitting must have taken place in Egypt, and Murray may even have suggested Maddox come out there in the first place; soon after the sitting, the 40-year old artist died of a fever in Pera, Constantinople, in 1853, twelve years after David Wilkie. The Cairene location would also explain a disturbing and crucial element in Maddox's portrait, which greatly complicates the elegant aura. I thought at first that the figure on Murray's right just behind him was a sculpture, a prize collectible of the mid-century, such as one of the portrait busts of Aboriginal Tasmanians sculpted and cast in bronze in 1835 in Van Diemen's Land by Benjamin Law, or one of the polychromatic marble carvings of North Africans by the French artist Charles Cordier. On a closer look, however, I realised this figure isn't an effigy, but a real child, posing like a slave in oriental costume, as if for an eighteenth-century plantation-owner portrait. The page is holding a letter in his right hand, and a folder with clasps tucked under his arm, which might be a portable writing desk; he is waiting perhaps for a signature on the document. But he is indeed in waiting, standing very stiffly in attendance, keeping his gaze lowered, the mien of deference. That is why he doesn't look altogether alive.

Law's bronzes are highly controversial, being the earliest captured likenesses of Aboriginals by a white man. With the strong rise in appreciation of orientalist art (spurred on by the collectors in the Gulf), Cordier's sculptures are no longer looked at askance as florid expressions of colonial condescension. However, in both cases, the artists stage their subjects standing on their own, in charge of their own presence. These images convey – at least to my eyes – an enthralling sense of their dignity and spirit as persons. But Murray, with his attendant child, has staged a social spectacle of hierarchy and erasure, almost two decades after Abolition.

Abroad, playing the foreigner could give access to other traditions no longer countenanced at home; affecting a foreign aesthetic style might issue a defiant defence of cosmopolitanism in the metropole; but in the elsewhere of a country under foreign control, it could turn into *çi-devant* nostalgia.

In 1849, Murray organised a hunt in the south. In pursuit of a baby hippo, the hunters duly shot a mother, bathing near the island of Obaysch on the White Nile, but they failed to kill her and she struggled to protect her pup in the bushes on the shore. One of the men 'gaffed it with a boat-hook as it was about to enter the water' but this account is euphemistic, as the baby hippo was probably speared in the traditional hunter's way – the puncture hole on his flank can be seen in the photograph taken many years later at the London Zoo.

In Cairo, the Consul General was delighted to take delivery of the 'little monster' and, the following May, in exchange for a gift of greyhounds and deerhounds to the new ruler, Abbas 1, Muhammad Ali's grandson, arranged for the animal's passage to London, in a boat specially equipped with a pool and a herd of milch cows. Two former snake charmers were hired to attend the baby animal, alongside a keeper who had looked after him from the time of his capture and would continue to do so for the twenty-eight years of the hippo's years of exhibition at the zoo.

Named 'Obaysch' after the place where he was captured, Murray's prize, the first hippo in Europe, created a sensation: visitors flocked to the London Zoo to see him – numbers doubled the year he arrived. There were no less than five royal appearances at his side. A craze for a dance, 'The Hippopotamus Polka', broke out. Abbas 1 captured another hippo and, as he had promised, sent Obaysch a mate, Adhela. After sixteen years of miscarriages, a baby hippo finally arrived.

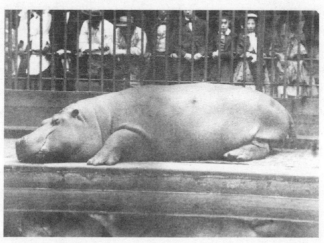

Visitors to the London Zoo crowd behind bars to see *Obaysch*, aged one and a bit, 1852.

The hippos in my memory have been misplaced – there weren't any in the Nile in Cairo, but we used to go to the zoo not far from our flat, on the left bank of the Nile at Giza. There are photographs of me sitting on the ledge of the lion's cage, beside my young mother who is smiling into the Box Brownie. She is wearing a lavish lace-trimmed summer dress, shining white in the photo, and accessorised with a wide-brimmed straw hat and gloves; I am in a short, pretty frock of dotted poplin, white shoes and socks, with a smocked bodice, which she has made for me, and a trimmed sun bonnet.

～

In her furious essay 'Three Guineas', written in 1938, Virginia Woolf savages the heedless assumption of legitimacy by historic institutions – the army, the law, the academy – and she included photographs of establishment and empire on display: Black Rod leading MPs into Parliament and a Chelsea pensioner, wearing a cuirass of medals. Here Woolf is being contradictory and contrary at once – the veteran looks abashed by his conspicuousness, and, to my eyes at least, his eyes have slid sideways as if disowning the heavy panoply of glorious and deadly deeds which loads down his narrow chest, his slight shoulders. He has trimmed his moustache carefully and polished up those medals, but it's not impossible to sense something hovering beside him, a ghost, a sound of a cry as someone is hit, the artillery, the scurrying by of a rat.

Woolf asks, 'What connection is there between the sartorial splendours of the educated man and the photographs of ruined houses and dead bodies? Obviously the connection between dress and war is not far to seek; your finest clothes are those that you wear as soldiers.' The argument then opens out, to connect those gleaming festoons on the veteran's chest to the restrictions on women's education and access to public platforms – from which to oppose war, among other things.

Two years before, in a piece she wrote for the Bloomsberries' Memoir Club, Virginia Woolf asked herself 'Am I a snob?' She answers in the affirmative, but so glancingly and allusively, with so many vignettes and sallies about hostesses and their pretensions that the wit at others' expense dissolves her self-inculpation, and another dazzling performance as satirist and social chronicler of mores remains.

I have always feared that I've inherited my father's anxious snobbery, which went with a kind of quick touchiness over social slights, imagined and other. I worry that I bear the stamp of colonial ambivalence, the creep and cringe of those exiled from the metropole, combined with the brutal superiority of the official class, so painfully observed in memoirs of that era of British power in Egypt, such as the diaries of George Seferis, and the novels of Fausta Cialente, an Italian from Trieste who fled Mussolini's regime for Egypt, where she stayed for nearly thirty years. I fear that something I do or say will betray that early imprint of empire yarns, my childhood saturation in derring-do adventure stories by Captain (Frederick) Marryat, G.A. Henty and Rider Haggard, in Anthony Hope's *The Prisoner of Zenda*, the Hornblower books and John Buchan. I devoured their books as a child bookworm, for they filled the shelves of my grandparents' and parents' bookcases. They painted a world in which the villains are foreigners, often Levantines and 'natives' of Samarkand, Calcutta, Khartoum – orientals, a term which covered Jews and Arabs regardless, like 'the Smyrna merchant' in Graham Greene's early novel, *Stamboul Train*. Or they were generically 'Indians'. Indeed the breadth of this term, embracing peoples from the North to the South Pole, the Caribbean to the subcontinent, discloses the blanket sense of otherness that issued from the vantage point of imperial London to demarcate most of the rest of the world. I have always been scared of this, as I read my way through the books of my father and my grandparents in which the navy, the army, the empire were heroically paraded by the writers I was reading. Later, in Enid Blyton, dark, sinister and crafty foreigners are unmasked by the doughty young heroes.

They were the authors I loved in my formative years. I don't remember the stories, just a mood, a pace. But I know the authors don't conceal their attitudes: they make no pretence at being anything other. And their glorying in the derring-do and brigandry are part and parcel of Admiral Walker's much decorated 'gallantry' in battle, of Charles Augustus Murray's triumphs in the chase.

In another of her essays, 'The War from the Street' (1919), Woolf extends a striking, self-wounding, cold picture of humanity: 'Soon your mind, if one may distinguish one part of the jelly from another, has had certain inscriptions scored upon it so repeatedly that it believes it has originated them; and you begin to have violent opinions of your own . . . so that there is a very marked sameness throughout the jelly.' Her metaphor is one of her culinary flourishes, but it also evokes the jelly of bone marrow, stem cells, DNA. Woolf's excoriation touches my live fear that I too have been inscribed, and the script has sunk all through my jelly without my being aware of it, making me part of thoughts and values that are not my own but come from the cellular mitochondria of my father and his tribal loyalties.

Plum Warner, like many young men from former slave and sugar families, went to school at Harrison College in Barbados, which had been founded with money from the same sugar-plantation owner whose fortune established the Codrington Library at All Souls, Oxford. Later, Plum was sent to school in the motherland – to Rugby, and then to Oriel College, Oxford. But Plum was a West Indian, the twenty-first child (two mothers) of Charles Warner, Attorney General of Trinidad. We used to test him, in old age: 'Go on, Grandpa, tell us the names of all your brothers and sisters! In the right order!' Three had died as babies, so weren't included. We also liked him to repeat how very old he was and how far back he went: he would tell us with pride how his father had been born before the Battle of Trafalgar.

Plum first played for the West Indies (the team was captained by his brother Aucher), and he always remained attached to Trinidad. One of his memoirs – there are several among the score and more books about cricket he wrote – opens with a scene in his father's house in Port of Spain: 'My first recollections of cricket are batting on a marble gallery from the bowling of a black boy who rejoiced in the name of Killebree.' The phrase is filled with the unconscious racist patronising of the era (the 'boy' named after the Creole for hummingbird was probably a grown man), but Plum never disavowed his Trinidadian roots. I once met the historian Hilary Beckles, author of *The Development of West Indies Cricket*, among other works, and was extremely relieved that he greeted me warmly, against all my forebodings, informing me of my grandfather's track record in integrating cricket for the first time.

The history of the Warners in the Caribbean went on rumbling under the story of my father's attitudes: his Britishness was cadenced by the long, deep roots of the family in the empire; I have been writing throughout my life in response to this background. Edward Said drew controversy when he pointed out that, in Jane Austen's *Mansfield Park*, slave plantations in the British West Indies are the source of the Bertrams' wealth, and the adulation of the Royal Navy throughout the closing words of the same author's *Persuasion* similarly stirs uncomfortable associations with the history of the nation's gains: 'Anne was tenderness itself, and she had the full worth of it in Captain Wentworth's affection. His profession was all that could ever make her friends wish that tenderness less, the dread of a future war all that could dim her sunshine. She gloried in being a sailor's wife, but she must pay the tax of quick alarm for belonging to that profession which is, if possible, more distinguished in its domestic virtues than in its national importance.'

Austen's last completed novel was finished in 1817: Baldwin Wake-Walker, the father of the little girl in the Ottoman dress who inspired in me such a longing to be like her, was then 15 years old and already a naval officer, headed for a posting 'on the Jamaica station', where he would enjoy the sweets of life among the plantocracy.

Early memory iv

My fairy doll

I vividly remember forgetting things – it seems paradoxical, but there was a word which I tried to recapture by retracing my steps back into the kitchen where I had left it, it seemed to me. Abdel and Mohammed raised themselves from their mats with smiles and warmth and wanted to help me – did they start up as I came in for some reason? I liked them both; their bright faces looked at me as if amused by me, but kindly, and when they were resting in the heat of the afternoon, they faced me levelly, I remember, since they were now on their elbows on their sleeping mats asking me what I needed. They had strong feet, dust mapping the wrinkles, but supple and lively, like all feet that are rarely shod or only wear slippers when they are.

The word or words that I was trying to find in the kitchen never came back to me and the sensation of missing them persisted as I turned and went back into the passage that ran down the centre of the apartment, which was where the dusk and the cool were deepest. Walking into a shuttered dwelling place in a hot country, touching a floor that's hard and smooth and still and cold under my feet, seeing the only light haloing the edges of the windows, pressing to gain entrance and spill through every space in this interior darkness that resists its blaze still gives me the sensation of quiet and happiness of those times when I roamed our Cairo flat when everyone was having a siesta.

I suppose losing a word and chasing after it would figure strongly in a psychoanalytic session, and it is indeed the first time I experienced the absence of something that had been a part of me – a magic word that caught something particular that I wanted to retrieve, and had been lost with the naming of it. I see now that I have lost their voices and their words: I no longer speak even the childish Arabic I knew then, and it lies beyond my range to project thoughts and words into their minds at this distance; although I believe writing should roam beyond the writer's experience, it feels wrong now, with these unequal relations in the past, to lay claim to knowing how Mohammed and Abdel – and Nanny – thought and felt. At least I know their names: she, whom I loved for the atmosphere she wrought around her, was not called by us by her own name.

Later, I also lost something else besides words, something which seems absurdly apt – to the point of self-parody. My fairy queen dropped her wand.

I searched up and down the sandy path leading to Gezira Sporting Club, poking in the mangy grass that edged it; Nanny urged me on, but I refused to allow her it was a lost cause. My doll's hand was a stump with no fingers, but a flap stitched over a narrow aluminium stem with a silver paper star on the end. This hadn't been done tightly enough, and you could slip the wand out of her grip and wave its star over other toys, playing the fairy. She was soft-bodied, with stuffed pink cotton limbs, a perky pink-cheeked face and another star on her forehead, a white tulle and satin dress and tiny gauze wings on her back. She had begun, poised on her tiny narrow stitched feet, at the top of the Christmas tree, but she had become mine after her descent, and I carried her with me every day.

Later, Mummy made me a fairy queen fancy dress; a family snapshot shows me, a podgy child bedizened in white lace and satin, yet glorying in the gauze moth wings on my back and the magic wand in my hand.

15

A Pocket Dictionary

ictionnaire Français–Italien; Dictionnaire Italien–Français.
Condition poor, covers falling off. Ilia didn't bring this
book with her from Italy; a stamp stuck in the flyleaf says it
came from Le Papyrus, another bookshop in downtown Cairo.
W.H. Smith's can't have started doing business with Italy, I
suppose. Perhaps they never did. The Italian community in
Egypt had been suspect: the men had been interned by the
British when Italy was fighting on the Axis side, and, afterwards,
by the Italians, and they were still suspected of hostility to
British interests, and even to entertaining communist sympa-
thies. Their numbers were also down – the many writers who
were born there left before the war (the poets Giuseppe Ungaretti
and Eugenio Montale had gone, while Marinetti, like them born
in Alexandria, had died in 1944). Leaving Cairo became a feature
of those post-war years for every foreign community: in my
father's address book names are regularly crossed out with the
single word 'Gone', written across them. The Art et Liberté

group, some of whom, like their leader, Georges Henein, had Italian connections (his mother was Italian), wrote in French and Arabic, never English.

~~~

Ilia must have needed such a dictionary immediately on arrival in Cairo, because the lingua franca of much of the community was French. I remember once overhearing someone praise my father's fluency and comment, with a chuckle, on his Levantine accent. Speaking French when you weren't from France was another way of dressing up. French was chic, whereas Arabic was of the people. French was the language of prestige in Egypt and in the eastern Mediterranean and a kind of code. Esmond acquired a little Arabic, Ilia too, and I picked it up a bit more because I was a child and went to kindergarten and played in Gezira Sporting Club with other children, some of them Arabic-speaking. After tangled negotiations with Britain, the Egyptian government had succeeded in stipulating that all business be conducted in Arabic alongside other languages, and that foreign-owned firms, like W.H. Smith's, had to employ a certain proportion of Egyptians on their staff; complaints continued that non-Arab Egyptians – from the cosmopolitan community – were still preferred, but when Esmond recruited the staff for the shop, he kept to the new laws and put together a strong team with locals, Arabic-speaking as well as French. George Nahas, the accountant, was a Copt, and he was assisted by Labiba Zaki and Ziza Botton the bookkeepers, hard-working, scrupulous; Pauline George was his secretary, and like Labiba and Ziza, a charming and efficient young woman. Ahdam Mohamed Alim, who drove the van, was also a local, while Nasrallah, his partner in the delivery van, was originally from Syria – and so on. Ben Mendelssohn, who was from Manchester but had been teaching English literature at the university in

Alexandria before the war, was part of Egypt's large Jewish community. Ben had wanted a change, as there wasn't much of a future for him in academe any longer, he felt. (We used to sing to his wife, Maisie, 'Daisy Daisy, give me your answer, do . . . But you'll look sweet upon the seat of a bicycle made for two'. Except we changed the name to hers – I liked the power of the rhymes and imagining the unknown object, a tandem.)

Ben spoke some Arabic and acted as Esmond's deputy in the office behind the scenes while he, with his sociable tendency and his contacts, and that undefinable something that his background conferred on him, worked front of house. The staff of thirty was a world within a world, a convex mirror in little of the larger horizons of the Middle East.

W.H. Smith staff outing for the visit of Arthur Acland (centre, hatted), board member. Cairo, 1950.

My father did pick up some Arabic, but French was still a sign of polish, a way of displaying sophistication and elegance, ever since the Khedive Ismail built his modern capital over the Ottoman city of Muhammad Ali. Khedivial

Cairo was to be Paris on the Nile, with beaux arts department stores, art nouveau cafés like Groppi's, international luxury hotels – one of them (now the Marriott) is still a perfect orientalist fantasy of a pleasance, and was put up for the visit of Empress Eugénie for the opening of the Suez Canal. Above all, the grand opera house would rival le Palais Garnier. It was built for Verdi's spectacular pharaonic opera *Aida*, which had its premiere in 1871 before the beau monde of Europe, assembled at Egyptian expense.

The khedive's profligacy placed his country deep in debt to foreign creditors – who exacted their dues. The repercussions for Egypt and its citizens went on rumbling through the Suez crisis and on and on.

Pas devant les enfants: this was a catchphrase as I was growing up. Forbidden subjects came cloaked in this idiom of the elite, of the international community, the Copts, the wealthy. In 1949 Jean Cocteau arrived with a large troupe – twenty-two actors, stage technicians, wardrobe mistresses – and put on plays as varied as Racine's *Britannicus* and Sartre's *Huis Clos* as well as his own *La Machine infernale*. The journal he kept at the time gives an impression of triumphant, packed houses everywhere the troupe went, playing before audiences of schoolchildren and *le gratin* of Cairo and Alexandria. One schoolmistress, he records, has 'for twenty years moulded Egyptian youth to our language and our culture'.

At another point in the journal, Cocteau takes note of the English agreement to withdraw their military presence to the Canal, and comments, 'The English in their wisdom have only left in Cairo some highly intelligent men, who pretend to be dilettantes . . . I would like to read their secret reports.' Had he met Donald Maclean, I wonder, the young, handsome, wild-living head of Chancery in the Cairo Embassy from 1948 who from this key position in British diplomacy was reporting to his Russian control? His secret reports would have indeed been worth reading. Perhaps Cocteau also met Lawrence Durrell, who was at the British Council in Alexandria. Or Olivia Manning? He doesn't mention anyone by name.

The film-maker, poet and playwright, who had notoriously remained in Vichy France through the Occupation and the war, was awed – and hollowed out – by the hedonism of Egyptian society: 'The life of the leisured classes of Cairo is harassing,' he writes. 'They gossip and eat standing up, a glass of whisky in their hand. The richest house is a branch of the metro, an interminable journey which goes nowhere.' Cocteau kept a doctor on hand to give him injections of vitamins.

At home, my parents spoke to each other in English and my mother would use Italian with my sister Laura and me, but in that world of whisky soirées, they spoke French, and their conversation, alone together and with friends, was liberally ornamented with Gallicisms, intended to add class and indicate social nuances; it included words for social structures and types (*bourgeois, le beau monde, élite* itself as well as *le gratin*), for shades of acceptability – and fascination (a *roué*, a *voyou*, a *soubrette*, a *coquette*, a *cocotte*, and of course, a *femme fatale*; and there were also certain people who were *racé*). The language of love likewise adopted certain proverbial turns of phrase, of course. In the beau monde of Cairo after the war, *le cinq à sept* meant the hour for trysts, between leaving the office and returning to the domestic hearth, when a beau or a *soupirant* – a lover or would-be lover – would come to call. *Amitié amoureuse* was an indispensable phrase.

French made snobbishness super sophisticated and naturalised it by setting its dictates in the language of urban, Enlightenment culture, gilded by association with Paris, that metropole of *savoir faire*. In this dandyish macaronic which my parents adopted – until my mother's death, she would still say, disapprovingly, 'He's a *poseur*'; or, 'Oh, she suffers from such *folie de grandeur*' (or, in relation to another friend, from '*nostalgie de la boue*'; or, enviously, 'She's a *jolie-laide* but still, she has a *je ne sais quoi* . . .') – I can now read, as if in a faded and stained etiquette manual (*etiquette* itself being one of these French terms) a whole world of relations and values (*comme il faut, noblesse oblige, de rigueur, convenances*, and *goût* itself, that all-important element – taste). Certain characters who had *goût* also had *cachet* and *allure* and attracted more French expressions: *à la mode, chic, soignée, distingué/e, raffiné/e, correcte, bien dans sa peau, en beauté, haut ton, bon ton, mignon/ne, gamin/e*; these French terms conferred on them covetable privileges which gave them permission to behave in certain ways, ways that were fervently envied, while others were to be mocked at best, shunned at worst (*louche, arriviste, parvenu, outré, rusé, capable de tout, nouveau riche*, or simply, with a look down the nose, *nouveau*). 'Isn't that a bit *risqué*?' was a way of pointing up a code of conduct not to be flouted. Ditto *mal vu* (very *mal vu* to bring your floosie to the club). A *mésalliance* meant disgrace. A *bonne affaire* was shady. *Pour épater les bourgeois* was a favourite axiom, used alongside such swipes as 'keeping up with the Joneses', and jokes, like she has ideas '*au-dessus de sa gare*' (above her station). *Trop prononcée* was another favourite term of disapproval – especially for females with opinions (later frequently directed at me).

Déclassé and so *passé* were useful put-downs. I did a cruel and terrible thing when I was beginning to write, and actually described my father in an article as *déclassé*. (How could I have done that? How could he have chuckled that way he did when he told his friends?)

My father loved Proust chiefly as a guide to social niceties and the rich comic contretemps they brought about – in the book and in the world. *Anglomanie* in *A la Recherche* presents a mirror image to the gallicising tendency of the Egyptian bourgeoisie: *le Jockey Club*, *le smoking*, *snob* as a term of praise (Esmond loved to repeat the legendary sign for an outfit in a draper's on the rue Saint-Honoré, '*Très Sport, Presque Cad*').

I'm told these phrases have a strong whiff of mothballs these days (they're a bit *passé*) as the language has moved on, along with the *poules de luxe* and the *petits rats*. The structures it underpinned were already even then subject to a subtle distancing, as if the pageant were always a little absurd, the foreign lingo serving to italicise the concepts, to deliver them with an ironic shrug. She has such *élan vital*! He's rather too *rastaquouère* for my taste. The speaker was only playing. French wasn't a brogue, but a code between initiates.

Any such glossary of class freighting, however, should begin with that adage, *noblesse oblige*, as it provided a fundamental ethical principle of my upbringing, invoked by both my father and my mother whenever they weren't themselves keen on doing something. The repetition of the phrase raised my rebellious hackles, provoked my teenage sulks, and made me quarrel with my father again and again, but until I began thinking about what it meant, I realised that I had misunderstood it all along, and that the meaning is even more complacent. I'd heard *oblige* as transitive – that is, 'nobility is obliging'– and I resisted indignantly the condescension in this. But *noblesse oblige* doesn't mean that; it doesn't evoke an action towards another, but applies only to the subject: nobility requires something of the person who is 'noble'; nobility entails responsibilities; the speaker is presuming nobility on his/her own behalf and is regretting, vaingloriously, that this involves responsibilities.

This phrase made a claim based on class affiliations which I wanted to delete from my own family's sense of itself. But the motto also embarrassed me because I wasn't at all convinced that my family could make such a claim (in this sense the snobbery of it all was coiling me into its premises). This parlance that my southern Italian mother adopted turned her into an impersonator, a foreigner posing as an insider. Yet women enjoyed more licence to practise this form of social ventriloquy than men: a wife could pass, as it were, when a man might be viewed askance as an impostor. A class infiltrator. Not rich and successful enough, perhaps, to be labelled *parvenu* or *nouveau*, but still not entitled. The French phrase, adopted as different from native parlance, was part of a role, another kind of fancy dress.

That odd-sounding word, '*rastaquouère*', was one of my father's and mother's favourites, used on and off to brand an acquaintance or a friend, uttered with relish at the scandalous nature of the individual in question. It belonged on the same spectrum of meaning as other derogatory but somehow seductive terms – with *poète maudit, enfant terrible, monstre sacré*. It evoked piratical, scapegrace, much-travelled men, steeped in self-delusion, living on the edge of respectability, often only just this side of the law, unpredictable, morally dangerous, and with an unreliable relationship to credit. Scoundrels. Women couldn't be described as *rastaquouères* – though there were exceptions in the case of Sarah Bernhardt and Rachel, probably because both of them were actresses and Jewish. A *rastaquouère* was not a *gentleman* (in French the term has a certain extra *je ne sais quoi*); a *rastaquouère* was dashing, with a tendency towards sexual unscrupulousness. An *aventurier*; a fancy man, on occasion.

Current French–English dictionaries, I see now, give 'flashy foreigner' as the definition. *Le petit Larousse* offers 'a stranger living in grand style whose means of existence are not known'. Francis Picabia, who in 1920 published an exuberantly outrageous Dada rant called *Jésus-Christ Rastaquouère*, thought God qualified. Today Wikipédia glosses '*rastaquouère*' as '*un personnage exotique étalant un luxe suspect et de mauvais goût'* (an exotic character displaying suspect luxury, with poor taste), and goes on to state that in the 1880s it was used to stigmatise a parvenu, and has come to be synonymous with a gigolo. The word is derived, it is thought, from Spanish/Portuguese for *rastrar* (scrape) and *cueros* (hides), and was contemptuously used of the super-rich Argentinians and Brazilians who'd made their money in fur and leather and, arriving in Paris for the Exposition Universelle of 1889, created a splash: they were arrayed in splendiferous jewels and clothes and spent freely. In Portuguese, by contrast, *rastacüeros* are closer to poor 'good-for-nothings'. Used by Englishmen like my father it has the appalling effect of distancing the true Englishman from the Levantine of British nationality, holder of a British passport, who formed the majority of the community in Cairo and Alexandria.

After Cairo, and a short interval in London, we went to live in Brussels, and there I began reading *Tintin* – Hergé was a kind of national treasure in Belgium, and as a child in the mid-1950s, I heard nothing against him then and can't recall if my parents ever discussed him or expressed a view on my enthusiasm for his adventures. Tintin himself, Milou his little dog, the endearingly vague Professor Calculus, the explosive Capitaine Haddock with his wild torrents of expletives, the Tweedledum and Tweedledee detectives Thomson and Thompson and above all the locales (Caribbean piracy, the pyramids, Aztec human sacrifice, Andean sun worship) gripped me, made me laugh and gasp and keep reading. When I've worried, as I often have in the past, that my colonial background and the adventure yarns of the empire have corrupted my mind, when I've looked at my appetite for exotic places and ripe language, I overlooked what a crucial part the *Tintin* books have played in this story. Tintin doesn't present an obvious fit with the profile of the colonial oppressor; he is meant to be a journalist and acts like a sleuth, but Hergé pitted the boy hero in plus fours against various figures of malignant power, including his arch-enemy, Roberto Rastapopoulos, who makes an appearance as a principal character in *Cigars of the Pharaoh* (1934) and expands into full-blooded villainy in another orientalist adventure, *The Blue Lotus*. I had completely deleted this antagonist from memory: but I now realise his exploits are set in Egypt, and are steeped in European attitudes to that country, ancient and modern. *Cigars of the Pharaoh* opens on a cruise ship called MS *Isis* which has docked in Alexandria; on board, Tintin comes upon Rastapopoulos as he is beating up the Egyptologist Sophocles Sarcophagus. Tintin recognises Rastapopoulos, commenting that he is 'the millionaire film tycoon, king of Cosmos Pictures'. The tycoon's private yacht is called *Scheherazade*, and a fancy-dress ball is being held on it the night of one of the darkest deeds which Tintin manages to uncover and foil.

Rastapopoulos' appearance accords with many cartoon images of Jews, the stuff of Nazi propaganda. Hergé protested that the character wasn't Jewish and that he himself wasn't anti-Semitic, but readers may have their doubts. Hergé reworked his own opinions and writings over and over, as his interpreters have carefully tracked, but 'despite these careful rejiggings, Hergé's sense of guilt keeps pulsing through'. Sidestepping open racist or anti-Semitic feelings, Roberto Rastapopoulos, Marquis di Gorgonzola, has been strongly flavoured Italian and Greek by his creator, but these handles of the comic villain serve as a form of disguise, adopted by a personality capable of infinite deceptions, a figure of many wiles, *polytropos*, and many faces.

Spoken in English *rasta* belongs in a sound cluster of words beginning with *ra* – *rascal* and *rapscallion*, *rackety* and *raffish*, *rabid* and *rank* (strong-smelling), *rattle* and *roar*; *hurrah* and *ra-ra* reverberate on the outer rings of these chords. In French today, *rastaquouère* is usually shortened to *rasta*, as Francis Picabia had done when he coined *rastadada* in the titles of paintings he made in 1920. But as *rasta* it overlaps with – on no etymological grounds – a wholly distinct cultural milieu, the Rastafarians, which may have given it a racist tinge against blacks as well as against 'Levantines' – Ali Smith in her 2016 novel *Autumn* remembers an American cereal that featured a happy-clappy black figure called Rastus. But now the reverberations of rasta have shifted again, through contact with the magic aura of Bob Marley.

My father and his friends adopted the term *rastaquouère* for certain figures of their acquaintance – who always provoked him to chuckle with delight at their delinquencies. They were glamorous, often subtly Levantine, or 'oriental'. One such was Ivar Bryce, whom he'd known from Eton; he was dubbed 'Burglar Bryce' (behind his back, of course) because he'd sailed for America to make his fortune, and on board the ocean liner met an heiress and was mysteriously able to present her with a magnificent engagement ring. That is one story, but there were several others.

Ivar was handsome in a way Ilia called 'louche'; as he lived some of the time in the Bahamas, he had a sheeny hazelnut tan all over, except his lips which were full and purplish, like his feet, where the veins bulged. I was fascinated by the overall sensuality of his body, and for a time, when I was a teenager, he'd invite me to stay in Moyns Park, the Essex manor house that had once been in his family and he'd bought back and restored luxuriously. His invitations to me were a kind of grooming, it would now be recognised, scoping me for a future as eye candy for one of the wrecked aristocrats he collected at weekends. He had thought up special refinements of pleasure for his surroundings: in the park, homing budgerigars flashed by, lime-green and sky-blue, returning to chinoiserie aviaries in the interior courtyard at dusk, and wild strawberries from the kitchen garden appeared on matching breakfast china on my tray in bed in the morning. In the Caribbean, he devised a beach house called Xanadu, a crescent-shaped pavilion where all the furnishings and decorations were made of coral and mother-of-pearl, and the posts of the bed were narwhal tusks.

The Burglar's exploits provided my father and his friends with endless entertainment – he'd been a spy in the war, active in disinformation tactics which played a part in undoing US neutrality. They speculated that since Ian Fleming, another school chum, had remained a close friend of the Burglar's, the charms of his hero James Bond were cast in Ivar's mould.

Ilia didn't find any of this amusing, and didn't like going to lunch there, loathing the lazy corruption he and his friends exuded – I was drawn, I was wary, but when you are young, curiosity overcomes fear. Significantly, Ivar collected forgeries, and explained to me at length one day how they were an excellent bargain, being much cheaper than the real thing but impossible to tell apart. He was especially admiring of Elmyr de Hory, the tragic hero of a clever and disturbing late film by Orson Welles, *F for Fake*. Though Esmond chuckled and Ilia frowned, they both agreed that the word for Ivar's character was *rastaquouère*.

In the past, this strange word conveyed a tight knot of tension, in which the seduction of the strange and a flight from tradition remains tangled up and streaked through with repulsion and anxiety about newfangledness. A desire to be foreign, so marked in the passion for costume and the pretence of being French, struggles in the colonial past with a loathing of the foreigner; the figure of a *rastaquouère* is packed with that historic ambivalence, in ways that still lie deep down inside the present increase in hostility to outsiders and to foreigners.

In a book called *Rastaquarium: Marcel Proust et le 'modern style'*, the cultural historian Sophie Basch identifies *rastaquouère* characteristics with a crucial, distinctive sphere of the *fin de siècle*;

her play on words takes a leap, however, and attaches the term
to aesthetics, and specifically to the bizarre, aquatic obsessions
of late nineteenth- and early twentieth-century decorative arts.
While art nouveau effloresced with terrestrial forms, burgeoning
into luscious fruit and flowers, leaves and grasses, its offshoot,
le 'modern style', transformed interiors into mysterious sea-caves,
covering wallpapers and fabrics, street furnishings and theatre
sets, book bindings and fashionable apparel with marine wonders
– seaweed, jellyfish, polyps and octopus, crustaceans, shells, sea
anemones, et al. Rastaquouère style, as evoked by Basch, gives
this 'modern style' a distinctive, even grotesque strangeness: it
was intended to be mixed, impure, monstrous, and was received
as such by admirers and detractors.

English was the idiom used in the phrase 'modern style'
because the London furniture-maker Maple's was one of the
innovatory suppliers, as Liberty's was of le style Liberty. But
the use in French of the foreign expression does something
more: it again helps to exoticise the idiom of the design – to
estrange it. After the invention of bathyspheres and underwater
photography, the world beneath the sea beckoned as a zone of
supreme, undiscovered mystery – twilit, surprising, inhabited
by rare, monstrous creatures, irreducibly alien and fascinating.
The aquarium was a prime surrealist realm of le merveilleux,
explored by the film-maker Jean Painlevé, who turned underwater documentary into a new artistic genre when he recorded
the doings of hermit crabs, octopus and seahorses; his films
count among the weirdest and most wonderful examples of
the surrealist quest for convulsive beauty.

Colette's husband, Willy (Henri Gauthier-Villars), claimed
to have made up the word in the first place, but Basch traces
it, far more significantly, to a journalist who became a Dreyfusard.
Her inquiry leads her to Proust, taste, foreigners in general, and
specifically anti-Semitism and the Dreyfus crisis. It seems to

me that her view of the 'rastaquarium' intersects very uncomfortably with my parents' usage of the category *rastaquouère*, and the combination of deep prejudice and envious emulation which she diagnoses reflects their attitudes. They would absolutely recognise the elements of exoticism, luxury, aesthetics and fantasy (the Burglar and his crustaceous scene-setting). Just as giving up English in favour of French added tone to conversation, sparkle to wit, so *le style rastaquouère*, usually combined with a dash of performative fancy dress, offered a way of self-fashioning that singled someone out from the crowd.

In Paris, as reflected in Proust's novel, upholders of tradition who loathed the new aesthetic also deplored the defence of Dreyfus. Basch presses more deeply into the politics of strangeness on home ground, and comments, 'the condemnation of "modern style" by the Duke and Duchess of Guermantes and likewise by Charlus is a facet of their anti-Dreyfus feelings.' As Proust's characters see it, 'Art nouveau, an unsettling force of national alignments, an agent of socialism, of Belgian–Jewish cosmopolitanism, and the Ballets Russes, which reflect all these currents, betrays tradition in the same way as Captain Dreyfus betrays the Nation.'

In the British Empire, the *rastaquouère* aesthetic also set rippling conflicting emotions, and curiosity – and repressed identification – necessarily grew differently from unquestioning xenophobia and anti-Semitism at home. And yet, in the social context of Egypt in the post-war era, much as I would like to discern a progressive dynamic in the cult of the exotic, it eludes.

Early memory v

At the Great Pyramid

On an outing with my parents to the Great Pyramid, the carved blocks of stone were so huge that I couldn't keep up with them as we were climbing up together, when all of a sudden, I found myself lifted from one to another of the steep steps. An Egyptian – possibly a guide – had come to my rescue. 'Memory is movement,' the neuroscientist Chris Frith has said, and certainly the sense of soaring lingers, and with it the delight I felt as the warm firm strength of the man in a long white tunic, who picked me up and set me down again one block at a time, changed me from a hot clumsy child, clambering unsuccessfully on the stones, into some fledgling winged creature, as if he were the sparrow I once watched as she propelled her fledglings off the edge of my roof until they found themselves aloft, startled that they hadn't tumbled to ground but had become one with the air.

Another time, I was being taken on a donkey ride near the foot of the Great Pyramid, and a friend of my parents was laughing beside me. He was somehow a handsome and uncomfortable presence – and though I was too young to know this, I wasn't too young not to feel his confidence in his own charm. He was holding the reins and striding ahead, turning back to look at me now and then. His attention was exciting but also a bit peculiar – grown-ups who were *visitors usually didn't play with me. My mother was fluttering as we drew away from her where she stood. Later, she told me that she was scared when this friend of theirs took off with me at a trot; Donald Maclean was a senior and admired figure in the Embassy, but Ilia knew about his crazy routs. She didn't trust him, and she didn't like him: his drinking made everyone around him tense, yet they pretended, it seemed to her, to find it funny and normal, too scared to check him. On the other hand, she thought of Melinda, his wife, as one of her friends. They had a lot in common: Melinda was stylish, social, lively, and had several children, and she too was an incomer in the circles of British influence – an American. Both women were foreign wives, and Donald was, like Esmond, another English gentleman very high on the spectrum of that condition.*

A snapshot my father took of me on the donkey, Maclean leading the animal, and the pyramids for backdrop, was borrowed by a programme about the Cambridge Spies on the BBC; my mother lent it, without the means in those days to copy it or scan it. The empty space in the album is captioned, 'Marina with Donald Maclean, 1951', the year he disappeared.

During the long months after Maclean vanished, Melinda became ill and was admitted to the London Clinic where, after we had returned to England, Ilia went to visit her. My mother was brimming with sympathy for her plight. Later, Ilia would often recall, and her perplexity never faded with repetition, 'I went to see her. She was sitting up in the bed, and she'd just had an operation. "I haven't the foggiest," she said, when I asked her what had happened to Donald. I believed her completely and I felt really sorry for her, she had been left just like that, with no news of his whereabouts or anything. She was very frightened: he might be dead. They had children, and he had just disappeared into thin air, it seemed.

'Then, just a few days later – can you beat it? – she was gone. To Moscow, too. To join him there.

'And I'd thought we were friends and she was telling me the truth.'

16

A Powder Compact

In a sleeve of blue watered silk, the box was a solid mass like an ingot, the gold of the case and the amethysts which framed the image on the lid adding to its bulk. This picture in the centre, painted on enamel, showed an odalisque reclining on a daybed, fanned by dark-skinned attendants waving peacock feather fans. A card included in the packaging declared, 'My most esteemed Mme Emilia, Please accept this small token of my appreciation. The lady reminds me of you.' The embossed name on the card was M. Georges Dimitrino. When Ilia gently prised open the small, precious receptacle, she found it was a powder compact: there was a mirror on the inside of the lid, a small pink puff, and a film of waxed paper, which, when peeled off, released a scent of roses, fresh and cool and vital.

~

'What shall I do?' Ilia asked Sadika. 'It's so pretty! Do I have to give it back?'

Sadika was a new friend, whom she'd met at a ladies' charity do when they were both wearing picture hats they had made and trimmed themselves. She replied, 'No, no. But they're always trying to go to bed with us, don't worry about it. It's a point of courtesy with them.' She turned the compact over in her hands, impressed by the lavishness of the present. 'Just be careful! Don't let him get you alone with him, anywhere. You can tell Esmond about it, and I don't expect he'll want you to send it back . . . he likes you being such a success. It reflects well on him.'

Esmond in fact laughed when she showed him.

'Yes, I can see the likeness,' he said, taking in appreciatively the painting on the lid.

He wasn't jealous of men friends, she would find. He often befriended them, instead. But he was unpredictable. Unless they were Italians. He would get cross, for example, if he thought she was being spendthrift, and though in her early life she and her mother and sisters had learned to be far more careful than he had ever had to be, he was on the watch all the time. His anger at this was a diversion, she learned, from its true source, and that wasn't something she could help: he sensed, perhaps, without bringing up into full awareness that she did not love him as much as he loved her. Or perhaps, that their ways of loving were taking different paths.

In 1948 Smith's had given him a rise, but his salary was still only £437.10.0 a month, and with his taste for high living (and the card table), it didn't go far enough – even with Ilia's clever needle and frugal ways.

'Nanny eats like a horse and the darling little woman [me] has a terrific appetite,' he wrote home to his parents plaintively as he totted up the household accounts. The order book at the shop was proving so much slower to fill than he expected, not that sales would affect his income, at least not directly. But one trouble after another was preventing what he had happily imagined, his business swooping down to the Sudan, and marching east into Palestine and beyond, to Syria, repeating in civilian clothes the Allies' advance in the desert when he had fought under Monty before and after Alamein.

Of course, they'd known from the start that things were turbulent. But Michael Hornby had assessed the risk and decided the business was worth a go. Who would have expected Israel to be declared a nation and Palestine abolished, just like that – with all the ghastly repercussions? The Palestinians, the best of the bunch in the region, industrious, clever, culti-vated – and the Jews, weren't they the energy supply? – not much between either of them when all was said and done – capital fellows, the lot of them, and their women even better, as was so often the case, attentive, clever.

And now this, another war. Just the last thing the region needed was fighting between themselves, and the wound inflicted by defeat festering. Moreover, the influx of refugees was putting a strain on local resources – Cairo was bursting at the seams and prices were climbing.

Sadika had come round one afternoon that week, during Ilia's usual time for visitors, and they were drinking iced tea on the terrace overlooking Gezira Sporting Club, with the racecourse to the right just in view and the whitewashed block of the Anglo-American Hospital to the left; it was there Ilia would give birth to my sister Laura, in the summer of the following year.

They'd met soon after Ilia arrived at a ladies' luncheon in the Heliopolis Palace Hotel, which was being given by Princess Faiza, King Faruq's eldest sister, in her role as president of La Femme Nouvelle – she was raising funds for her humanitarian causes. The two young women instantly recognised each other, and not only because they had, with their understated hats and gloves, a certain chic, but because they were both married to Englishmen, and a certain sort of Englishman at that – public school, officer class, club members – Christopher was a regular at the Turf Club downtown. Both young wives were penniless and had reached the society they found themselves in through the men they had married; tacitly, they valued them and the status they conferred. Life had handed Sadika, who was half-Egyptian, half-German, a similar laconic playscript in a new language; she and my mother were practising its precepts as they went along, improvising.

'Christopher is thirty-four years older than me,' said Sadika.

'Esmond is fifteen years older than me,' said Ilia.

'I am Christopher's fourth wife, but nobody's meant to know, so we don't talk about it.'

They found much to discuss.

Sadika, Ilia's close friend and confidante, half-Egyptian, half-German, wife of Christopher Tancred, c.1945.

Sadika had met Christopher Tancred OBE, formerly of the RAF, when he arrived in Cairo as the representative of Dunlop's tyres across the region from Jordan to Eritrea – a lucrative and none too arduous post, and one which, like Esmond's job with W.H. Smith's, had enough class, in that colonial society, to give access to trade representatives in the national regimes, and to the cocktail parties and charity raffles to make useful connections.

'Admirers – like this chap who's given you this expensive gift – they like to show off, and they'll say things to excite one,' said Sadika. 'It's all phoney.' She was waving a cigarette, not exactly smoking it. To her new friend, the ring of lipstick on its tip, between her painted fingernails, looked very sophisticated.

Ilia wasn't so confident. 'Don't they mean it?' she asked.

'It's a charade! But if they ever get close, they'll have a go. And you mustn't even think of it, because they'll forget all about it, immediately. Let them dangle. Always. All's lost otherwise.'

Although Sadika Tancred (née Miligui) was born in Berlin the same year as her new friend Ilia, she was very much more worldly-wise about Cairo and its ways, since she had lived there ever since the war started. Her Egyptian father while he was in Berlin did 'nothing much', said Sadika, disparagingly, 'he never did do much'. There, he met and married her mother, who was German. As soon as war broke out, he was interned, one of a tiny number of Egyptian nationals in the country whom the Third Reich rounded up in protest against Egypt's declaration of neutrality. On 22 July 1940, her mother was given an official permit to leave the country and go back to Egypt, and she brought Sadika and her brother to Cairo for safety; the British there had decided not to bother about the women or children of enemy aliens.

You couldn't really choose between the two young women for elegance and glamour. Both stood tall and therefore neither of them wore heels; dark red polish gleamed on their fingertips. Sadika's build was more powerful: she had a square-shouldered set to her upright slenderness that Ilia envied (Sadika did not have to add shoulder pads to her outfits to improve their hang). The arcs of Sadika's brows were as harmonious as if drawn by twin compasses, her irises grey-gold and green, her brow high, her cheekbones too, her hair dark and gleaming like a blackbird's plumage; her voice was lower than her new friend's, far less girlish and gay. Above all, they were foreigners from the Allies' enemy nations, and had married Englishmen before Italy changed sides and Germany was defeated. Furthermore, they were both fatherless: Sadika's father, Radwan Khalil Miligui, though he was still alive, had disappeared from the family's life and she had no feeling for him except antipathy. She had however remained a Muslim, spoke Arabic, not fluently, but far better than most of the British colony. In spite of the differences in their origins and nationalities, when the two young women met in Cairo, they had so much in common they were to remain friends the whole length of their days.

~~~

Not long before Sadika met and married Christopher, she was invited to Tehran by her aunt, Sadiqa (after whom she was named – the word simply means 'friend'), and who, among her Egyptian relatives, was the only one she felt close to. This Sadiqa's husband was highly placed in the Persian civil service, and during the course of her niece's visit, H., a top diplomat and courtier, came to dinner and was charmed by the young woman from Cairo whom he was sitting next to.

Born circa 1881–1883, this small but elegant figure was English-educated, well-connected, highly placed and destined for power in his own country.

Sadika confided to Ilia several years later as they remembered those days when they sat on the terrace overlooking Gezira, 'At first I thought, he'd want something, and it's not right. But he never did anything except write me these long long letters. The first one arrived as soon as I got back to Cairo and to Christopher, and I'm telling you, ever since I left Tehran, he wrote to me almost every day.' Sadika paused. 'He'd mention my mother and my granny but never Christopher! And he'd send gifts, too, so many! They'd come with the diplomatic bag from Tehran and the driver would bring them round to us from the Embassy.' She laughed. 'Lavish gifts,' she touched her ears. 'These came from him, in the official car with diplomatic plates.'

H. would write to her, she remembered, 'in English and French, switching between them. He sometimes talked politics – he was a big shot, you know – but mostly music and books. Always addressing me as Dea – Goddess!' She paused. 'Imagine. It was lucky he stayed put in Tehran. I think he'd have to have had a go if he'd come to Cairo. They always need to.' She chuckled. 'The caviare was delicious.'

'Caviare?'

'Yes, heavy pots of it . . . At first Christopher looked a bit put out, but then, you know, he likes caviare, and he's rather happy with the supplies he sends . . . Besides, he knew my suitor was a long way away . . . and besides,' she lowered her voice, 'he was even older than Christopher . . .'

~~~

Sadika gave my sister Laura and me the letters her longtime swain had written; she had copied and listed them, with notes about their contents. I began reading; they are fervent, frequent, gossipy, solicitous, extravagantly flattering. He makes gallant compliments about the beauty spot on her cheek, quoting a poem by Hafez in support. He tells her the family circle misses her lively and glamorous presence. The decorum is a bit stilted, even scholastic. He is never less than impeccable in his manners; he sounds lonely. The letters strike me as the outpourings of someone who has nobody to talk to. They open, 'My dear Dea' or sometimes 'My <u>very</u> very dear Dea'; he goes on to report on books and plays, on current affairs near and far. Sometimes he apologises, on the lines of 'I hope you are not bored by my pedantic elucubrations . . .' Every letter ends with a declaration of endless love.

H. is a significant historical figure in the history of Iran but is now forgotten except by specialists in the field. His presence in the letters to his goddess brings a deep shiver of the past into the ambit of this story of post-colonial Cairo; with him comes the cold breeze of the spectral empire under Victoria. He was the son of the Persian minister in London at the end of that queen's reign, and became a senior diplomat (London, Washington); his two brief periods in power in his country coincided with the turmoil over the oil industry before the election of Mohammad Mosaddeq and the US-led coup that ousted him and consolidated the shah. In 1952, for example, he resigned in protest against the nationalisation of the oil industry. Yet his political longevity, as he negotiated through chaotic upheavals and retained his calm, showed a similar, persevering tact, in the same vein as his courtship of his beloved Dea.

These were the last years of his life. H. was over forty years older than Sadika. In his photographs, he cuts a dapper figure, with a trimmed moustache and swept-back hair; small, trim and upright, in court dress dripping with decorations, he has the look of a dancer, controlled but light on his feet.

'What is it about me? Always the really old boys fell for me . . .' Sadika wondered, when I went to see her to read to her what I was writing about her (in her old age her eyesight has dimmed).

During those days long ago, Sadika confided to Ilia, 'I now expect the letters, and I'm no longer alarmed. It's all very strange, but I don't think I shall ever see him again, and even if I were to go to Switzerland to meet him there – that's what he has suggested – I am sure nothing would happen. With these men, the longing is all. They run away from the real thing. It is all a fantasy. I am his fantasy.'

'Look, I brought you one or two to show you.' She handed Ilia a sheaf of silky onion skin pages embossed heraldically. Endearments drifted from the spiky script, intermingled with allusions to his rose garden and lines of Persian poetry.

A kind of melancholy came over Ilia – so much unfulfilled yearning.

Sadika was no longer laughing. My mother looked at her thoughtfully. 'Would you have preferred something more to happen?'

'It used to worry me sometimes,' said Sadika, 'when he sent me jewellery and flowers and sounded so passionate.'

'But you must have liked it, being a goddess?' The powder compact Georges Dimitrino had sent Ilia felt smoky hot in her hand as she contemplated the painting on the lid, puzzled. 'What will happen if I accept it?' She clicked it open again and inhaled the scent. Her questions to Sadika were subdued, because she couldn't help feeling that the long courtships and long-distance amours her friend was describing must be a bit unsatisfactory.

She wished she could ask her sisters what they thought she should do, but when she wrote to them, it was hard to convey her puzzlement, and her mother wouldn't approve, she knew, of any thought beyond her husband. Would she ever see her mother again? The thought cast a shadow across her, as she considered Georges Dimitrino and what she had done to inspire him to this sudden gesture – they had talked of books, and writing, and her favourite writers. They'd exclaimed together over their shared love of *Un Amour de Swann*. Had that set him off?

> This morning (Sunday) we motored [Esmond reported], with Marina to Seddiqi's country place and the Delta looked quite lovely. So did his garden. An orange bignonia and a mauve thunbergia ramping all over the pergola there and now it is the season of the large red poinsettia flowers.

Ahmed Seddiqi Pasha, one of Esmond's new friends and 'a very important customer', was giving a party in his villa in the country. He was also another declared, fervent 'admirer' of Ilia's.

An elegant figure, tall, with a long straight-backed stride, he was one of the few Egyptian – Arab – friends my parents made. In a photograph of him with Ilia, he is definitely making bedroom eyes at her. It seems he was happy mixing with the British or perhaps it was the other way around. Seddiqi Pasha's wife Ulla was German and Jewish, and maybe that made him a cosmopolitan.

Cairo nights: Ilia in one of the evening outfits she made, with Seddiqi Pasha and an unidentified friend.

He had started buying books and other things from the shop as soon as it opened and would invite Esmond and Ilia out to dinner in restaurants in town or in his summer retreat, Tara – antebellum *Gone With the Wind* was the theme of a famous fancy dress party in 1943, and the fashion hadn't faded; there, in the large garden, the Pasha offered whisky and soda, beer, lemonade and Coca-Cola, with dishes of meze and fruit.

As Ilia was standing quietly in the shade of a large magnolia tree, their host brought over another guest and introduced him: 'Georges Dimitrino, one of our melancholic spirits, a writer of distinction.'

The poet waved a hand slowly in dismissal and gave Ilia a small bow: 'The Pasha is my rival.' He paused. Did she catch a twinkle in his eye? 'He's a keen book collector. How can I compete? But together we are making the fortunes of your delightful husband!'

Georges was 'well preserved', as Ilia liked to say of older men, with a moustache sparking with silver under a high arched nose; he wore round spectacles like Esmond's and his eyes behind them looked sad, with the lid of his left eye drooping. She noticed his hands, and his pale pink gleaming nails (a man who goes to the barber's and has a manicure, too, she noted).

'My chief interest is in Egyptian archaeology,' their host Seddiqi was saying, 'and yours is flora and fauna. So I think, my dear fellow, you have very little to fear from me in this regard. Besides, you are truly literary – I know you read all the young terrors . . .'

Ilia wanted to know more — she asked Georges Dimitrino to tell her more.

Remembering this brief conversation, Ilia turned over the compact wonderingly.

'But this present? Surely Dimitrino – Georges – can't be serious?' Ilia was genuinely perplexed.

'Oh, he'll be writing about you, before you know it. A special rare flora . . . isn't that so?'

Ilia opened the gift and inspected herself in the mirror inside the lid, lifting the flat puff and powdering the tip of her nose.

'Don't you think Esmond will mind if I keep it?'

Uneasiness stirred inside her, at the thought that he might even be pleased.

'If he's anything like Christopher,' said Sadika, 'I don't think so. He might feel relieved – takes some of the pressure off him when it comes to presents.'

~~~

In 2016, a letter arrived for me from Cairo, handwritten on heavy paper, from the diplomat's great-grandson. He had heard about the letters Sadika Tancred had kept all this time and he was coming to London and hoped to be able to look at them: 'Our family lost all records of our history in the revolution of 1979,' he told me, 'including every document relating to H. These letters are the only thing that remain.'

Laura and I gave him the sheaf, and he made another set of copies. Sadika had given the letters to us in the first place because she sensed their historical singularity, and she hoped they might be used in some way. Perhaps H. himself wrote them for the future, this future in which he lives on as a lover of great refinement, as a man of delicate courtesies mixed with ardour rather than the broker of the shah's oil policies. Sadika would like the story to be told – and his great-grandson will tell it in a different way from me. He is a journalist and lives in Cairo; his articles – on literature and other aspects of Iran, Egypt, and the Middle East in general – have appeared in various papers and on various websites. Though he is much taller than his forebear, he seems to be cultivating a resemblance to him, and with large, almond-shaped eyes and curving eyebrows, he looks like a figure in a Persian miniature. He was most elegantly dressed and wearing an astrakhan hat.

Recently, he sent me a message about a trip to the Sinai he had made with a friend, and added, 'I have frequently returned to H.'s letters. They have brought together many family memories, which I have been writing down.'

~~~

In the notebooks my mother kept all her life, she copied out quotations, most of them about love, coming at the question of what it is and what it demands through the words of many novels she read. Her reflectiveness on the topic is a sign of the gap ever widening between my father and herself. He was pragmatic, extrovert and cared more about their social contacts than any fine-textured inner feelings. It is sad but perhaps not harsh to say he was oblivious to her hunger, not exactly for love, but for talking of love and coming to understand better its mysteries.

From *Swann's Way*, she picked out 'One's ideal is always unattainable, and one's actual happiness mediocre.'

And the Egyptian novelist Naguib Mahfouz offered her this thought: 'For love is like health. It is taken lightly when present and cherished when it departs.'

Early memory vi

Learning things

The back terrace gave on to the desert and Giza to the west; on a clear day, when the wind wasn't swirling sand into the air, you could see the Great Pyramid and, as if podded from its parent's underground roots, its two smaller neighbours. Towards sunset we'd gather to watch the sun go down beyond the startling green of Gezira Sporting Club, with its bars and tables under parasols, swings and slides, lido and croquet lawns, racecourse, snooker room and golf course. This terrace was an outside room, shaded by awnings and fully furnished with wicker chairs plump with cushions – the fabrics flowery and lush but faded from the brightness of the light. It was my father's favourite part of the flat, where he could stretch out in the shade, or sometimes, with a cigar clenched between his teeth, tend to his pots and trellises, where he was growing flowers and rambling vines, mustard and cress, nasturtium, chilli peppers and many herbs.

It was there I learned to count, by watching the sun set: when the bottom edge of the burning disc touched the horizon, we would start . . . one, two, three. The orb slipped down very very fast. Were we dispatching it into the welter of orange, flame and gold, or tugging it back from disappearing? Every night we wanted to *beat the time made the evening before, either dipping below the horizon more quickly or more slowly. Whichever it was, I learned to count to ten by watching the sun set in Egypt. 'Night falls quickly in the tropics,' Daddy would say.*

When the sun had disappeared, its afterglow cast up in the few ribbons of vapour just above the slight bulge the earth, the ebbing light settled over us, over the city. There must have been lights in night-time Cairo, but I don't remember them.

I learned to name and recognise colours when I went to school. I was first enrolled in a French convent, where the nuns — perhaps Sisters of Charity? — wore the full fig. On my second day, a sister asked me to hold out my hand. I recall being puzzled by her request, but even more astonished when she whacked me across the palm with a ruler. I remember her mouth tightened with a kind of pleasure. I told Mummy, or maybe I was just crying when I came home, and I was taken away from that establishment forthwith (I was lucky, a much-loved and petted child), and sent instead to a small cheerful play school a few stairs down in the same block of flats where we lived. There, I learned the words 'red', 'green', 'yellow' and 'blue', from the low painted tables each group of children sat around for our lessons.

Daddy taught me to swim: he placed me face down on a stool in our sitting room and flexed my legs and arms in the correct froggy shapes for breaststroke; every day I went to the pool with Nanny to the Club behind our block of flats. She was from the Sudan, I was told. It was the custom in Egypt in those days for the servants to be black, as were Abdel and Mohammed in the kitchen. Nanny was comfy and giving, bringing me back sticky sweets after her day off. She would watch from the side of the pool as I splashed about inside a rubber ring. My swimsuit's wet texture still wriggles under my fingertips: scratchy wool — why did the English abroad wear woollen clothes to swim in? — which slumped slimily when taken off — and, delicious and fascinating, the stretchy little pockets of air

*created by the lighter, elasticated fabric of my far preferred outfit —
'ruched' as my mother called it in the precise terminology she learned
from the sewing patterns she used.*

*When Daddy joined us, he took me on his back which was flat
and large and smooth, like a fat dolphin's, and hooted as we made
lumbering and splashy progress through the water.*

*His body was round and solid underneath his tropical suits
which were pale in colour but also solid, the linens and cottons
lined and interlined so that he truly felt like a tower of strength;
but on the inside of his right arm he had a scar that was terrible,
a rope of raised flesh white as a fish that twisted all the way from
his wrist to his elbow where he had been cut open as a small boy
to scour the infected part and drain the pus that was building
there. Something had happened that began small and grew
devastatingly, until his whole arm was full of streptococcal
poisoning; and this sepsis took hold of him in the days before
penicillin, and before anaesthetic. The drastic surgery was the only
way to save his limb. It was 1917, he was 10¾, it says, so very
precisely, on his fever chart, which has been kept for all these years.
He was lucky to survive: for weeks through the summer that year
he had a raging temperature.*

*It still gives me shivers when I remember him lifting his sleeve
to show the scar; later, seeing engravings of écorché figures in
anatomical books would bring on the same fluttering fear in my
guts, one body responding to another's past and its ordeals with a
flow of feeling through our separate matter that needs no actual
contact to feel real. The other side of his arm was freckled, rather
like a fish that lies unseen on a sandy bottom, and silky with long
hair that had been red-gold and, when I was young, still seemed
fair. His head was already grey, though, when he married.
Because he was bald and white-skinned as a dried cuttlefish, he
could not go out in the sun at all, and always wore a hat, often
with a coloured band.*

Only later did I begin to know these ribbons were signs of his tribe: the MCC, the Eton Ramblers, the Guards, the Garrick . . . These insignia could be springlike in mood, coming in pale pink and powder blue. In the same old suitcase where I found Mummy's clothes, there was a fine silk twill tie, with blue and white diagonal stripes, punctured with tiepin holes, yellowed and stained all down the front. His Bullingdon tie. A relic from Esmond's salad days. Another tribal sign, another clue to those expectations foiled, to the world he thought was his which eluded him and which he did not live to see return. It lay where I found it, looking alive enough to bite me.

For a while it had seemed as if that world were over, the playground of deposed princes, the likes of Faruq, playing with baubles, with nobody wanting to join in. This was an illusion. Against all odds, this sign from the past, a revenant from a class that is once again swollen with office and, perhaps, in command of the future, unless something changes.

At the height of the summer, when Cairo became torrid and sand-laden dust from the desert lay thickly on every surface, furring eyes and noses and throats and ears, we would go to the sea at Alexandria with the rest of the foreign crowd – those who hadn't travelled home to escape. One morning when my father took me with him to the beach to swim, we found a tideline of jellyfish. A school must have been cast up on to the pebbly part of the beach by a fierce storm, as there's little tidal rise and fall in the Mediterranean. Daddy didn't take me away straightaway but keeping me close to him and warning me they were very poisonous, he wanted to have a closer look. We picked our way between their slimy loose fronds and hooded bells – like plastic bags today, they were smeared over the sand, which was a gritty greyish kind of sand, I seem to remember, and the jellyfish lay over it in blooms of pale goo but grey to match, shrivelling in the heat. Or perhaps, my mind's eye retains a glimpse of translucent blue.

This was one summer — in 1950 or 1951? I am not sure how often we went. When I was growing up and racked with the kind of anxious snobberies that English boarding schools seem particularly good at stirring up in children, I used to think 'Alex' had more tone than Cairo, and when people inquired, 'Ah, did you live in Alexandria?', I'd feel a twist of envy of that city and its population. Alexandria was more European: even as a little girl, I was sensitive to these unspoken currents. Cairo was an Arab city, by contrast, and I picked up even then on the ambivalences that excited snobbery and triggered desires to claim this label or that aura, be allotted rank and elected by the right club.

A postcard among the papers is addressed to Mother Rat in South Kensington from the Hotel Beau Rivage, Ramleh, showing the garden with parasols and rattan tables and chairs and loungers, set around a pond with lilies and many other flowers I can't identify at this scale. The scene is waiting for visitors, presided over by a single black attendant in a long white gown and sash. On the back, on 9 June 1950 Esmond wrote to his mother: 'This is the garden (and a very flowering one) at the back of our hotel in Alex. The front looks over the sea. Marina is never out of the water.'

I have forgotten this paradise, but not the jellyfish. Or the cats, stringy and dusty too, and the birds, many birds, ibis riding on the backs of hippos and crocodiles in the Nile (I know now this can't be true), and those hoopoes whirling down to peck at my mother's breakfast crumbs, the flamingos whom I used to watch hoping to get a glimpse of their second legs. The term 'pie-dog' for the strays and mongrels who marauded the streets stuck in my father's vocabulary afterwards for many years; a term from the 8th Army, not exclusively used of animals.

PART IV

1950-51

Balm in Gilead

Early memory vii

Being ill

When I was four, I caught something and couldn't breathe; long
words shivered in the spaces between my mother's crumpled face and
my father's. He carried me to a nest he had made under the
dining-room table and draped it with a Persian rug big enough to
reach the floor on both sides, leaving just starry chinks through
which I could see them – Nanny, Abdel, Mohammed, Mummy
and Daddy – as shadows against the light, bending down and
checking me where I lay on a pile of cushions. My mother was
bringing one kettle after another of water so boiling hot it filled
the space under the table with steam; she told me not to move, and
I remember that in the moist steamy darkness under the carpet,
which pricked my eyes, I began to scrape air in and out of my
body. My parents were whispering I'd caught 'diphtheria', by
always playing outside in the dirt, which was why Abdel and
Mohammed had to be always scrubbing and mopping the flat,
beating the rugs so nothing would lurk there to make anyone ill.
    In this mysterious, darkened shelter, I couldn't yet smell
anything, but I know the steam was laden with starbursts that
went up my nose and cleared it, and today, when my passages are
all blocked, I still cover my head with a towel and inhale the

sharp, perfumed steam of an infusion from a bowl of hot water sprinkled with drops of friar's balsam.

Later, when I used to make my parents' beds — they slept in twins with blue satin upholstered bedheads and matching coverlets, exactly like the beds in my doll's house — I sniffed the pillowcases to know which one was which. Daddy's was laced with the spices of Bay Rum; Mummy's held the perfumed warmth of her skin as did her hand-hemmed lace petticoats from when she lay down each day after lunch for twenty minutes to half an hour, during which time she would sleep and then wake refreshed and vigorous. (I have never trained myself to copy her.)

Friar's balsam still exists, its name remembering medieval apothecaries, their stone pestles, tall mahogany cupboards and majolica flasks; in some monasteries in Italy, a dun Franciscan with his knotted cord or a sooty Dominican with rattling rosary will offer visitors phials and lotions that his shrinking community have made according to old recipes, announced these days with ecumenical, esoteric accents, invoking holistic principles. These remedies — for sore feet and phlegmy chests, droop and decay — will be on sale alongside the rosaries and miraculous medals and holy pictures (with prayers) and postcards. Friar's balsam is pungent and sticks to the side of the bowl in a kind of scurf which is hard to rub off. Its resinous origins are palpable in ways that its far more medically up-to-date derivatives have managed to eliminate, by suspending its minty hit in glycerine, as with the Vicks inhalers which my father was always sticking up one nostril while holding the other.

17

An Old Map

Map of Cairo included in a job lot with seven picturesque prints of Egypt and North Africa; various artists, early nineteenth century. Views of the pyramids, the mosque of Sultan Hassan, and other sights, Cairo, Alexandria, Philae, by O.B. Carter, L. Mayer, Robert Hay et al. The *Veduta* or panorama by Matteo Pagano (Venice, 1549), nineteenth century, reproduction; this is the earliest rendering of Cairo as a vast and teeming metropolis, packed with services and wonders; Pagano captioned the scenes, his attention trained on the astonishing urban infrastructure, the impressive extent of the city, its serried streets, mosques, enclosed gardens, ordinary dwellings and palaces, the horse traders' corral, the sultan's 'Castel', the magnificent aqueduct, the Nilometer, warehouses and waterwheels, washing places for laundry, and luxuriant gardens of emirs; he also identifies several ancient monuments – the Sphinx, obelisks, the pyramids, and the City of the Dead. Written in the dialect of the Veneto, his inscriptions provide a guide to pilgrimage sites; the cartouches invoke Faith (Fede), floating above the scene on a cloud with a chalice in one hand and a cross on her shoulder. The stations on the Flight into Egypt of Mary and Joseph and the baby are marked to the west of the city in 'Matarea': an enclosed garden behind high walls is identified as 'The lodgings where the Madonna stayed when she fled into Egypt for fear of Herod'; beneath this scene, the artist labels a tree ('Pharaoh's fig') and declares, 'This is where the holy family rested in the shade.'

The garden where the true balsam is gathered, with an obelisk.
Matarea on a map of Cairo, Venice, 1549.

In the fifteenth century, a healing shrine flourished at El Matareya, which was originally part of Heliopolis, the old city which was replaced by the new capital, Al-Qahirah, the Victorious or the Vanquisher, in the tenth century. Near another enclosed verdant garden, the inscription declares 'In questo se cava el vero balsamo' ('This is where you find the true balsam'). The true balm, a sweet, fragrant remedy and solace – prepared as an unguent it can seal wounds, and inhaled in fumigations (as I know), it clears congested lungs and heavy heads, it sweetens stale linen and stuffy rooms, renders flesh intoxicating, and prepares a mortal body to last for ever. It has helped preserve queens and pharaohs, viziers and overseers, and many officials and their families among beloved familiars – cats, shrews, ichneumons, falcons and mice – found, swaddled in cerements, among the treasures in the tombs of ancient Egypt.

I have passed old women in the street in the south – in Naples, in Palermo – and caught that sweet balmy scent from their warm skin, often tinged with light violet or jasmine. In London today, you may be enveloped in a small cloud of myrrh as a woman goes by in the street, swathed head to foot in her black abaya, with her Gucci or Dior sunglasses masking her face.

According to one of the many apocryphal gospels about the Flight into Egypt, this balm was no plant, but the sweat of Jesus.

~~~

One day in 1949, Esmond was putting together some especially beautiful books for the Christmas catalogue – for his new antiquarian section, specialising in rare books about Egypt – and browsing through a small volume he had found in his rummaging about the bookstalls in Ezbekieh Gardens. It was an Italian traveller's account of a visit to Cairo in the 1860s, with finely drawn engravings (a zebra, the water wheels at Fayoum, an oryx, fellahin picking cotton, turbaned nomads of the Oasis) and lovely fold-out maps throughout, illustrated with more vignettes of typical sights. One map was a panoramic view of the city, and when Esmond had spread it out – eight folds of it – it aroused all his reconnaissance officer's delight as he fitted what he found there with the city as he now knew it.

The 'garden where the true balsam is gathered' would have made little impression on my father had he not come across the story in another old volume, the handsomely illustrated memoirs of Monsieur Benoît de Maillet, a 'Gentleman of

Lorraine', Consul General in Egypt of the French King Louis
XV and ambassador to the court of 'the king of Ethiopia'. The
author's portrait showed a shrewd potentate in parade armour
and full periwig. His *Description de l'Egypte* came out in 1735,
half a century before Napoleon would use the same title for
his ambitious survey of the country.

Esmond pencilled in a stiff price – he was confident he
could sell this well to the growing number of Egyptophiles
among his customers.

Benoît de Maillet, the learned Lorraine gentleman, was also
a pioneering evolutionary biologist (Esmond was to discover)
and set down an awestruck account of his visit to the part of
the city now called 'El Matareya'. The name means 'fresh
water, new water', Maillet writes, and claims that the spring
was the only running fresh water in the whole of Egypt –
'perhaps', he adds, sensing caution is needed. Others suggest
it comes from *mater*, mother, and is named for the Virgin Mary
because the holy family stopped there when in flight from
Herod. M. de Maillet relates how Joseph gave the baby a drink
from the miraculous spring that gushed from the rock for
them, and Mary could also wash the nappies of the baby Jesus.
The place was, he added, held sacred by Christians and Turks
alike. There was a mosque there, and a church, served by
Coptic priests.

In a handsome engraving, the miraculous tree stands beside
an obelisk, and the author declares the balm was used for the
chrism with which babies are anointed at their baptism, and
laments that the species of plant is 'absolutely lost'. Pilgrims
reported, he continues, that Muslims prescribed the balm for
nasal problems, lumbago or pain in the knees, while Christians
recommended it particularly as an antidote to snakebite and
other poisons, as well as a remedy for toothache. Monk apothecaries at the shrine did well from the proceeds.

Esmond had never been to El Matareya, a popular, over-crowded, poorer part of the outskirts of the city; indeed, he'd rather avoided going, as it was likely to be insanitary and possibly dangerous. But when it turned out that Florence Nightingale had also visited the shrine, he became very curious indeed. 'We were loath to leave the garden,' she wrote. 'We rode about it and found a broken stone of my friend Rameses, and the well where Mary rested – for Heliopolis has recollec-tions from Moses to Pythagoras and Plato down to Mary – a man with an ass was coming out at the time just like old Joseph. Then we rode home through long avenues to Cairo, the very way Mary and her baby must have come on their road to Fustat; and I thought of her all the way, how tired she must have been.'

The Bible pressed up very close and its dramatis personae became very real. Florence Nightingale was time-travelling back into the wisdom of the past, its philosophers and evan-gelists and prophets; she felt Plato near, Moses likewise. Egypt was ancient and sacred past, pharaonic and biblical, as it had been for Napoleon and still is for tourists today.

She does mention the fellahin whom she saw as she made her way, and she expresses pleasure at the heartfelt loyalty several of her guides and helpers showed her and her party. But real-life Egyptians around the British, when they were the de facto rulers, remained mostly invisible or, when visible in the old engravings, they're extras, picturesque Bedouin, or Cairene shopkeepers, in the scenes by visiting artists like Louis Haghe and David Roberts. They aren't the prime subjects. And I too have found, as I piece together this book of memo-ries, that the Egyptians themselves remain shadowy; to draw them out of the wings is hard. I remember how habitual it was to discount them: a memoir like Lord Edward Cecil's *The Leisure of an Egyptian Official*, from 1921, is ruthless, in the comic malicious mode of Evelyn Waugh. The attitude percolated on, right through to my mother, who would say, when Abdel and Mohammed had a long siesta in the heat of the day, 'That's Egyptian PE for you.'

The pyramids and the sphinx, as seen on the *Veduta* or view of Cairo, Venice, 1549.

Esmond, showing the books to Ben Mendelssohn, 'What d'you think – a staff outing thereabouts? A picnic? Sometime next spring?' Ben liked the idea: Maisie would enjoy it, he thought. At home that night, Esmond took off his glasses to look closely at the mapmaker's sphinx: 'Looks rather ladylike, what?' He drew Ilia's attention to the coiled hairstyle and puzzled brow of the sphinx in the map's engraving. 'A bit like Lady Killearn on a good day, what? One can't believe he'd really seen the real thing.' Then he added, giving his wife a squeeze, 'We could go for a jaunt and take in the shrine – you'd like that, I think. And it would be just the right thing for Christmas, no?'

～～

Balm expresses a hope for solace against discontent, for grace, for a way to ensure or return to health; it's a broad-spectrum panacea. Shakespeare uses it in relation to anointing, to healing, to grace, to sweetness, to desire, to fair speech and caresses – and tears: 'I'll drop sweet balm in Priam's wound,' weeps Lucrece. Balm was a prize, long coveted and cultivated, but its range is wide, its meanings fluid; it's synonymous with balsam, but more strongly redolent of fragrance, health, solace, voluptuousness, luxury, bliss: George Herbert taps it in his ecstatic poem, which climaxes on the promise of 'the land of spices; something understood'. The poem gives a feeling of touching something blissful, but what it is eludes: like the smoke from a smouldering crystal of resin. While the substance itself figures less prominently in everyday life, its meanings have not vanished: the philosopher Agnes Heller, resisting the repressions of Viktor Orbán, wrote from Budapest in 2018 – her ninetieth year: 'I also participated yesterday at the demonstration; a kind of balsam on our wounds.' During the Covid-19 pandemic, the voices of Jessye Norman and Kathleen Battle's performance of the spiritual, 'There is a balm in Gilead / to heal the sick sick soul' poured consolation on the nerves of the locked down and isolated, even if I/we weren't believers.

Sometimes the word acquires a tinge of luck, and is used interchangeably with 'manna from heaven' – a sudden windfall, the pot of gold at the end of the rainbow (calls for funding from supporters sometimes invoke it: the magazine *Cabinet* asks donors, 'Please mark the envelope, Balm from Gilead'). It's one of those biblical phrases, like 'eyeless in Gaza', 'Gadarene swine', 'apple of my eye', 'the golden calf', 'the widow's cruse', 'a horn of plenty' and 'the voice of the turtle', which contract their claws into the mind because they're so odd.

This solace, this dew of grace, this balm of Gilead, was what Esmond wanted when he left – when he fled – post-war England with his family for Egypt, abandoning cold, bomb-scarred, soot-laden and ashen London, where there was little prospect of a job for him. Although the dust of Cairo was also thick with sand from the desert, it didn't carry with it the cinders of corpses.

In a wet country like England, rain isn't often longed for as keenly as it is in the Psalms (at least not until recently when climate change has brought drought). Yet the many verses casting God as a generous rainmaker, plumping the harvest, bedewing the flowers, reflect wishes in arid conditions. Many examples could be given of depths of disconnection between the imagery of the Bible and the climate and circumstances of its readers, in, say, Surrey. Yet the lines are thrilling: 'I *am* the rose of Sharon, *and* the lily of the valleys. / As the lily among thorns, so *is* my love among the daughters.'

Balm grew there, on thorny bushes, among the roses and the lilies. Balm would flow for him here, in Cairo, his second home.

~~~

Esmond was one of the many visitors who romanced the south – North Africa, Egypt, Sicily and southern Italy, where the war had taken him. For him these landscapes and their culture were bathed in colours and scents and sensations that his own world – which is still mine – has beamed on to the region through Herodotus, the Bible, Napoleon, Florence Nightingale, on and on. Balm belongs in this story of Esmond and Ilia and their lives in Egypt because, like so much of the imagery of the Bible, it infuses the territory where the sacred stories happen with sensuous, voluptuous pleasures: the ultimate sacred places are conjured by strange substances, and paradise itself is clothed in incomprehensible words: 'Take unto thee sweet spices, stacte, and onycha, and galbanum; these sweet spices with pure frankincense: of each shall there be a like weight: And thou shalt make it a perfume, a confection after

the art of the apothecary, tempered together, pure and holy'
(Exodus 30:34–5), says God to Moses, while the vision of the
New Jerusalem, arrayed as gloriously as a new bride, dazzles
with exotic phenomena that I for one could not match to
anything real when I first met them in the course of readings
during the Mass: 'Thou hast been in Eden the garden of God;
every precious stone *was* thy covering, the sardius, topaz, and
the diamond, the beryl, the onyx, and the jasper, the sapphire,
the emerald, and the carbuncle, and gold: the workmanship
of thy tabrets and of thy pipes was prepared in thee in the
day that thou wast created' (Ezekiel 28:13).

What is sardius? What is that carbuncle in Eden?

No matter what it means or refers to or how it could belong
in reality; the scene seduces, it palpitates with life.

~~~

The phrase 'balm of Gilead' first appears in one of the prophet
Jeremiah's loud protests at the fallen state of the people of
God: 'Is there no balm in Gilead,' he rails, 'is there no physi-
cian there?' (Jeremiah 8:22). Berating the Israelites for faltering
in their beliefs, the furious holy man compares them to a sick
girl needing treatment: 'Why then is not the health of the
daughter of my people recovered?' He was writing this from
Cairo, as Florence Nightingale noted with a frisson of pleasure
when she visited the synagogue in the old fortress, and remembered that the prophet had been living and working there. 'If
I can believe,' she writes, 'that here Jeremiah sighed over the
miseries of his fatherland – that here Moses, a stronger character, planned the founding of his – that here his infant eyes
opened, which first looked beyond the ideas of "fatherland"
. . . is not that all one wants?'

The people in Gilead have as much balm/rosyn/sweete
gumme/triacle (translations of scripture vary), Jeremiah

thundered, as needed to heal every ill – the presence of the one true god. But can they see this? No. They're faithless, and on top of this, murderers of their neighbours the Ephraimites for not speaking proper (though the prophets don't usually preach loving kindness across ethnic differences). You have the one true god, Jeremiah thunders, you scoundrels, just as you have delicious precious balm/rosyn/sweete gumme/triacle, so why are you so lazy, unbelieving, sinful, weak and wicked?

When Myles Coverdale renders the phrase as 'Is there no *triacle* in Gilead?', the word he chose comes from *theriacum*, from the same Greek stem as '*ther*apy' and '*ther*apeutic'. Before there was treacle tart and golden syrup, 'treacle' was a medicine, especially for eye diseases, snakebite and menstrual cramps. Like ancient Egyptian mummifying ointments it could preserve and reinvigorate. It described sweet-smelling substances, such as the precious oil Mary Magdalene pours on Jesus' feet, and which she carries to the tomb after his crucifixion, in preparation for tending the dead body. Mixed with sulphur, it was a widespread remedy well into modern times: a dose of 'brimstone and treacle' is favoured by Mrs Squeers in *Nicholas Nickleby* and much feared by her charges. The miraculous 'treacle well' wasn't a joke, as Lewis Carroll knew, during that summer afternoon on the river in 1845 when he started telling Alice the famous story of Wonderland. A deacon talking to the children of the dean of Oxford Cathedral, he was fully aware that he was making a kind of clerical joke, poking fun by drawing on a word now obsolete, but which had been used for the holy spring at Binsey, which helped sufferers from eye diseases and sexual problems. The well is still there, a mossy puddle like a cyclopean eye in the ground of the cemetery, and seems no longer in use.

When the angry Jeremiah uses the phrase 'balm in Gilead', he's reaching for a figure of speech; it's not certain that Gilead itself, a large territory in east Jordan, beyond Galilee, was a prime source of the healing stuff. But the phrase stuck.

Look up 'balm of Gilead' in dictionaries and the terms go wandering through the column lists of plants, untethered to exact species. Besides frankincense and myrrh, there's terebinth, storax, spikenard (which just means 'spicy ointment'), all fragrant, all essential to the art of perfumery. They derive from multifarious *commiphora* and *opoponax* shrubs, yielding fragrant gums and resins, and the bounty they give seems all the more wonderful because the plants are so thorny and the terrain they grow in harsh and dry. Balm is from Latin *balsamum*, from Greek βάλσαμον meaning 'balsam-like' in the sense of 'restorative' or 'curative'. Arabic *tzeri*, close to Hebrew *tsori*, words for balm, simply mean to flow. Kew Gardens' Plant List for 1913, under *Commiphora gileadensis* offers a rigmarole of synonyms as successive flower hunters kept bidding for a moment of eternity through naming specimens after the biblical phrase. Towards the end of the eighteenth century, a self-styled wise man, Samuel Solomon, concocted a proprietary 'cordial' to a jealously guarded secret recipe, called it 'Balm of Gilead', and marketed it as an infallible and very expensive cure for 'the consumptive habit' – that is, male masturbation. It made him a considerable fortune. Meanwhile, balsamic vinegar, now a staple of the modern kitchen, doesn't include any botanical balsam at all, and that goes for the most expensive vintage decoctions from Modena.

The word Gilead means little to most people now – or didn't do so until Margaret Atwood adopted it as the name of her nightmare state in *The Handmaid's Tale* (1986) and *The Testaments* (2019); she is playing with heavy irony on the word's associations of comfort to capture the regime's double-speak, as its Commanders promise protection and well-being to the women they enslave. And now, as I write, during the full onset of the Covid-19 pandemic, a pharmaceutical company called Gilead Sciences is starting trials on a cure.

~~~

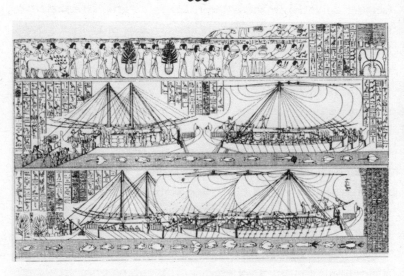

Queen Hatshepsut's boats being loaded with monkeys, panthers – and balm trees, wiith their root balls intact (upper row). Bas relief from Deir al-Bahari, Luxor.

Hatshepsut's funerary temple at Deir el-Bahari, on Luxor's West Bank, is decorated with an intricate and crowded frieze of bas reliefs, showing the expeditions 'the female Pharaoh' organised to the land of Punt – Punt's exact whereabouts are still a mystery – to bring back treasures such as sweet-scented myrrh trees. The paintings have faded to wraiths, but an archaeologist made drawings in the nineteenth century, and they show Hatshepsut overseeing the transshipment of specimens. This ruler, her botanists and plantsmen, were the first people ever to think of transporting living mature plant specimens across great distances and replanting them. Two of the ships are being loaded with precious cargo – monkeys, panther skins, ebony and, the inscription proclaims, 'all goodly fragrant woods of God's Land, heaps of myrrh-resin, with fresh myrrh trees'. The queen ruled over a prosperous and largely peaceful kingdom for fifteen years, from *c.*1473 BCE to *c.*1458 BCE. As the first plant-hunter on record (setting aside Gilgamesh's quest for the plant of immortality), she made Egypt a prime cultivator and trader in such goods. She dispatched her most learned court botanist, supported by two expert plantsmen, to strike a deal in Jericho, where gum-yielding bushes and trees grew in abundance, and bring back specimens. She planned to plant them in the equally stony soil of the desert on the outskirts of Heliopolis, terrain as dry as the bush's natural habitat in Judaea. A millennium before the star led the three kings to Bethlehem, Hatshepsut had understood the preservative power of the sticky scented stuff and the consequent riches it might reap for her treasury – she was ruling over a people for whom overcoming decay was a paramount concern, and who knew how to futureproof so cunningly that their corpses remain the prime attraction in museums in Egypt and elsewhere. When Jacob is planning to ransom Simeon from captivity in Pharaoh's court, he tells his other sons to take balm to the Egyptian official in charge, who is, unknown to them at this stage, Joseph, the brother they left to die in a well.

The threads of the story of the true balm are all entangled with several other female rulers: the Queen of Sheba who, when she came from the south to put hard questions to Solomon, presented him with, among many other treasures, slips of balsam which the king planted in a *hortus conclusus* (an enclosed garden) near Jerusalem; later writers described it as part of Herod the Great's palace in Jericho. And according to Josephus, Mark Antony confiscated Herod's garden where the trees grew, and handed it over to Cleopatra, in 34 BCE.

It seems that the land of spices must be a queendom.

The garden of the True Balsam in El Matareya doesn't claim Hatshephut or the Queen of Sheba or Cleopatra as its founder, but instead it gives the Virgin Mary the role as its genius loci. Another Mary – the Magdalene – also plays a leading role in the story, when she pours her oil on to Jesus' feet – provoking the enviers and hypocrites at the dinner party to object loudly that she was squandering it, and besides, it was ill-gotten gains, the wages of sin. Mary Magdalene, the prostitute who repented her ways, takes a prominent place in the tight historic inter-twining of women, power and perfume (at airports, in an early morning daze before your flight leaves, you will be led through a gleaming meander, past crystal phials and gilded stoppers, and you will be solicited by beauties, male as well as female, with their speaking looks and gold-dusted skin, to buy mysteriously expensive perfumes with oriental names – Samsara, Shalimar).

Ilia knew her saints – and among them many whose bodies drop balm (they are technically termed myrrhoblytes – myrrh-givers). In her home town, the body of San Nicola still oozes a precious 'manna' from an orifice in his sarcophagus. When my mother and I went to Bari for what would be her last visit, I accepted the sample from a priest and tasted it – it was odourless and without flavour, neither redolent of rotting corpses nor the perfume of sanctity – unlike mumia or 'mummy' which was a popular pick-me-up from medieval times into the nineteenth century. It's said that François I, King of France, never ventured out without some.

San Pantaleone is another saint who still yields a life-giving balm. The patron saint of Ravello, he was a Roman doctor martyred in one of the great persecutions. On his feast day every year – 27 July – his blood liquefies. I came across the miraculous vial behind the high altar in the duomo there, as Esmond and Ilia may have done when they were there on their honeymoon in 1944.

The saint and her precious jar of balm, Jan van Scorel,
Mary Magdalene, c.1530.

A jar of precious balm is the attribute of the Magdalene,
and although it changes from artwork to artwork, setting off
artists' most lavish powers of invention, she always carries a
variation, often fantastically opulent. Museums display these
precious flasks for oil from ancient times, and label them
'alabastron', 'unguentarium', 'lekythos', 'pyxis' – these special
words, their elaborateness matching their subjects, add to the
aura, especially as they're now 'obs.', out of time, like the vessels
themselves (though in the fight against plastic, they might
make a comeback). In many pictures Mary Magdalene has set
down such a vessel on the floor beside her at the banquet in
the House of the Pharisees, to wash Jesus' feet with her tears,
drying them with her hair and then pouring out the unguent
in her jar over them, and kissing them again and again.

The tree which bleeds this precious scented balm is no beauty:
the scaly bark, a sickly yellow, desiccated and peeling, is studded
with long, sharp needles, to repel all predators. Only the toughest
goats nibble it (and goatherds then comb the precious nuggets
from their beards). As hedging, the thorny branches provide
humans – and their herds – with spiky defences against all

intruders, a natural bulwark or *chemin de frise*, but they are also cruel to handle and harvest, and can inflict deep gashes on the unwary. They have a stringy taproot that plunges deep into the loose dry listless soil; if you slash at the branches with a cutlass, they aren't as dry and dead and brittle as they appear, but sinewy, and where the blade slices through the stem, drops of gum bubble up through the lesion and collect there in glistening beads. What soothes and cures and calms stems from a wound.

This gum is dull, sticky, and sallow like the bark, and dries into pellets like crystallised sugar, the kind that Ilia served with after-dinner coffee and used to let me spoon up from the bottom of her cup just before it dissolved: a delicious crunchy sweetness. But you can't eat the amber nuggets of incense, only burn them for their fragrant smoke or grind them to suspend them in another medium. You can sniff them and savour them, and the resin can be rubbed, warmed, mixed, dried and burned, to give out the sweetest scent, light and fresh as dew, gentle as a baby's skin, pure as fresh water, a perfume of rejuvenation and beauty, promising conquest over the ravages of time and the putrefaction of flesh: a scent of paradise.

Accordingly, *Commiphora myrrha* (the current favoured botanical term) became very sought after indeed. Its price per ounce rose accordingly, the trade was keen, and the garden of the true balsam, even as it struggled to survive in the middle of a hectic and populous outer district, remained a key supplier to the perfumiers and traders in spices from the suq of Old Cairo. Today, this dry, fierce and spiky bush is the only thing that grows in Dadaab, the largest 'Refugee Complex' in the world, a vast temporary/permanent improvised conurbation in Kenya, which gives shelter to more than 300,000 refugees, most of whom are Somalis fleeing war. They fence their homes using the only effective means available, which happens to be the thorn bush, in more peaceful times a source of revenue and luxury, but now simply organic barbed wire: Dadaab has become known as the City of Thorns. Yet these barbed and scraggy growths produce myrrh, that most luxurious of substances. What an irony that myrrh should drip from gashes in their bark.

During the parish priest's sermon on the Maddalena's feast day, Ilia wondered how the saint could have wept such a quantity of tears that she washed Jesus' feet. But the thought was still thrilling – as it was for me, when I was growing up and the scene was painted and praised by Mother Bridget during lessons, explaining that the Pharisees didn't understand anything about goodness, especially when they objected to the Magdalene's actions, saying that if Jesus was a true prophet, he wouldn't let such a woman come near him, let alone touch him. But Jesus liked to forgive women – he was tougher on men like the centurion, and hard on fig trees – but if you had a flux of blood, he could stop it, and if you had had seven husbands, he wouldn't turn his back on you, and if you had been taken in adultery, he wouldn't join the mob who wanted to stone you to death. He bent down instead and wrote in the dirt, 'Let him who is without sin cast the first stone.' (He could write! Is this the only moment in the Gospels when we see him doing so?) Likewise, Jesus dismisses the outcry against the woman pouring the expensive balm on his feet and drying them with her hair and her kisses. He makes that famous statement, 'Wherefore I say unto thee, her sins, which are many, are forgiven; for she loved much' (Luke 7:47).

But what kind of love? Ilia wondered. What did Jesus mean? I wondered, too, later on when I was struggling with my faith and its ideas about sin and the flesh. Love was tangled up with generosity – indeed with prodigality, it seemed, and that gave rise to an expectation. Presents were the guerdon of love, and Ilia, who was so thrifty that she picked out from her discarded outfits the zips and buttons and even sometimes pulled out the thread from the seams and wound it on a spill of paper in order to reuse it, still felt that lavish gifts were a true expression of love. And Esmond had begun so strong and indefatigable in his hunt for *gages d'amour*, love tokens, for the shining bale of exquisite, featherweight tulle, for the diamond rings his mother had given her, which she nearly lost.

Recently, there'd been episodes; she didn't want to linger on them, but they would buzz in her consciousness, like a fly that, swatted, still spins upside down on a tabletop, refusing to die. It was a Christmas party – 1949 – and they'd been invited to a supper dance at the Auberge des Pyramides (in a photograph, **Ilia is wearing a conical party hat**), and she'd been dancing to the big band, with Seddiqi Pasha and Jamie Chantry and Ben Mendelssohn and others. Esmond would dance, occasionally, but he liked her to dance more. He was a poor performer, he would say, though this wasn't strictly the case; the reason was, she knew, that he preferred to play cards.

Esmond, waving, with friends, and Ilia, right, in party hat and gown. Christmas party, 1949.

She was going back to their table, laughing, a bit puffed, when one of the waiters in his maroon tunic and sash came up to her and with a small bow whispered, 'The chef would like to thank you in person in the kitchen for your kind congratulations.'

Ilia was startled, and as her lips parted to exclaim that the message couldn't be for her as she had not thought to congratulate the chef, though he did indeed deserve such; even as these words were forming on her tongue, she caught a slight widening of the pupils in the *nadil*'s eyes, and it stole the breath from her lips, and she dropped her head in response; yes, she would follow him.

She put on a brave smile as she passed knots of other guests; some at the small round tables, some standing waiting for the band to begin the next set, many of them in funny hats like hers, and the drifting smoke from their cigars and cigarettes wreathed about them. Where was Esmond? She hadn't seen him for some time, she realised.

She followed the waiter out of the ballroom and into the corridor past the door to the card room and down more of the corridor till they reached a pantry and there was Esmond sitting on a chair groaning, his tie pulled out of his stiff collar and everything, everything undone.

'Thank God you've come, baby,' he said. 'Take me home.'

She fled to him and then turned to the man who'd been with her, but he'd been replaced by two others, the *suffragi* from the foyer, and another of the hotel front-of-house staff – maybe the concierge, she realised, because both of them were in full hotel uniform with tall turbans and long maroon coats. She began crying, as Esmond muttered choppily at her, 'Oh, don't cry baby, don't cry, just get me home.'

'We've told the driver to come around to the back entrance,' one of the men told her. 'We can leave through the kitchen.'

'What happened?' she cried.

'Bloody fool, can't count to thirteen.' He was trying to shout, she could see that, but the words came out in a kind of croak instead.

'Oh, it's just the gentlemen's ways, my lady,' said the footman. 'Nothing to worry about.'

She tried to tidy Esmond a bit before they hauled him to his feet, a dead weight, his head rolling as he moaned again.

Back at Soliman House, she woke Abdel and Mohammed and brought them downstairs in their pyjamas to give the doorman a hand in bringing Esmond home.

They too did not seem surprised or perturbed, and this reassured her. Perhaps, growing up among her sisters with her mother a widow, she just didn't understand much. She thought Esmond would explain, but he never mentioned it, though he did keep away from the card room for a while.

But later, the flow of Esmond's love would change course, and he'd spend his money on his clubs in London and on the subscription to a livery company and doing the rounds of the salesrooms and buying pictures and silver and china which he liked. There would be terrible quarrels: 'I would like a new overcoat this winter,' she would ask him. 'It's been ages since I bought mine, and I have to wear it every day . . .' Unspoken, her sadness at the long lightless winters; unsaid, the cold inside the house which meant she wore it inside, too.

He would pull at his jacket and turn out the breast pocket to look at the tailor's label: 'Look, my dear,' he would say, with a gratified chuckle, 'Cairo, 1948, and still going strong. Why want a new coat! Absolutely no need. Pure nonsense.'

These stand-offs, which would leave my mother shaking with tears, determined me never to be in the position that she was in, having no money of her own.

～

My young mother was taught a woman's body is dangerous, filled with powers that she could use: it radiated from her like a fragrance, but it was devil's work – she was an occasion of sin. Her dressing table displayed her scent bottles and cosmetic jars, some of them glass with silver lids engraved with the coat of arms of Mother Rat's father (they had come from his gentlemen's toiletry box); to her delight, she was given a bottle of Miss Dior for Christmas the year it was newly created to accompany the couturier's sensational post-war collections. Esmond couldn't afford the perfume itself or the eau de parfum, but only the eau de cologne, which was packaged in black and white houndstooth – a sporty touch, at variance with the light heady perfume. (By the way, this was another class shibboleth: she taught me, 'Always use the word scent. "Perfume" is vulgar.' Euphemisms, as ever, conveyed suspect genteel pretensions to be condemned as 'phoney'. Later, when Diorissimo came in in 1956, she switched – she was a mother of two daughters by then, and Miss Dior was for a bachelor girl.)

The priest in San Nicola whom the 14-year-old Ilia heard giving the sermon on the Magdalene's feast day, 25 November, explained that Mary Magdalene pouring out the oil that was so expensive showed that what matters is love, not money. The Pharisees overvalued money when they muttered that she should have used her ill-gotten gains to feed the poor. Magdalene's tears gushed so profusely they made enough water to bathe the dusty feet of a man who had been walking in the hot desert and the stifling streets, her hair flowed so abundantly she could use it as a towel and then she lavished on him the oil and the kisses, and he liked it, he said she was forgiven all her sins. The salve she did not stint on her beloved master was to bring about her salvation. But when they said she had loved much, did they mean she had slept around? It sounded like that. We women are all occasions of sin, Ilia knew. The Devil's gateway. The saints had been tempted and managed to resist the overtures of 'bevies of wanton girls'.

The sinner who lavishes the precious oil on Jesus' feet has

no name in Luke's story, but from the beginning she was conflated with the woman who had seven devils conjured out of her by Jesus, and with another, called Mary Magdalene whom Jesus was very close to and, yet again, this Mary was bundled together with the Mary who is the sister of Martha and Lazarus, who all lived in Bethany. This composite persona was also thought to include the woman who goes to the tomb to care for the body of 'her lord' after the crucifixion, who, three Gospels report, has the exceptional privilege of being the very first person to see the resurrected Christ. But on this occasion, she mistakes him for the gardener, and when he reveals himself to her as her beloved master, who has risen from the dead and left the tomb where he was buried, she tries to embrace him, crying out *'Rabboni'*, my lord. But he holds her off: *Noli me tangere*. Do not touch me.

Did Jesus wave away Mary Magdalene because her touch would have sullied the heavenly body of the risen Christ? Like an oily fingerprint smear on a clean glass? She was a prostitute, that was assumed, and she was rich because she had sold herself, gaining her great wealth in the process, and she bitterly repented her sins for the rest of her days, stripping herself of all her jewels and finery which lay scattered about her as she wept over her jar in the rocky cave where she withdrew after she was changed, altogether changed, by meeting Jesus. It was all very puzzling.

Much later the same scene was described to me by my father's friend, my godfather Frank who, as a Catholic convert, would all of a sudden remember his pastoral role. I tried to point out that there was no reason to assume that Mary Magdalene's money could be made only through sex or that she could only afford that expensive oil in its expensive jar because she was putting herself up for sale. Frank looked startled. 'She had loved much,' he said, 'and a sinner who loves much can't be anything else than a tart – not that I am condemning her for that, you understand. I know what the world is like for women who have no chances in life.' This was the time when he was cleaning up Soho, campaigning against the growing freedoms of the 1960s and making common cause with the protestor Mary Whitehouse, who attacked foul language on the BBC. He wasn't a Puritan, but more of a sympathiser, and he identified with Jesus and had a very soft spot for sinners, especially sex sinners.

Frank and I always met in Soho. He'd resigned from Wilson's Cabinet when they didn't raise the school-leaving age as they had promised to do, and become director of Sidgwick & Jackson, a publishing house with a historic interest in Catholic matters. He'd invite me to one of the old-established restaurants near his office, which were, literally, plush, all muffled in velvet and linen, as if no conversation should ever be overheard: Kettner's in Romilly Street, the Gay Hussar on Greek Street, Quo Vadis on Dean Street. I was beginning to earn some precious money of my own, but I still had no grasp of what things cost or how valuable time is, and Frank's generosity towards me didn't surprise me as it should have done. We talked about Esmond and his exploits: how he had broken a golf club in a rage at a caddy one time when Evelyn Waugh was present and had cowered in terror in the nearby bushes . . . how Esmond was so clever he should have done more with his life . . . and so on. At the coffee stage Frank would remember his duties to my spiritual welfare. When we left the restaurant and were walking together down the street, friendly cries rose here and there, from doorways and passersby. 'Lord Porn!' they cried, 'How are you doing today?'

During the years of his alliance with Mary Whitehouse, he was also a passionate advocate of prison reform and instituted the parole system. As a Catholic, he believed in personal redemption. Most famously, he took up Myra Hindley's case, believing she had repented. In the early 1960s, when another series of sex crimes began spreading terror through Cambridge, Frank was agog that Esmond had employed the man known as 'The Cambridge Rapist' – these were the words the perpetrator had painted on the zipped leather hood he wore when breaking in on nurses' hostels and student digs. By a twist of fate, he turned out to be a van driver for a local wine merchant's, who, on dropping off an order, lingered and asked Esmond one day: 'Any odd jobs needed round here?'

There were, several, and thereafter Peter Cook – that was his name – became a regular at our house in Cambridge, cleaning out the gutters and drains, trimming the roses rampant up the walls. When the attacker had been identified and arrested, Esmond took to enthusing that he could now outdo Frank in the notoriety of his acquaintance. The Cambridge Rapist was almost as notorious an offender as some of Frank's dubious protégés. He immediately wrote to Frank to inform him. He imagined he would get to see Peter Cook before Frank, and he wanted to; the man was a mystery and, as his occasional employer, he felt he had a right to understand more. A policeman came to vet Daddy, and I heard his guffaw, as he told the sergeant, 'Peter Cook's a very fine chap! A hard worker. Can't imagine that he's done such things.'

The police sergeant nodded and wrote it all down in his little black book. This visit was followed up by an official letter denying Lieutenant Colonel Warner permission to visit the prisoner, who was now in Broadmoor.

We – the women in the family – were spooked by this strange twist of fate. Ilia remembered with a shiver how Peter Cook tossed rose cuttings at her from the ladder he was using to prune. 'Here comes another, Mrs Warner, watch out!'

'That's not funny, Mr Cook. Now stop it.'

He was whooping with delight as he lobbed another thorny stem at her.

'I told you to stop. I mean it. Stop.'

But my mother had to move her garden chair to get out of his reach.

Worse, Laura had been sometimes alone in the house, doing her homework, while Peter Cook was there, and the police had found a photo of her in his wallet. She was then a willowy teen in tiny skirts, with huge eyes and long wavy hair which she wore in an Alice band for school but let loose on other occasions: a Pattie Boyd lookalike at the height of Beatlemania.

Later, from Broadmoor, Cook petitioned to have a sex change to control his urges, he said.

~~~

When Ilia was growing up, not loving meant not letting men touch you . . . there or there. Yet Mary Magdalene's hair flowing down and covering the man's calloused heels and soles, the unsealing of the jar and the stickiness that must have covered her hands and her mouth and all that hair after she poured out its fragrance – the scene made Ilia's insides squirm, for reasons which were not clear to her yet, but would be when that body of hers, inside which her spirit struggled like a moth between a shutter and a windowpane, became visible to her through the admiring eyes of men, who would bring her perfume, nylons and jewellery.

The jar of fragrant oil was alabaster, Luke tells us, and when she carries it to the tomb she is known as a myrrhophore, a myrrh-bearer; when artists imagine it, they borrow from the luxurious flamboyance of the Magi's vessels – the wise men or kings who followed the star were also travelling a trade route in spices from the East, and artists vie with one another to represent the jewelled receptacles which enclosed their gifts.

Mary Magdalene in Roman Galilee would hardly have owned such a fabulous jar, however successful she'd been at her (reputed) trade. But the paintings are telling us that what we are seeing is a miracle, the outer sign of inward grace. She carries the miracle she is about to take part in – her own conversion through prodigality and love – in the form of a jar, a jar that is usually lidded, since it holds its precious contents safe, and prevents their perfume from being squandered into the air like bottles of expensive scent left unstoppered on a careless diva's dressing table. ('Always remember to keep your powder compact closed,' Ilia would tell me, 'so the lovely, delicate fragrance doesn't fade.')

Artists rarely choose alabaster, as specified by Luke. Instead they conjure up vessels coruscating with gems and bristling with gold knobs and spires and finials; the penitent saint holds it near her body or displays it by her side or sets it on the ground next to her as she kneels and bends to minister to Jesus' dirty feet. It's sometimes a chalice, or more specifically, because it has a lid, a ciborium, as used to conserve hosts inside the tabernacle, after they've been consecrated – transubstantiated into the body and blood of Jesus – and so mustn't be trifled with. The treasuries of rich pilgrimage churches and cathedrals often display 'chrismatories' too, special goblets for a travelling priest to carry to a sickbed or a deathbed. Such vessels belong in a range of luxury wares – table pieces, épergnes, and extravagant 'salts' with bathing nereids, dolphins and palm trees . . . If Mary Magdalene and her rich dresses don't look sumptuous enough, her jar makes up for it, signalling the ultra-preciousness of the balm that she brought to soothe Jesus' feet and, at the same time, beaming out the fabulous promise of her body.

Like Pandora, whose charms are all mixed up with the box she opens, Mary Magdalene is identified by her jar. From one work of art to another, it shifts and changes. Bernardo Luini, a follower of Leonardo in his love of soft, sfumato shapes, shows the saint pinching the knob on the lid to lift it, as she eyes us, as if daring us to come closer and have a peep. Under that half-lifted cover and her delicately splayed fingers holding the knob, the concealed contents take on a mysterious, secret character. '*Acqua cheta*,' Ilia would warn when she was talking about someone who put on every appearance of demure virtue. '*Acqua cheta rompe i ponti* – it's the quiet ones who are dangerous,' she'd say. The proverb's not quite the same as 'still waters run deep', but close. She'd also say, meaningfully, '*In bocca chiusa non entrano mosche*' – literally, 'no flies go into a closed mouth'; she translated this as 'silence is golden'. But it verges on 'butter doesn't melt in her mouth'.

All unconsciously, Luini is touching on a highly suggestive, nigh lewd correlation between Mary Magdalene's body and the sweet juicy balm inside the pot. The motif recurs again and again in pictures of this saint: Jan van Scorel's well-rounded (an Ilia term) Magdalene, seated with a very large, tall jar on her lap, regards us foxily sidelong, against a craggy landscape of clefts and hollows.

~~~

As I moved among my ghosts and rummaged about in the past and tried to find my way back through the darkness that wraps them, these scents rose all around me – fumes of rose water, pistachios and icing sugar from the Mouski, chlorine in the swimming pool at the Club, seaweed and stranded jellyfish drying out on the beach at Alexandria, the sand and dust tang of the wind from the desert. Frankincense and myrrh burning in censers inside the flat and the houses of friends. The dust from the desert gently powdering the surfaces all around. Sugar melting in pans to make syrup. My mother's dressing table glinting with glass. I knew it was an illusion, but the painting on the lid of the compact is an illusion: Georges saw Ilia through smoke rising from shared dreams of oriental pleasure, 'all the perfumes of Arabia', which Lady Macbeth cries out 'will not sweeten this little hand'.

The Virgin Mary rises from her tomb to ascend to heaven in her body, and drops her *sacra cintola*, or belt, to convince the apostle Thomas. Cola dell'Amatrice (Nicola Filotesio), triptych of *The Assumption of the Virgin*, 1515.

While I was trying to understand the uneasy excitement Mary Magdalene's jar set off in relation to Ilia in those days, I came upon a triptych of the Virgin's Assumption into heaven by Nicola Filotesio, known as Cola dell'Amatrice after his birthplace, a small earthquake-shattered town in the hills inland north-east from Pescara. During his lifetime, Amatrice was riven by gang warfare, and the artist ended up on the losing side, and had to flee. Vasari condemns Cola's art as irredeemably provincial, but relates how, when Cola was being hounded out by a furious crowd, his wife threw herself over the edge of the mountain road. It was an act of despair, Vasari says, and he is very moved by it. Her action gave their pursuers such a shock that their fury subsided, and they abandoned the chase: 'thanks to the sacrifice of his beloved, without doing Cola the harm they had intended'.

Cola twisted his figures and painted grimaces of agony on their faces, and these contortions might arise from his own troubles. (But they're also stylistically typical among artists in the region – Carlo Crivelli and Cosimo Tura, for instance.) Cola's Mary Magdalene does however suggest some deeper disturbance: her throat and forehead and bare feet uncovered, dressed in shades of red – pink to ruby – she's holding the jar below her waist in her left hand and the tall knob on the lid is topped by what can only be seen as a glans-like protuberance; this pokes up towards a deep cleft in the heavy pink labial folds of her overgarment, preposterously arranged in an open inverted V, and tucked into her belt. Fleshy in hue and texture, a lighter pink than the rich ruby reds of her outer clothes, it seems to display a tender vulva opening to the upstanding lid of the jar of ointment, while her upturned gaze and bared throat recall the amorous expectation of Danae irradiated by Zeus in a golden shower or the blissed-out face of Santa Teresa of Avila receiving the burning point of the angel's lance.

The Devil's gateway!

The penitent Magdalen, left, gazes in awe at the incorrupt Madonna. Cola dell'Amatrice (Nicola Filotesio), *St Mary Magdalene and St Gertrude / Scholastica* [?], left-side wing of the Assumption triptych, 1515.

Redness carries associations – with heat and flesh, with beauty and danger. Mary Magdalene is a scarlet woman. Blushes and flushing, those rushes of blood to the cheek, bring rubies quickly to the poets' imaginations. 'Who can find a virtuous woman?' asks the writer of the Book of Proverbs (another cynic about sex and love), 'for her price is far above rubies' (31:10). I may have a prurient mind and be seeing things, but I am reminded of the title of the book by the unhappy actress Carrie Fisher, called *Surrender the Pink* (1990).

Cola's painting, which glows with crimsons and scarlets, offers us carnality as its implied subject: female flesh redeemed, made radiant by sanctity and freed from mortal troubles, as promised by the imperishable body of the Virgin going up to heaven.

Throughout her life Ilia kept the gold medallion of Our Lady that her mother had given her to wish her luck in her marriage. She believed she would be rewarded if she tried to be good. She did try to be good, especially as a wife and mother, often to her great cost.

~~~

'The muse has left me,' Dimitrino said, with a frown, 'since the war, since all this . . .' he waved at the company and turned to Ilia. Had she seen anything of the landscape beyond Cairo? he inquired. Yes, she told him she had visited the pyramids and the Mena House Hotel. She was always drawn to a sad person and her sympathy spurred her on to gaiety to cheer them up.

'Esmond is planning a staff outing to the Nile barrage in the Delta,' she began.

He nodded approvingly. 'You will see heron . . . and egrets of course, and falcons . . . kites . . . vultures.' The birds hadn't changed, these were the same species that the ancient Egyptians had soaked in balm and then wound in basket-weave mummy bands: time was racing past now, and only last year and last month and last week seemed to have vanished to a far horizon, while the past, the past of Canopic jars and their treasured contents, that past was still here. Dimitrino wasn't able to write such things any more, couldn't find room to breathe in the post-war jangle as rival forces pulled at Egypt this way and that.

Noticing the medallion at her neck, he asked her about it, and Ilia told him she was from southern Italy where everyone was Catholic. He replied that there was an old oasis in a faraway part of the city near the old capital Heliopolis, where there was a shrine to mark the spot where the Rest on the Flight took place.

'Yes,' she said. 'I think Esmond . . .' she paused, she was always careful with a man not to know more than he did, and he was loosening up, unexpectedly. He offered her a cigarette, but she never smoked.

'Your husband likes this brand, I know.' He was smiling. 'No? You don't share your husband's tastes? Ah well. The tree that bent down to offer dates to the baby, that is there, I can show you.'

She felt he was mocking her, but flirtatiously, and she was enjoying herself.

His expression turned serious. 'There is a cave there, where the holy family hid. A spider wove her web over the mouth and so their pursuers passed on by, deceived into thinking nobody had entered it for years.' He was looking at her, still straight-faced. 'I think the same miracle helped the Prophet when he was in flight from his enemies. Maybe it was the same spider? They live a long time, I believe.'

Ilia laughed.

'No, it is not funny. It is wonderful. And the ointment Mary Magdalene uses when she washes Christ's feet, it was brought from Cairo, my dear Madame Ilia, from the garden of the true balsam, where monks prepared it to a recipe that remains secret.'

~~~

Later, Esmond confirmed, Dimitrino had recently purchased an expensive album of Egyptian birds, by a certain G.E. Shelley, a captain in the Grenadier Guards and a keen shot who had reconnoitred the hunting grounds of the Nile. It was filled with species that were less common sights today, said Georges. 'You know the book has marks in the margins: a Greek delta against a bird he had bagged, and an S when he's had a skin prepared, and three crosses for birds he "very much wanted" to see . . . the sacred ibis! But these were already pretty nearly extinct then – fifty years ago.'

Esmond felt a genuine affinity; it was after this outing to Seddiqi Pasha's that Esmond told her approvingly, 'Georges is one of the better class of Copts. The family's in tobacco. You know, those cigarettes I like. The family's . . .' he rolled his eyes and left a word hanging in the air, then whispered, '*richissime*! But Georges I think is the black sheep – an intellectual. Never married. Takes an independent line.' He had asked him to keep an eye out for comparable volumes – in English and French. A kind of Egyptian Catholic, Ilia realised, with a stir of curiosity as well as relief, though she had made friends with some Muslims, her friend, Sadika, for example.

'He was one of their leading writers, though nothing much has been appearing recently. Some journalism, reviews, that sort of thing. I said we'd stock the papers he wants if he gives us the gen. Has some real standing in some of the top literary circles, here. Part of a group who don't hold with the current situation – with us being in charge, what? But he's a fine fellow all the same. Very cultivated.'

~~~

When Georges looked at Ilia, smoothing his moustache, and offered his car and driver for the excursion to the garden where the true balsam once grew, she basked in his attraction, though he was far too old to be of any real interest to her. He was saying, in his deliberate English, with strong rolling Rs in the Arabic style, 'They say that this balm was the finest – and the costliest – fragrant oil in the world. Hatshepsut, the woman pharaoh, who wore the sacred beard to fulfil her offices . . . my dear child, this is really true, why are you laughing? . . . it is no laughing matter. Her beard was a sign of her high status . . . she brought the art of distilling the leaves to Egypt from Jericho, where the plants were first planted and flourishing in the time of Suleiman. She used them to preserve her own body in immortality.'

~~~

The winter of 1949–50 brought beautiful weather, as Esmond noted in his diary:

> Suddenly today it is quite gorgeous. Lovely sun, no clouds, but not 'baking'. Shade temperature only 62 [degrees], but quite perfect to sit out. The <u>visibility</u> astonishing – objects such as the distant Sakhara pyramids which normally we can hardly see from the terrace are now clear as crystal. Delta looked quite lovely.

An outing was planned for soon after Christmas – the first staff party for the bookshop. The numbers grew larger than expected and Esmond drew on his old army expertise to arrange the transport: Ben Mendelssohn in one car, with Maisie, George and Labiba, the accountants, and Esmond's secretary Pauline; we were to come in our car with Jamie and our driver Nasrallah, and another car would take several other members of staff – the other bookkeepers and the front-of-house manager. But there were still others who wanted to come. So, when Georges Dimitrino made his offer Esmond was happy to accept. Ilia could then travel in comfort in his car, with . . . maybe Sadika would like to come? If she could persuade that clubman Christopher to leave the city.

With Best Wishes for Xmas and the New Year

From W. H. Smith and Son. Cairo House, 1949.

Christmas card from the bookshop, 1949.

Esmond was unfolding the map decisively: 'Always keep to the original creases! Don't force it any old how . . . that way you preserve its life. Respect a map. It's a wonderful thing, a good map.' He was in his element, plotting the route, the stops for revictualling, etc. . . . 'There's a place near the barrage that's been recommended . . . with facilities for you ladies . . . let's hope up to snuff. We'll take a picnic . . . this time of year, it'll be very pleasant by the river. El Matareya might be a bit stifling but still bearable. We can take some refreshments and sit in the shade.'

Ilia was also growing excited at the prospect; she would wear the broderie anglaise tiered skirt she had made recently, trimmed with cerise and black ribbons, with a matching detail on her wide-brimmed white straw hat. It would keep her looking cool even if she weren't feeling it. For her footwear, she'd choose her darker crimson sandals, with long laces tied around her ankles.

On this occasion, Esmond was encouraging, which took her by surprise, as he had forbidden her to go anywhere on her own and it seemed to her that going out with a man who was a stranger (and an Egyptian, besides) surely was more dangerous. She would have preferred her husband to warn her against travelling in the car with him, or utterly reject the very thought of it, but he seemed amused rather than jealous. She wanted to suggest Jamie rode with them but Esmond was adamant he should travel with the rest of the staff. 'Dimitrino's even older than me,' Esmond had commented when she showed him the compact. 'A pussy cat, I think!' (It was a different matter, however, when she developed close ties with someone she had met on her own – especially an Italian.)

At the last moment she decided, if she couldn't have Jamie near, she would take me with her, and Nanny. Our being with her would help to . . . she didn't formulate what the future might hold, not exactly. But Esmond said Nanny should have the day off, as there were too many people piling in. So she told Nanny to put me in my best dress, the one she had smocked for me in green and blue thread following the lessons Nic, Michael Hornby's wife, had given her before they left for Cairo.

Nanny adjusted my sun bonnet and fastened my white sandals and whispered, 'Don't forget, say a prayer for me to holy Mariam, peace be upon her.'

Surviving photographs reveal that pretty clothes didn't suit me, but that I tried hard to live up to them, getting myself into dainty poses I'd been shown at my dancing class, that bumped up against the sturdiness of my limbs. When Ilia looked in on this class, arriving early to collect me, and I tried my hardest to do my pirouettes and curtseys to please her, she could not control the dismay and disappointment in her face: I was my father's child, and none of her willowy grace had passed on to her first daughter, as it would, later, to my sister.

When I think of her, it is often in contrast to myself – she felt a kind of rivalry, envious of the chances Laura and I had, so very different from hers.

We took the lift down to the hall, and the car was waiting with Georges Dimitrino in the back. If he was startled to see me, the child as chaperone, he gave no sign, but put me beside him, between my mother and himself in the back seat, and we set off.

I can follow my child self sitting in the back seat of the car, between Georges Dimitrino smoking and my mother, with the driver at the wheel and another servant in the passenger seat in the front, who would serve the picnic from the basket in the boot of the car, as we made our way towards the garden and the shade of the old fig tree by the spring which watered the date tree that angels bent down to feed Mary, Joseph and the baby.

Ilia, apprehensive, began chattering.

'You are very gay today,' he said, 'but I fear that even though it is January, it will still be a hot drive and the dust will spoil your beautiful dresses – yours and Marina's.'

The car's fan laboured, but a pleasant breeze came in through the car's open windows, bringing the scent of donkeys and dried mud as we drove down the Nile and eastwards; very very few other cars. As we entered the quartier of El Matareya – Dimitrino explaining the route – we slowed down as the crowd grew denser.

'Ragpickers, I am sorry.' He spoke to the chauffeur in Arabic, clearly ordering him on, faster. 'This is the only way to the shrine, through these wretches. But we shall be past them soon.'

I saw and my mother saw, glimpses cropped by the car windows' frames, a busy populace crawling over heaps of rubbish, some children and many women with babies tightly wound to their bodies – on their backs or clasped to their breasts – going over the waste and sorting it, like worker bees from a hive, nuzzling the entrails of the body of the city to transform its leavings back into a new habitation, inspecting discarded materials of the recent war, clothing and scrap, leather trappings and horseshoes, canteens, kitchenware and pottery, old uniforms, other items of clothing and furnishings, throwing what they chose to keep into cloths which they bundled up into bags and loaded on to their shoulders alongside their offspring before dumping the contents in front of one of the traders, sitting under an awning by the side of the road.

Dimitrino banged on the driver's seat, 'Move, Move . . .'

'I am trying, Monsieur Georges.' The driver was hooting, intermittently at first, a polite cough, then sustained, hand on the horn.

The crowd on the side of the road were mostly men, with only a few women, and they were waiting for the women dredging the trash heaps to come down; they then opened the bundles the women laid down before them, and poked through them with a stick . . . lifting a garment here, knocking upright a piece of furniture there. Avoiding lice and fleas – and rats, Ilia realised. Their leathery faces, if not expressionless, were aggressively disdainful as they dropped a coin or two into the women's hands. A lemonade vendor, squeezing the bright fruit from the pyramid on his cart and shaving a block of ice with a saw-toothed scraper, was doing fine business.

One of the women turned away from the press of the market, with a baby asleep on her back, and holding another child, a little older than me, by the hand. She came towards the car as we inched along and thrust a hand into the back, supplicating – it was unmistakable, that high-pitched cry of want. Ilia's mother and her sisters had very little when Ilia was growing up, and she had seen many poorer than themselves in the stifling *bassi* in the old city of Bari, but never so destitute as these women and their babies knee-deep in the city's leavings. She sensed the proximity of the woman, and all those other women at work in the rubbish; she intimated rodents and sores and lice and mange, and though she didn't mean to or want to, though she wanted to be otherwise, she shrank back in horror. I squeezed myself closer to her, a whimper came out of my mouth. The driver said something, loudly, and dipping his hand into a box on the car floor under his feet, fetched out some loose change and called the woman over to his side of the car and dropped it in her curled, dry, cut-about hand.

'There, there, don't cry, little girls,' said Dimitrino to my mother and me. 'The fellahin are God's children. I am a Christian, but in this regard, the ways of Islam are superior. We must give to the poor, always.'

In the low-slung dark grey car, flinching from the approach of beggarwomen at the windows whenever they drew to a slow speed, when the driver would reach into a box by his side on the floor of the car and fish out some coins to pass to the suppliant, Ilia remembered how another writer, Fausta Cialente, had said to her, with light flaring in her pale eyes, when they had met at a party, 'I used to work for the British Army, all through the war here in Cairo, I used to talk on the radio to the soldiers – Italian prisoners of war – about poetry and novels. I was working for the English because at least they weren't Fascists. They gave me the opportunity to talk to my fellow countrymen about how I thought about things, what I was trying to write myself. But now, what's to be done? Levantinismo! All this . . .' she had gestured around the party of elegant society women, Egyptians and Europeans and some Americans, in the airy room with the light falling through the slatted blinds at the hotel and slanting through the amber iced tea in their glasses. 'Levantinismo!' she'd repeated. 'This supposed tolerant, mixed, wonderful society! We Europeans, we Levantines of the old world still enjoy conditions which we have crafted to our own advantage, which makes our life from day to day very sweet and easy. But I have seen, in all these years I have been in this country, the atrocious misery of this people, who are so gentle and pacific, so meek and mild. It is all destined to disappear. And it must.' She looked at her new young acquaintance: 'Soon,' she said. 'They' – she gestured vaguely out of the windows – 'won't accept it – or us – for much longer.'

Ilia watched her lips close on her cigarette, and her eyes close in heavy-lidded warning, and she shivered at Fausta's prophecy.

'You will see, *cara*, what you will see.'

Later, after Fausta Cialente returned to Italy and produced her novel *Ballata Levantina*, a book drenched in its author's sorrowful nostalgia at having left Egypt, one of her characters remarks on the wretches that crowded up against the cars, the shops, the bars and restaurants, the clubs, hotels, parks and gardens which were forbidden to them. The indolent, cynical Matteo tells the heroine, 'But the peasant *is* Egypt, Daniela! It's the fellah with his donkey and his bundle of clover, the same peasant of two thousand years ago. Nobody has done anything for him, for two thousand years.' Then, prophetically in our present time of coronavirus, he goes on, 'In fact, you'd think that epidemics and scarcity were devised just for him!

And when they pass on the road, the pasha's car and the peasant on his donkey, they don't see each other . . . the two worlds brush past each other and never meet.'

Georges was soothing her – and me; he was setting up a distracting accompaniment of compliments and history, social banter and nostalgia . . . I was the butt of his flirting jokes: 'You will grow up to be a heart-breaker, just like your mother . . . you are a very special little girl, anybody with eyes in their head can see that. But it's hardly a surprise, is it, when you have a mother like yours . . .? Tell me, *habibti*, what do you like best to do . . . I am prepared to do anything to please you . . . for your mother's sake. Look at your feet, are they like your mother's? She has long slender toes, with the second digit longer than the big toe, always a sign of depths of feeling . . .'

Then with a wave at the scrolling view outside the car windows, he said,

'All this part of Cairo used to be date palms . . . but the fellahin have been leaving the countryside and their oases and their fields and pouring into the city, swelling its size, obliterating its boundaries, strangling its natural beauty and its life . . . but let's not dwell on the dark side. I am taking you – my dear Mrs Warner and dear Miss Warner – to a very ancient and mysterious place: you will feel the presence of the past there very strongly, the pure and holy past . . . not all this rubble and sprawl.' He waved at the tangle of shacks and carts on the side of the road as they rolled slowly on.

The journey had probably taken only half an hour, but Ilia was almost asleep from the greasy slow hot air in the car and the strange flattery he was enveloping us in, her drowsiness mixed up with hallucinatory anticipation as to what Georges might do next. She was stiff with anxiety – was he going to let a hand fall on her thigh, was his support to her arm as she stepped out of the car more than courtesy, why was he giving the driver instructions in Arabic, now that we had finally arrived at a gate in a low white wall where bignonia, plumbago and bougainvillea were intertwined? A man in a white wool galabiyya, soft and clean, came out and greeted Georges, hand on heart, with a slight inclination, and then acknowledged us, his guests, dropping his head deeper, as the driver opened the trunk of the car, out of which he hauled a picnic basket and a broad parasol.

'Come, we shall have some fruit and drink some water – they will quench us,' said Georges. 'I think we have reached here ahead of the others. Let's hope they join us soon. I regret the discomfort of the journey, but now we have reached the destination of our pilgrimage, we shall go in and you will feel restored.'

Georges supervised the spreading of the rug on the ground in the shade, set out a small drum-like stool for my mother and himself, and we settled down to eat the oranges and sweets he handed round in boxes powdery with sugar, and began drinking sherbet from a thermos (it tickled me, fizzing up my nose).

'The others will catch up with us soon,' he said. 'But they have to find their way.'

'This is the fig tree of Pharaoh [...] where, we are told, the Madonna often sat in its shade.' Matteo Pagano, *Veduta*, 1549.

The holy tree was at first very disappointing, its main branch propped up on a crutch and sparse foliage sprouting from its withered limbs, its split seams trussed against further damage, some of its joints bandaged, with some feeble leaves giving signs of lingering survival. The trunk was so thickly knotted, gnarled and swollen as it sprawled, in its creaking cradle of branches, that it exuded antiquity as potently as the far more massive stone monuments of Luxor and the Sphinx; the tree was indeed very ancient and sphinx-like, an ancient and sacred beast, ravaged as a longtime chain-smoker or one of those shrivelled, clinker-like relics that would be lifted up high in a monstrance for the congregation to worship. It did not seem impossible, after all, that it had seen Mary and Joseph and the baby stop to rest under its shelter all those hundreds of years ago.

Or so Ilia was feeling, as the eerie charge of the place sent pleasurable quivers through her.

Where was Esmond, though? And Jamie? And the rest of the party? Ilia kept turning to look at the entrance to the shrine where I was playing with a little girl there . . . the daughter of the shrine's custodian who was older than me, which I found exciting. She showed me some rabbits in a hutch, and we fed them stalks of something while Georges and my mother talked and laughed. Yet beneath the enjoyment Ilia felt as his pleasant melancholic conversation flowed around her, letting her into his ideas about books and art, about the writers he enjoyed reading, her sense of unease grew: what had happened to the staff? If they didn't arrive soon, they would never reach the Nile barrage in time for lunch as planned.

Yet, as he confided to her how wracked he was by writer's block, which he'd been suffering from for years, she felt a wish rise in her to help him, to inspire him. So the words would flow again – she could be his muse.

Then she called me to join them as they wandered through the garden to the little chapel at the end of it. The miraculous spring which an angel had raised beneath the tree to help the holy family was also meagre: paintings of the Flight into Egypt give an expectation of a gurgling stream, abundant enough for Mary to launder the baby's swaddling clothes, and Joseph to dip a bowl to drink from and offer to Mary. But this muddy trickle, deep down in a cleft in the sandy rocky terrain, had almost dried up. Ilia looked into the depths and tried to think back to the images she knew. When Georges gently laid a hand on her upper arm, she jumped.

'No need to be frightened,' he said, and laughed.

Was she apprehensive that he would make advances (Sadika had warned her so clearly against them)? Were fears bubbling up from the depths that he might pin her against the wall in the chapel and press himself against her, his hard thing on her . . . did she cower? Did he kiss her, perhaps, when they were out of view inside the shrine, his lips brushing her forehead, lightly, and did he hold her steady till she looked back at him? Did she like the unexpected bristles of his moustache, and feel their impress long afterwards?

But the past won't shape itself into a page-turning story, not for me. And I remember nothing of this kind – the memories of children can't penetrate others' feelings since we can hardly do that even with far more experience and understanding. We can't go into the chapel with my mother and Georges Dimitrino any more than into the Malabar caves, however much the mystery of what happened there forms the fantasies that continue. I can't eavesdrop in make-believe any longer.

All I can surmise – and the surmise has a basis in later events, as they were to become apparent – is that Ilia was changed, utterly changed by the attentions of the Cairene world and its climate of worldly flirtation, which she had never experienced before. Hers was an ugly-duckling tale: the gawk-iness and height which had inspired that teasing pet name, la Giraffa, were now found utterly irresistible – Katharine Hepburn and Rita Hayworth and Greta Garbo were adored in Cairo, a city of cinemas and magazines, and after the war, Ingrid Bergman's long limbs added to the transformation of the ideal female silhouette. Besides, the social codes that had ruled her life in Italy were dissolved – superannuated by a mode of approach that flouted her upbringing – when she had learned to avoid the aggression of some soldiers and to coax the inhibitions of others, like Esmond. But now, as a married woman, she was caught up on invisible currents like one of those most wanted, delicately feathered species of bird which were suspended on invisible laminae of heat in the summer light over the pools. It glimmered in her consciousness that she need not have married Esmond. That she was desirable in herself and could be so to others. The thought was only a feeble undercurrent at this point; of course this old Egyptian writer held out no real attraction to her and would not have 'done' anything, in spite of her (my) feverish anticipation, as, Cassandra-like, we both foresaw calamities which could not be averted.

But anyway, Dimitrino wasn't the kind of man who's inter-ested in women . . . however much he lavished gifts on a young new arrival like Ilia.

Later, when she came to know him better, she realised why, but during that outing she was assailed by anticipation of . . . something improper, something terrible.

He had laughed at Ilia's tremulous anticipation, because his donjuanismo was a *façon de parler*, a mask to idle away the time when he couldn't write – or love.

My father had known that.

Flustered and hot, a group of staff arrived to join them; they had got lost and stuck in the milling crowd. They flopped down, a bit damp and dusty and crumpled, in the scant shade of the withered tree, fanning themselves and accepting the oranges with sighs of relief.

Jamie came over to her, with an orange in his hand. He offered it to her and caught her eye. She was glad of his clear anxiety that she'd been separated from the larger group. She felt a wave of tenderness towards him, his slight figure, his tousled head and sad eyes. He was her type; indeed he was.

At last, Esmond arrived, with his companions from his car. He was cross; he was hot and bothered from the traffic; his straw hat with the MCC ribbon looked limp. His smart new linen jacket which a local tailor had made for him was looking a bit tight, she noticed, across his shoulders.

She prayed he wouldn't erupt.

'Bloody map,' he cursed, 'and what a melee in that market-place! *Odi profanum*, what? At least we're all here and in one piece.' He accepted a piece of orange from Ilia. 'What have you been up to?' he asked her. It was a rhetorical question. 'Have you had the low-down from our learned friend?'

~~~

Nothing had happened, nothing. But something inside her felt different, as if she had grown another organ. The attentions Georges had shown her had lit a craving in her. It was a double craving, as it happens: for courtship and caresses, for admiration and for igniting manifest desire in others' eyes, yes. But also, for a world of literature that lay beyond the bookshop. This she shared with Esmond: a subtle longing for the world angled through writing and writers. Georges Dimitrino was attractive to Ilia because he had written many books. She would begin to read what he thought about his country and his people, and she'd ask Esmond to track down Fausta's stories in Italian. The mystique clung to the activity of writing, and they both passed on this feeling to Laura and me.

She left many journals behind, after she died, mostly written in Italian in her characterful spiky handwriting that is rebarbative to read. They are filled with recipes, notes on books she was reading, teaching notes about Italian literature for the classes she began giving, and lists of proverbs; also many, many pages about love affairs, mostly unsatisfactory – there was the one with Jamie Chantry which began when he was still uncertain whether he was gay and went on and off till he died. That was a sweet and precious and long-lasting *amitié amoureuse*. Another was very painful. But most of this happened later, after Cairo.

〜〜

You move back through the shadows of the past, you listen to the voices of the dead, and if you are trying to reimagine what they did and what they thought (if you are writing a book) you can go some distance, but only so far. If the ghost you want to speak to is your mother's, then, like Odysseus, you try to touch her, hug her, but your arms clasp nothing but your own hallucinations. It's not only that it feels sacrilegious to press too far into the private life of your own mother and father. It is also frightening for the same reason, and you shrink away from it. Rather, I shrink away.

Early memory viii

'Tiger'

One day, Daddy came back home, chortling. He'd been called in by the
Gezira Sporting Club manager to discuss my behaviour. There had
been a complaint from another parent: I'd bitten a boy because I
wanted my turn on the swing and he wouldn't get off. I remembered
doing it – I still remember doing it. I had a favourite swing and
every afternoon when I was taken by Nanny to Gezira Sporting Club,
I'd swing on it, working it up higher and higher. Daddy had taught
me both methods: sitting on the seat and stretching my legs out in front
of me and hanging my head back till like a living pendulum the
swing began to mount in the air. But this movement made me feel a
bit sick if I misjudged the angle and dropped my head too far back
and opened my eyes, and my stomach would begin to lurch; I preferred
the other way, standing up between the ropes and flexing my knees
while I hauled on the ropes with all my weight. I was impatient to
get on the swing that afternoon, and I asked the boy who was
occupying it for my turn, and he went on. I traipsed about in the
playground. I may have had a go on the slide – I never liked slides as
much because I was a girl who was always dressed up and the hot
metal chute threatened to scrape my bare legs, and though I liked the
little wooden merry-go-round which you could push round faster and
faster with one foot and then jump on while it whirled, I wanted my
go on the swing. I considered it my territory, I suppose, and he didn't

get off when he said he would, and wasn't swinging properly, as I was able to rush at him and bite his arm and I wouldn't have been able to do that if he had been flying. The rage that took hold of me is still vivid, and his howling as he ran away and I took over on the swing.

I wasn't punished: Daddy howled with his kind of laughter then, and later, whenever he referred to the incident, shaking his head at the outrageousness of this behaviour, but not censoriously. 'It shows spirit,' he said. He nicknamed me 'Tiger' and wrote it on the back of a photo of me taken at Gezira, holding hands in a ring of blonde, no doubt peaceable children.

He didn't know how to handle this child in his own image, and had no idea of discipline or punishment; he made me feel that if I had a temper, it was part and parcel of something else that made him and me close and separated me from my mother who never flared up in this vicious way, and found it, quite justifiably, very frightening, a curse on those who have it and on those who suffer its effects. I was myself bitten at school once, and I remember the ring of tooth-marks my attacker left on my arm: oddly neat and small, the imprint of a bracelet, with one place where she had broken the skin.

Marina (second child from right) with Nanny and friends. Gezira Sporting Club, 1949?

In the 'Tiger' photograph I'm with Nanny who is leaning over me; and now I come to a far more shameful episode than my biting a playmate. Many of the other children I played with in Gezira Sporting Club had white nannies from Trieste and the Balkans, who came to Egypt to earn enough to send back home and were known there as le alessandrine (the Alexandrians). For example, Claudia Roden, pre-eminent historian and chef, speaks Italian fluently after learning it as a child from her nanny, and she always acknowledges her debt to Italian cuisine and its cross-fertilising effects on Middle Eastern cooking.

I wanted a nanny like hers.

It is peculiarly horrible that I had learned such attitudes and was such a little tyrant that my mother and father produced another nanny. But the new one wasn't Italian or Slovenian. Perhaps my father thought I should speak more English? She was Northern Irish, dressed in a uniform, with grey curls stuck stiff to her head. My Sudanese nanny wore her own clothes, which were soft when she picked me up and held me close to her, as was her flesh, her cheeks, her breasts and her lips. I was very unhappy with her replacement, and besides, she smelled of 'perspiration', as my mother always called sweat. It was caught in that starched uniform, under her arms and around her neck.

Nor did Daddy enjoy the new nanny from England's ideas about decorum and discipline any more than I did, and she upset my mother's fastidious sensitivities, as I say, and I was miserable, so again, I had my way and she went. She came and went so quickly that miraculously, Nanny was there again and remained until we left Cairo. At least this is how I remember that time: how I was so happy she was back and with her return I could lick again the delicious powdered sugar from my fingers after I'd picked out a bright cushion of lokum from the twist of paper in which she brought them back from the market.

But when I look in the photo album my mother kept, I realise

*once again memory plays tricks: this nanny who replaced the one
from Britain was an Egyptian, perhaps from the city, not from the
country, and she came when Laura, my sister, was on her way.*

*One morning she held me to the window of the nursery at the
back of the flat.*

*'Your new little sister's just arrived over there,' she said. She
pointed out a long white building, the Anglo-American Hospital.*

*Soon afterwards we went to visit my mother: she was on her
own in a huge bed in a huge room and was wearing something
lacy and satiny and was surrounded by vases of flowers, like an
effigy of a saint on her feast day. She was smiling, and happy;
light flowed through the window. I was relieved she was alive.*

*Daddy then took me to another part of the hospital, below, and
there were rows of cots in pink and blue, each one with a baby
swaddled inside. I wondered how they knew which one was ours.*

*'We put a label on them, silly,' said the nurse, picking up
Laura and showing me the ticket on her wrist, saying 'Warner';
she had not yet been named.*

I remember I was relieved, but not entirely convinced.

*'She came out long and thin like an Egyptian figure,' Mummy
would say. She was always superstitious and believed that her
visits to the National Museum, when she'd pored over the crowded
array of gods and goddesses in the museum's halls, had had a
profound effect on Laura.*

*I don't know the name of the first or second nanny but under N
in my father's address book a name appears, **Adriana Barakat**,
which means 'blessing'.*

18

A Silver Photograph Frame

Item: one plain, solid silver photograph frame, c.1949; hall-marked, with an ornamental scrolling line around the inner edge; interior lined with silk, formerly pink, faded to beige; back made of coarse-grained wood with ripple markings, clipped in place by brass hinges; a slanted flap at the back for support.

～～

At Esmond's urging, Ilia was calling on Beryl Wynne at her house in Garden City: she was a bright-eyed woman who rode every morning before breakfast at Gezira Sporting Club, and campaigned for women's polo; she was still, to Ilia's surprise, in her jodhpurs at teatime; they were close cut at the hips, and made of a smart, light beige canvas, Ilia noted. Beryl had a hunting stock at her throat, slightly loosened over a white cotton shirt, which was a bit crumpled from her exertions. She was struggling with her boots, a pair of high-tops with a dark band over light tan.

Beryl Wynne was the wife of the headmaster of the Cairo boarding-school branch of the 'Eton of Egypt' which had moved to the city from Alexandria during the war and stayed there. Esmond was eager for the school's custom: 'a terrific institution, quite along the lines of the old school, indeed Michael Barker says he's modelled it directly on it, except that it takes every sort of boy, absolutely, not only C of E, but certainly Copts, and Jews and Arabs – Catholics too, probably. My word! It's not religious at all in any respect. No chapel.'

This English-style school, where Edward Said spent some unhappy years, had been founded by the Barker family, who'd been running the Levant Company in Alexandria since the last century. It developed, under their ownership, into a vastly wealthy shipping enterprise, based mostly in the port city but of course crucial to Cairo and towns further south, into Sudan and beyond.

'Apologies, dear girl, for my informality,' Beryl was saying. 'I wasn't expecting anyone. But it's fine. Indeed, it's a pleasure.' She looked warmly at Ilia – her blue eyes had lights in them, shining even in the shade of her shuttered drawing room, 'I'm training this lovely young Arabian filly – what a joy she is! And I'm running late – with everything.' She chuckled contentedly. 'She's called Samara and she's *pur sang*, you know, direct line back to Crabbet – the splendid stud the Blunts established when they brought us in England our gorgeous Arabian bloodstock.

'Now there was a terrific horsewoman! Lady Anne Blunt – one of those enviable types who pick up languages just like that. Fluent Arabic, Persian, imagine that. *Racée*, as the French say. Not the same as our racy, not at all. She was straight as a die, whereas the husband . . .'

The Blunts often turned up in reminiscences in the table talk of Cairo. 'Lady Anne was widely admired – and greatly pitied, too. Blunt was a cad – worse, a traitor.' Beryl was rattling on about Byron the poet – Lady Anne's grandfather – and how Anne had saved the whole pedigree of the Arabian horse and how her undependable spouse used to hold picnics ('orgies, rather, ahah') out there in the desert on the khedivial estate he'd acquired after the celebrations for the opening of the Suez Canal bankrupted the country and the khedive had to sell up. Ilia watched her, the loose-limbed sprawl of a grand Englishwoman always inspired in her a mix of wonder and horror, as she pulled off her boots and stood them up by a sofa and rang a handbell. 'Blunt picked up this exquisite pleasance, Sheikh Obeyd, it was called, and he and Lady Anne established their stud farm there. But there was an incident – an unfortunate episode.'

A young *suffragi* came to her call and she pointed at her boots, 'Do take 'em away, Yusuf, there's a good fellow. But wait,' she fixed Ilia with her blue look, 'what d'ye like to drink, my dear? Tea? Coffee? Something stronger?'

'Coffee, thank you,' said Ilia.

She looked down for her boots, 'Oh, you've got 'em already. You know what to do? Dubbin! And tell Lila to bring me some footwear that's more suitable for receiving my lovely visitor.'

Ilia was wearing the dress of emerald-green slub with narrow pleats in the bodice to give some fullness to her breasts, which had shrunk, she thought, since she had been nursing Laura. The generous skirt, trimmed with a velvet ribbon a few inches above the hem, flowed over the sofa and the cushions as she sat down opposite her hostess.

'Some officers here had tried to get some hunting going,' Beryl went on, 'but the hounds scared the mares and merry hell broke out, with that scoundrel Blunt bringing charges against the men – can you beat it? Besides, there aren't any decent foxes round here. Just rat-like creatures – desert foxes, not the thing at all.'

Esmond mentioned Blunt now and then, but in a rather different vein. He wasn't much interested in horses and didn't ride. For him Blunt was above all an actor on the stage of history, and he was curious about his attitudes. 'He wasn't much of a poet,' he told Ilia, 'and he was a queer fish – but a man of principle; and in several matters, he had judgement. It was a complicated story,' Esmond went on; Blunt was tempestuous and hot-headed, and Esmond had a lot of sympathy with that. 'The truth is Blunt was impressed by the Egyptians he met when he was sent out here on diplomatic business in the 1880s, and he quickly formed a clear view that they should – that they could – govern themselves. He took his views to extremes, that was his way, and he failed to see how we – the British – bring the benefits of civilisation wherever we go. But Egypt is a special case – as is Ireland – and even I believe that Blunt's views really showed the way forward. Books, not bombs – on both sides. Roads, not guns. That's partly the reason I'm here, that we're here now, you and I, darling girl. We're part of this changeover – we're handing over the reins but staying in the picture. Blunt had an unexpected and unfashionably high regard for Indians and Arabs, but *au fond*, he was right, their cultures are older than ours and we should respect that. His was a lone voice in his time, but he saw the gravity of the consequences of certain behaviour in the past, and he was prescient.'

Esmond was referring to the Dinshawai incident, another episode haunting friends' and acquaintances' conversation, when a party of British officers out hunting shot some domestic pigeons local farmers were raising on their land. The fox-hunting debacle at Blunt's Sheikh Obeyd estate was nothing by comparison: it had ended up with a few injuries and the imprisonment of some guards and grooms on Blunt's staff at the time. But a serious riot ensued when the local farmers' pigeons were shot; and when one of the Englishmen was killed, the reprisals were severe and brutal on the fellahin, four of whom were summarily hanged in public. Floggings and hard labour and long prison sentences were ordered for the others involved. These acts of the British provoked outrage, and when Esmond and Ilia arrived in Cairo they had had not been forgotten. Tensions continued between the *afrangi* – the foreigners – and the *baladi*, the locals; the memory of Dinshawai decades ago lingered beneath fresh injuries; hostility to the British presence was gathering. Only the other day, one of the staff at the Sikket el-Fadl premises had been roughed up by a young man of the 'coat and trousers' party, an *effendi* – one of the educated clerical professional class who were vociferous supporters of nationalism – and Esmond had to call the police, though by the time one turned up, the assailants had all scarpered and the lone culprit they'd held for a time had struggled free and vanished, too. They'd taunted his staff member for working for foreign interests, especially the British. This was why Esmond had stopped Ilia taking the car and going into town as the fancy took her.

In Beryl's elegant sitting room, as Yusuf brought in a tray set for coffee, the ghosts of the Dinshawai incident skimmed into the room, made a sweep above them, dropping a cold breeze from the chandelier to the carpet, and then left, silently. But then, as ever when this happened, a trace remained, like the silvery smear of a snail left overnight on the mats on the terrace for Ilia to find in the morning.

The young man set the tray down in front of Beryl, who poured out the coffee from a small brass pot with a curved spout like a flamingo's beak, into a tiny glass painted with flowers in a silver holder.

'Sugar?'

Ilia nodded.

'I shan't join you. I'll have something later.' Her blue eyes danced mischievously. 'Something a bit stronger. Meanwhile, you, dear Mrs Warner, you must tell me all about yourself – and give me the name of your dressmaker.'

Ilia had completed the task of hemming the wide circular skirt only the day before, and she told Beryl that she made all her own clothes, and would be glad to help show her how . . . but even as she said the words, she realised her hostess was not going to be taking up dressmaking.

'I very much approve of Cicurel's,' Beryl was saying instead. 'Is that where you get your material? The firm – the company which began the school – does a great deal of business with them, so I often hear about special shipments from Paris – ahead of time. You look as if you understand fashions, so you need to keep up.' She laughed: 'Not only dresses but furniture, crystal chandeliers – frames, tableware, curtains from Paris! You name it. My new saddle, too, I ordered it from Paris through them. The French like tackle, you know. In their eyes, nothing as chic as a snaffle bit on a silk scarf.'

She went over to a side table on which stood crystal decanters and poured herself a pale golden drink – could it be sherry? Ilia wondered.

'Tell your little man to drop you off at Cicurel's – it's on your way back to Zamalek from here.'

Ilia hadn't been into Cicurel's again, the largest and most luxurious department store of Cairo, not since the first months of their life in Egypt. Esmond had begun to be very firm that she should stay at home, especially during her pregnancy, and keep herself busy with all her clever home-making abilities, out of harm's way.

When she was back in the car, she was excited, and she asked Nasrallah to drop by the store, and he made no objection but said he would wait for her. At the main entrance, the tall carved doors were held open for her by two bawabs in fezes and scarlet tunics with a sash and braid generously looped here and there. She thought she would stumble, as she stepped into the high-roofed shining hall, and moved on to come abreast the first glass display case, glinting and humming in the flaring illuminations on all sides. Perfume, cut-glass bottles, sprays – the attendant waved a flask in her direction. She shook her head, dumbly, and kept on through the glittering enfilade of glass counters, past the attendant standing by each of them – after her coffee with Beryl, it struck her that they were grooms and their wares were racehorses, going through their paces. She hesitated. The assistant half bowed and indicated the drawers behind him – every shade, every length, Madame, velvet, satin, suede! The softest suede – look, feel. He was talking in French, and she nodded but she must keep moving, since the sequence stretched on and on and above, far above, colonnades marched along further floors, a spinning infinity of mirrored repetitions, like falling into a kaleidoscope, feeling that someone invisible outside is twisting it and the lights and colours keep tumbling past and she is the eye in the centre of the whirl.

'Can I help you?' A woman's voice pierced through her daze. She pulled focus to take her in and found herself looking at a familiar face. Where had she seen her before? No, perhaps she didn't know her. It wasn't likely that she would have met her somewhere socially, was it? Or perhaps the uniform she was wearing misplaced her and they had been together somewhere?

But she found herself moving closer to the counter. Then she said, 'I am looking for paper patterns.'

'Signora Warner, isn't it?' the voice said, in Italian. 'You won't remember me, but I was on duty that day . . .' They did know each other – from one of the charity parties Sadika had taken her to.

'Paper patterns are on the first floor, Madame, next to the fabric department, which is very large – the lifts are over there. I'll show you.'

The ordinariness of the exchange steadied Ilia, and she was grateful and looked down at the goods displayed inside the vitrine of the counter and on the low glass shelves behind the sales assistant. Photograph frames. Every size and shape, single and double, gold, silver, silver-gilt, brass, glass, wood . . . she thought of the pictures which had just been taken of her with me, her firstborn, and of Laura the new baby, and fatally, she asked this saleswoman who was so courteous and helpful and a new friend, how much one of them cost. It would look so elegant on Plum's desk, or even in the drawing room if he preferred.

It'll be wrapped and delivered to you later today, she was told. She didn't demur – it would be a surprise.

Esmond was home from the office when the doorbell rang at the flat, and there stood their doorman, Ahmed the bawab, holding a package, beautifully swathed in blue paper, and tied with matching ribbon stitched with the shop's name.

'From Cicurel's,' he announced, beaming.

'What's this? Is there a card? Has someone sent this to Ilia? A new admirer? Aaha!'

She was on the front balcony and came into the room to tell him how Beryl had suggested she go to Cicurel's and look at the fabric department there, and how she had met this nice Italian shop assistant, who remembered where she had seen her before and was very helpful, and how she so liked the pictures they had had taken of her with me and with Laura that she would love to have one of them framed . . .

But she could see her words were falling in pieces between them even as she began uttering them, that his features were tightening and darkening and the lenses of his spectacles clouding.

~~~

The letters Esmond wrote to his parents during the war and afterwards, from Cairo, keep on about money. Again and again, he repeats his high hopes of a legacy from Aunt Dot, making no nod towards sorrow. But in the event, when Aunt Dot dies in December 1944, within weeks of her husband Basil's death, it turns out that there's less money than everyone imagined (yachting is an expensive hobby), and none of it has been left to Esmond. Only some 'things', lovely, precious things, the two Regency glass-fronted bookcases, and yet more silver bonbonnières. But as Esmond had given up the lease on his flat in London as soon as he went off to Staff College, he keeps fretting that he has nowhere to store them. He worries, too, that the things will go missing or that his younger brother John, who is one of those charmers who can lift the milk out of your tea, will somehow appropriate them as his, or, even, substitute inferior items for them. Esmond also returns again and again to the question of outstanding bills – his tailor, the club, the kennel where his terrier Arkie is still being looked after. He contests them bitterly; he swears he's being over-charged or even deliberately cheated. He also casts about for ways of generating revenue. He's delighted to be promoted to major – more pay. He begs his father to buy some shares in this and that; he keeps instructing him to acquire those foreign currencies that he's been tipped off – chiefly by C.M. Wells – will be a sure bet. In the middle of the fighting in Libya and then in Egypt, the flow of calculations and speculations does not let up. He wouldn't accept that he was short of means to live life at the level he wanted. Cairo was gloriously cheap by comparison with London – he could run up a tab at the Sporting Club and the Muhammad Ali and the Turf and, sometimes, play a hand or two of poker or bridge. Even at low odds, he could come out quits at the end of an evening. But, he reported home, he had rotten luck with his cards. Even when he won, money worries gnawed him. His tastes ran far beyond his means. That younger brother who would touch Mother Rat for a fiver or even a tenner whenever he went to visit her, was even more profoundly affected by the expectations that never materialised – and there were tense moments when he came very close to . . . well, keep it in the family. Better never to speak of such things.

Ilia liked to repeat, 'Do your washing of your dirty linen in private.'

Over the years, Esmond had learned to put up with dashed hopes for legacies from this aunt and that uncle, one after another bequeathing to him more silver bonbonnières, or a set of garnet and diamond dress buttons, those bookcases . . . So disappointing when childless Uncle Basil and Aunt Dot had seemed so fond of him. And Mother Rat . . . it wasn't quite clear why her fortunes had fallen so far (a gambling habit, undependable wartime stocks). Plum's journalism sustained them – but there was no surplus.

As a married man with one child and then another, the sharp edge of longing cut deep into him and he bled from envy, envy of others, who had money as almost everyone he mixed with seemed to have, and he raged from the thwarting of his desires to live as they did.

~~~

'You went shopping?' Esmond was shouting at her. 'You know I do any shopping that's needed beyond the usual. You went out and spent money on some . . . frippery? You think money grows on trees? You want to behave as if we're made of money? You think we can afford you to go dilly-dallying about in luxury stores? Shelling out my hard-won earnings on any fribbling thing that takes your fancy?'

Esmond took hold of the package and hurled it across the room at her, where she stood with the open French windows to the balcony behind her, and on it sailed, the package from Cicurel's, past her, shying just clear of her head, past her cheek, thank goodness, on past through the empty balcony and, keeping on going under the momentum of the weight of the silver and glass frame inside the compact parcel, with the lovely box and its tight wrapping paper, over the edge and down, down, hurtling down to the pavement of Sharia al-Gezira below where it crashed at the feet of a passer-by, narrowly missing him, at the same moment that the bawab emerged from the lift he had taken back downstairs after delivering it.

It so happened that the passer-by was a policeman, and though the bawab did not say that he had heard or seen anything, he agreed eagerly when the policeman offered to go upstairs to the penthouse flat. He picked up the now misshapen package, shook it gently and it tinkled: whatever was inside was now broken, they both realised as the policeman took charge of it.

'. . . and it was the tyrant father,' writes Virginia Woolf at the very end of her life, 'the exacting, the violent, the histrionic, the demonstrative, the self-centred, the self-pitying, the deaf, the appealing, the alternately loved and hated father – that dominated me then'.

I recognise this, horribly, and I also feel the underlying

current that flows between Leslie Stephen and male authority, even though Woolf's father was individually an unusual Victorian gentleman in many ways, far less of a routine upholder of establishment rules than mine. I recognise the next part of her memories of him, too: 'It was like being shut up in the same cage with a wild beast. Suppose I, at fifteen, was a nervous, gibbering, little monkey, always spitting or cracking a nut and shying the shells out, and mopping and mowing, and leaping into dark corners and then swinging in rapture across the cage, he was the pacing, dangerous, morose lion; a lion who was sulky and angry and injured; and suddenly ferocious, and then very humble, and then majestic; and then lying dusty and fly-pestered in a corner of the cage.'

Discomfort, unease, constraint, suffocation, these almost capture the sense of oppression I too felt, with a father also given to rage and then to bouts of abject remorse, who also kept everyone around him, most particularly my mother, in a fever of anxiety that a spark might fly at random and his ready fury catch alight. And then, in a blaze of righteousness, he would rail that things should be done this way, that only ignorant fool women could fail to understand how matters stood in the world and what the done thing was; he'd rail that we were all ungrateful spongers, and he was going to disinherit us – often me, in particular – for not wanting to behave as I should and do as I was told. After these explosions, he would then as quickly subside, and seem to forget, as if it truly were an illness from which you recover without a memory of the pain, but he left all the plans around him – the walk, the meal, the ride in the car, the visit from a friend, an outing to the theatre, a proposed new outfit – wrecked.

Yet this passion sprang from the intensity of his feeling for my mother and for me, too: he was a doting father from the first moments, when he filled a Baby Book with notes about my every step, and later, when he kept my milk teeth which skittered as he moved in the gold snuffbox that hung from his watchchain.

One of the most terrible quarrels, of the many that flared furiously between us, was prompted by the invitation he had secured for me, as a debutante, to go to the Garden Party at Buckingham Palace. It's astonishing to me at this distance, not how much he wanted it, but how strongly I objected. I hammered out a bargain with him, involving Paris and Italy in exchange, and I went, in a yellow shantung coat which Eulalie my godmother paid for, white strap shoes from Dolcis, and a floppy white picture hat, and he was beaming, so proud and happy. Inside, he pointed out to me a pair of Gurkhas in the thick crowd and told me what fine soldiers they were and how they had helped us win the war; he got choked up and tears dropped from his eyes behind his glasses. (Now, with a child of my own and grandchildren, I feel ashamed that I had been so resistant and indeed self-righteous about going.)

By the time the doorbell rang again, that evening in Cairo in 1951, my father was on his knees, his glasses now steamed up by his flowing tears, begging Ilia to forgive him. She would have been crying too, as happened many times when I was old enough to remember, though of course on this occasion when she bought the silver frame, I was too young. But this, my mother, sister and I came to know, was the abrupt pattern of his rages, and this was the first one that she herself had ignited, all unwittingly – she told me about it many years after Esmond was dead. When he exploded with these fits of fury, she would cry, but she was also terrified and her shoulders caved in over her breast and she quivered, her thin frame shaking. It was a curse that came upon him, a curse that in the stories takes hold to turn a husband into a werewolf, but Esmond had no recourse to claws and fangs and rank breath and bloody eyeballs and stiff short-haired pelt, and you could not tell when the transformation would come upon him, except – and this is the nub – except when it came to money and the lack of it.

The policeman who presented himself at the front door alongside the bawab and the delivery man was a local man, an Egyptian, as was generally the case in those days, when the local force worked under the superintendency of the legendary figure of Sir Thomas Russell; the bawab Ahmed rang the bell and they were let in by Abdel, and came face to face with Esmond and Ilia, the well-known jovial British gentleman and his vivacious and beautiful young wife, who lived in the penthouse flat, from whose balcony the package in his hand had suddenly fallen; they would have appeared oddly frozen at that moment, but the policeman felt the urgency of the errand in hand and carried on.

'An inch or two this way,' he began, wonderingly, 'the package would have brained me. Or the delivery man. Or the bawab. If he'd been back at his post near the entrance, or anyone else unfortunate enough to be walking by at that moment. It is very dangerous, what has happened. Thanks be to the All-Loving, the All-Merciful nobody was hurt. *Malesh.*'

'Yes, indeed,' said Esmond. 'That's the spirit. *Malesh.*'

Ilia told me about the episode with the silver photograph frame only a little while before she died, and though I had seen many such outbursts, she had kept this one to herself. It was the first bout of his rage she had herself provoked, and it was too terrible for her to speak of. Comparable fits, which we children also saw, would have remained from later years. Inside her, his rage had struck a deep wound which closed and congealed in scar tissue, gradually thickening to an icy numbness, as she realised what Esmond could be like and how he could do her harm.

My by now frail mother went on to describe what followed the fall of the package from Cicurel's: it seems that my father who, as a foreign national, was not subject to local Egyptian courts, was able to talk most agreeably to the policeman, the bawab and the delivery man, explain everything, drop the names of his friends in the Embassy and describe the occasion he met Sir Thomas Russell Pasha and what a fine figure he was, this long-serving commandant for the Cairo City Police, such a dedicated servant of the Egyptian people. He invited them to chuckle alongside him at the vicissitudes of newly-weds and clapped them both on the back and called them my good fellows as with his other hand he pressed some baksheesh into theirs.

Eventually, Ilia would find ways round my father's anger, his meannesses and anxieties: after we came back to England in 1959 to live in the countryside near Cambridge, she won over the deliverymen who came round – the laundry man, the milkman and the butcher's boy; she'd arrange to be billed for a little more, so she could have some spending money Esmond wouldn't know about. They did so, willingly. Perhaps they did this for other women, too? How many housewives in that period had to resort to some such subterfuge? Knowing these humiliations she suffered, I resolved I would never ever depend on a husband. Jo in *Little Women* was my lodestar and, though I would marry, I would 'paddle my own canoe'.

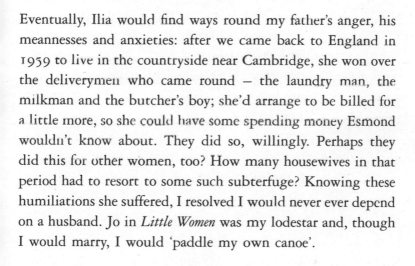

PART V

Revolution

ثورة

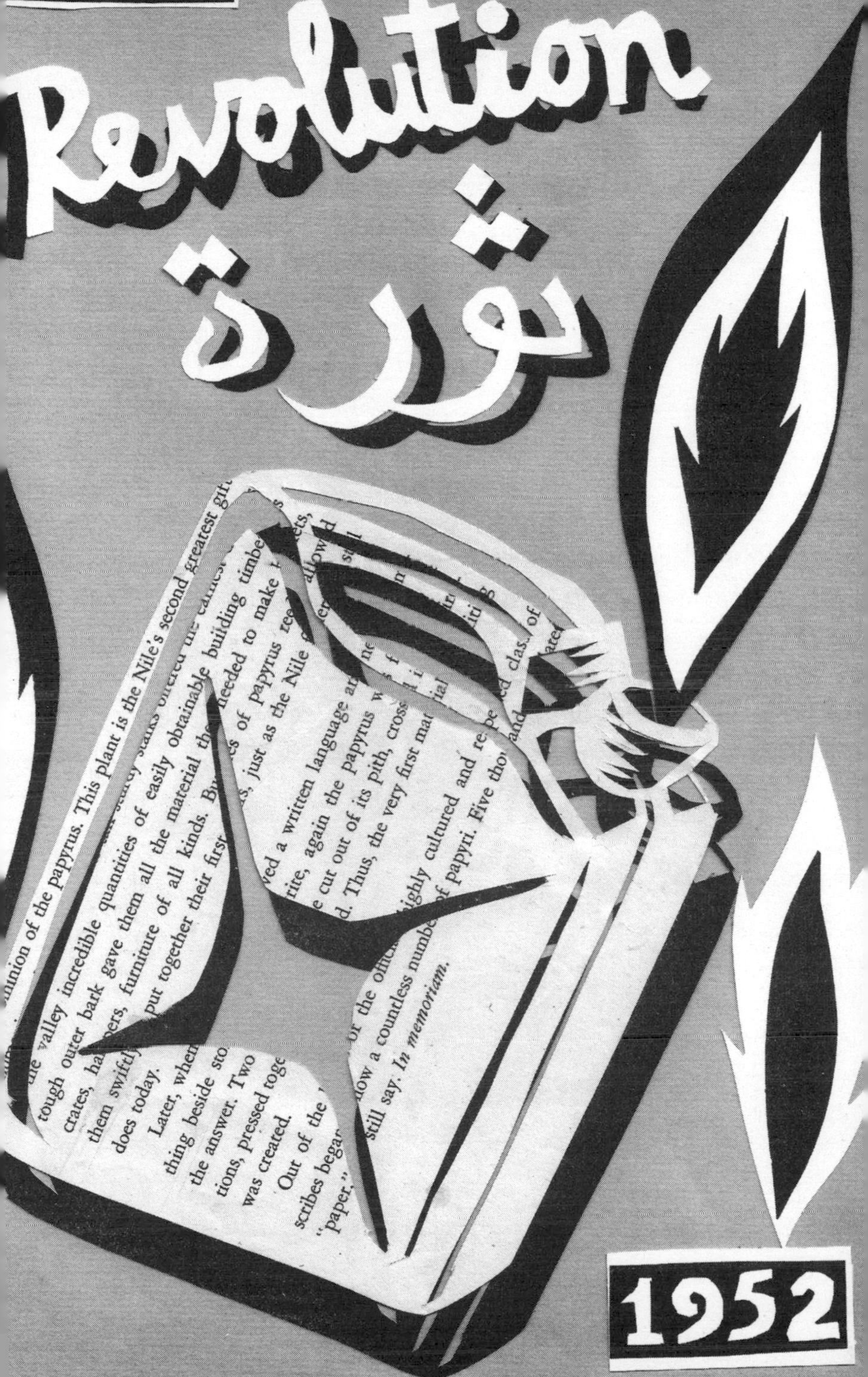

1952

Early memory ix

The burned-out bookshop

*This was the first memory I wrote down, and the point of
departure for this book, not because the burning city was traumatic
to me, but because my father's response to it was; he cried, and I
had never seen him cry and I knew something must be terribly
wrong to make him.*

*I was playing on the floor on the carpet in the large light-filled
drawing room that gave on to the verandah overlooking the Nile
and the Qasr al-Nil bridge where the stone lions crouched,
guarding the access. Mummy was sitting on the sofa, sewing, and
we were quiet and apart in a kind of still happiness that meant I
did not have to pay attention to her nor she to me; we were
wrapped in the harmony that lack of self-consciousness brings
about, when love can be taken for granted and no threat stalks it.
'Do you love me? I am never sure you love me unless you say so',
'Please say it, please say you love me': these are cries that rise from
the threat of fissures in the bond. In those days, I would often
throw out my arms as widely as I could manage, crying out, 'This
much? This much?' But that afternoon, I was calmly playing on
my own, safe in the knowledge she was there, and I only looked up
and across at her where she was sewing on the sofa after Daddy*

came home that day – it must have been earlier than usual, but after my mother's siesta. A row of windows formed one side of the room, with deep curtains from floor to ceiling; he walked in along this wall, looking out over the city, and put down his briefcase on a side table between two of the windows, which weren't open. He had a large tan leather briefcase with his initials EPW stamped on the flap that locked it; it went with him from Cairo to London to Brussels and later to Cambridge, becoming more and more baggy and bulging, the leather cracking. He said to my mother, 'There's trouble in the city, they've sacked Shepheard's Hotel . . .' He sounded tired and worried: these are the first words of my father's I can remember verbatim.

Then he turned to the window and looked out across the river and howled, 'Oh my God,' and fell down, hitting the carpet and sprawling there, his glasses off his face, saying more softly, 'It's burning.' Mummy rushed to him from the sofa, and as she rose so suddenly to her feet she tipped her sewing basket to the floor and a shower of buttons and cotton reels and beads and hooks and eyes skittered across the room, tinkling when they met the varnished floor at her feet beneath the sofa and rolling towards me on the carpet like so many marbles in a game.

She was helping Daddy to his feet, and his face was screwed up in a strange fashion. I got up too and went over to them – they of course loomed above me, but their unaccustomed disarray made them draw together, smaller, more fragile, and it frightened me very much to see them crying. There was a smudgy blast of black smoke rising from the sprawl of low-lying buildings, bristling with telegraph poles and wires, in downtown Cairo that lay across the Nile in the city panorama we enjoyed from our balcony on more ordinary days. I hadn't been aware before that you could see the shop from the balcony: it wasn't a high building and when it wasn't burning, it wasn't possible to pick it out from the rest of the surroundings. He fetched his field glasses from his time in the

desert war (Leica, two pairs, and my sister and I still have them),
and he watched that part of downtown go up in smoke.

Later, perhaps it was several days later when the trouble had
quietened and the ruins would no longer be smouldering, he took
me with him to see the shop. I am glad now he wanted me to see
it: it was an historic riot – a revolution. Mummy didn't come
with us, but one of the people who worked for Daddy was there –
one of the Egyptians on the staff, who stood slightly apart from us
as we walked around the site hand in hand and investigated. The
shop didn't have frontage on the street, but the photographs show
the display tables like looted coffins. It housed his office and the
storeroom for the stock, from which the orders for newspapers as
well as books were dispatched. The building was concrete on a steel
frame, and the steel frame was still standing: I remember looking
through an empty prison cage set over a vast mound of ash, as
huge a ruin as the tomb of Augustus in Rome, or a contemporary
artist's dreamed earthworks in a volcanic landscape after eruption.
Some carcasses of partly burned books were poking out like spars
after a shipwreck. Almost at the top, slightly to one side, lay
nested the bowl of the lavatory, untouched white porcelain with its
maker's name still legible: Shanks of Glasgow.

19

The Cairo Fire

One aluminium film cylinder, embossed with an emblem saying 'Perutz' in cursive relief on a pyramid inside a circle; on the lid, in black ink, 'W.H. SMITH & SON LTD'. Inside, Esmond coiled together the two rolls of negative film, the compass points of his life: the first is the one showing Ilia breakfasting on the balcony of their room in Ravello in 1944 and, again, in the gardens of the Villa Cimbrone, her hand on the gazelle; the second was taken in Cairo, late January 1952, a sequence of the burned-out shell of the bookshop at 3 Sikket el-Fadl, and inside, the hulks of the bookcases and bookshelves, the heaps of charred books.

~

On 26 January 1952 in downtown Cairo almost every British business and most other foreign interests, especially French, were set on fire: Barclays Bank, Shepheard's Hotel ('a fantastic ruin', Esmond reported), Cicurel's and six other luxury department stores, the Groppi cafés with their stained glass and mosaic decor and lucent counters of vividly dyed sweetmeats, all the cinemas and theatres, restaurants ('special thugs', reported Esmond, 'went out down the Pyramid road and burnt down the Auberge des Pyramides and 3 other roadhouses nearby'), every nightclub and bar ('any place associated with vice'), car showrooms (the agents for Rolls-Royce and Chrysler – 500 cars [the like of those which had awed Michael Hornby in 1947] – all of these establishments, around 750 in toto, which offered Western goods and pleasures and modes of living were set fire to. Very late that day, just before sundown, almost as an afterthought on the part of the arsonists . . . a little boy alerted a crowd of them to the whereabouts nearby of an English bookshop. It was one of the very last buildings to be attacked and burned down.

The modern city, as envisioned by the prodigal Khedive Ismail, a capital of getting and spending for the south, Paris on the Nile, went up in flames.

By nightfall the following day, forty-seven people in Cairo were known to be dead, or at least that is the figure given in historians' accounts so far – it is likely there were more, as these were predominantly foreigners or non-Arabs, and the archives of that time have not been opened. Much is left to explore and understand. Some of the known dead were killed in horrific circumstances; several more were injured. At the Turf Club, most popular drinking hole of the foreign crowd, nine bodies, heavily charred, were recovered afterwards, and several of the staff were wounded. One man tried to escape by throwing himself out of a window, and fell, his body seized by the attackers. An old Middle East hand, James Craig, who had devised a way of projecting maps which helped Muslims anywhere plot the direction of Mecca, died in the attack. Christopher Tancred was there as was his custom but managed to escape in time. A Foreign Office telegram to London estimated that the destruction led to 10,000–15,000 people losing their jobs.

The day came to be known as Black Saturday; however, for many modern Egyptians the day marked a historic revolution which brought about true national independence at last.

Among the targets that day were several buildings that were hardly fleshpots: the Livre de France, the British Institute and its library, and the offices of the British Council were singled out (the latter occupied the fourth floor of its building so must have been specifically targeted). One of the staff – not Robin Furness – lost his life. The Standard Stationery Co. was looted and burned ('a £200,000 claim, I gather', wrote Esmond). It stood a few blocks from Sikket el-Fadl, run by Wadie Said, Edward Said's father, who with his cousin (and brother-in-law) George Boulos, had secured the concession for the latest instruments – Monroe calculators, Sheaffer pens and Royal typewriters. (I seem to remember Edward Said saying his father sold Arabic keyboards, the first of their kind.)

Nadia Gindi, who still lives in the family apartment on Zamalek three floors down from the Saids, remembered 'Mr Said's granite-like exterior [which] never crumbled.' Even after this disaster, 'True to character, Mr Said set to and "All right Lampas," he was quoted [. . .] telling his old manager, "Let's roll up our sleeves . . . and begin again." And so they did.'

Born in Palestine, Wadie Said had served in the US army in the First World War, and become an American citizen; consequently, he was able to give his children citizenship and send his son Edward to a privileged boarding school in the US, where the future famous professor of comparative literature was indeed studying in January 1952. (When I first met Edward Said, we talked about the Cairo Fire, and I pretend-crowed over him that I had been there, whereas he'd missed it.) Was his father's shop attacked because the business was owned by Palestinians – many of whom, like the Saids, were Christians, and used to be among

Shepheard's Hotel, after the fire of 26 January 1952.

the most prosperous and influential peoples in the Middle East, and were consequently deeply resented? Or was the typewriter itself the suspect element? Out of intense reverence for the word, especially the word of God in the Qur'an, the printing press was long resisted in Islam; the aura of 'that which is written' mandated copying reverently by hand.

But it would be a mistake to think that religious ardour dominated the many different nationalist movements who combined to light the Cairo fires. Although Esmond reported that 'the Christians here of all races are terrified; in the poorer quarters their houses are already marked with crosses', and one of his accountants, a Christian, had immediately taken flight for Lebanon, there seems no evidence that any churches or religious institutions (and there were many Christian denominational schools like the one I attended so briefly) were targeted. The focus was more on ethnic identity than on faith, though the two overlapped at points: the attack on the Said family's office supplies business reveals how the Cairo fire-raisers were following a political definition of Egypt and Egyptians. The Swedish Consulate was attacked, and so was the Lebanese. The German bookshop Lehnert & Landrock was spared; so were Russian businesses. The label of foreigner was widening to include very long-standing communities – Jewish, Greek, Italian, Turkish, Armenian and Palestinian – communities whose members had lived and worked in the country, sometimes for generations, and considered themselves as belonging to it. Though much of the nationalism was secular, it was also predominantly non-Christian and ethnically and culturally Arab.

As Esmond noted bitterly, the bookshop was one of the last places to be set on fire, late that afternoon. It was an inconspicuous building, compared to the fabulous showrooms and department stores the insurgents attacked, and stood down a small side street; the books weren't even visible from the street through the grilles on the windows, and the premises were predominantly Esmond's offices and the wholesale headquarters of the distribution and supply business he was planning; in the basement, the display tables and shelves held the antiquarian stock he delighted in, as well as the latest publications. But you really had to be a known customer already, or a friend, to go to this address for books.

Esmond wrote: 'It seems our thugs came for Walker Vallois, the wine merchants on the corner nearby . . . but were persuaded it was a Russian business by a cute bawab. Then a small boy said, "but English library is up the street".'

On Zamalek there was a smaller premises, called Isis, which was entirely retail – but the crowd never crossed the bridge to Zamalek, nor did their feelings leap over the river and ignite other possible action there. Gezira Sporting Club was untouched – it had recently been nationalised ('an act of petty spite', Esmond thought, and I realise now the reason I was inside that day playing at home). Maybe that gave the Club immunity, although many of the burned-down enterprises were Egyptian-owned – privately, however. But the pattern of the day's unfolding violence was part of the mystery. Although Esmond commented 'Every gunsmith in town has been clean looted', on the whole there was little looting: destruction was the principal aim. The bookshop's contents were thoroughly and purposefully burned: the stock, the accounts, 'even the "imitation-marble" floors have burnt to dust & ashes'.

In the eyes of many locals who were angered by their country's subjugation by the British, English books – fiction, history, biography and above all newspapers and educational materials – could be infected by the bacillus of foreign ambition and arrogance. Rage against imported culture, indivisible from politics, had never been stifled, but had rather grown among many Egyptians under the violent measures taken by the British, often in collaboration with their own changing governments. Naguib Mahfouz, in his magnificent *Cairo Trilogy*, gives an acute and tragic picture of this long history of conflict. Kamal, the idealistic son of Al Sayyid Abd al-Jawad, the old-fashioned patriarch at the centre of the novel, embodies the passions felt by the younger generation against the burden of British military rule; partly a self-portrait of Mahfouz himself, he witnesses much violence in the city: his brother Fahmy dies at the hands of a British soldier during the violent protests of the 1919 revolution.

The causes of the Cairo Fire of 1952 run back deep into history, and disturbances had been increasing. It had been a while since Esmond let Ilia borrow the car to go into town. Months before, he'd told her, 'There's a lot of trouble these days. Here in Zamalek it's calm, but downtown . . .' Ilia knew he was worrying about money. A boycott of British goods had been declared. Esmond assured his board that the threat hadn't had an effect, but . . . 'The cost of living here is soaring,' Esmond wrote home to the firm. 'Custom duties are rising.' He was thinking he would have to let go some of the staff. 'At least your beau pays up,' Esmond told Ilia, talking of Georges Dimitrino. 'More than some customers. We're having the hell of a time getting our money in – the universities have placed big orders but they're still owing from last year.'

However, the spark of the Cairo Fire was a particularly violent response on the part of the last remaining British forces in the Canal Zone: where the tankers and liners seem to float like Fata Morgana in a shimmer of salt crystals. The towns of Suez, Port Said and Ismailia were the last bastion of a British military presence and had been in conflict with the local auxiliary police who had been posted there in October the year before: boundaries and curfews had not prevented hostilities. 'Even the YMCA,' wrote Esmond about the difficulties of doing business in the escalating hostilities, 'cannot physically collect from the Transport Company's depot in Ismailia.' In early January he reported, 'Law and order has nearly broken down in the Canal towns. We all feel that we are living on the edge of a volcano . . .' That was on 14 January. Ten days later, British forces in the Canal Zone, furious at the collusion of the local police with 'terrorists', as they saw it, attempted to disarm them: in the ensuing fighting, four British soldiers were killed and forty-two Egyptians, with many more injured on both sides.

Like the Dinshawai incident almost half a century before, this retaliation crystallised the foreign enforcers' illegitimacy. The British had overreached, and the locals were pushed beyond the limits of their biddability. Fausta Cialente grieved that Egyptians were so mild and docile, and for the most part they were, under their ruler King Faruq's carelessness, and his ministers' corruption. But they resented his weakness in the face of British high-handedness and when they suffered the deaths of colleagues and compatriots and were humiliated and exploited, they were hurt into rage, and then into revolt.

The deep-rooted colonial assumptions of the British in Egypt generally make this reader flinch, and although those *de haut en bas* attitudes dating from the period of occupation and rule had modified, they could still rise to the surface, just as the plan of an ancient settlement reappears after a drought, engraved in the landscape.

In one of his letters home after the riots, Esmond reported:

On the previous day, 25th January, early in the morning, the British Military authorities in the Canal Zone had inflicted severe punishment on the Egyptian Police and Auxiliary Police ('Bulek El Nizem') killing 40 plus before the remainder surrendered. This caused much tension and anticipation of trouble in Cairo.

In his long report to Michael Hornby and the firm about the loss of the bookshop, Esmond set out his analysis:

January 31st, 1952

Gentlemen,

I confine this report to the account of the destruction of our premises on 26th January last, Saturday afternoon, about 5.15 p.m. . . .

Here is a chart of how I think the plot worked:
Type of Target, Type of Thugs used

(a) British landmark, e.g. BOAC, Br. Inst. 'Peace movement' (Communists) &c. Fanner's [the firm's lawyers]
   office: Ahmed Husayn's 'Socialist' Party

(b) 'Rich business' so called. Stores, jewellers, motor-car
     agents, etc. Ditto
(c) restaurants, cinemas, bars, 'Pleasure', anywhere you
     can get alcohol or 'vice': Moslem Brotherhood

Esmond described the scene:

Next morning, Sunday, I went straight to the office; the
whole inside of the building is completely burnt out. The
bawab and neighbours say it was a large mob. It is tragic
that we were fired at all, as the worst fire-setting was over
by 4–4.30. [. . .] Anyway I understand that the mob first
broke through the shutters of the Subscription office,
dragged out the contents and made a bonfire of them in the
road, including the typewriters (I add this to show looting
was forgotten, as everywhere, in the passion of destruction –
the miserable BBC tonight was telling on the air of the
police, the police who assisted at many burnings and probably at ours, I gather, recovering actively the goods stolen
in the riots. What goods? Everything was <u>burnt</u>, except, I
suppose, jewellery and guns and cartridges. Later they made
fires in the basement and upper office. Everything is gone. I
enclose photographs.

These photos are on the roll I found in the canister: they show
the view from our front terrace very much as I remember,
miniaturised by the camera. But the smoke is far more pervasive than the exact column I remember, which I took to be
rising from the shop.

Cairo from our terrace was one great pall of flame-streaked
smoke [. . .] the last time I went on to town in the dusk at
a quarter to 6, like Dante's Inferno. So many cars and other

things had been pulled into the streets to burn as well as the burning buildings – if there had been a wind Cairo would have been destroyed.

'Cairo from our terrace was one great pall of flame-streaked smoke', Esmond's photograph, 26 January 1952.

The local paper *Al Assai* printed one of the photos and Esmond sent the clipping to his parents: 'captioned as I have translated. "Cairo burning and Nero minding his business"'. He has traced a red pencil arrow to the word 'Nero', and identified him as Fu'ad Siraj al-Din, the interior minister, and a leading force in the anti-British, nationalist Wafd Party. (Siraj would be arrested a few months later in the king's feeble attempt to restore control and then, in 1954, sentenced to fifteen years by Nasser's new revolutionary government, only to return to power briefly as leader of the New Wafd Party, under Anwar Sadat.)

～～

Needless to say, my childhood memories, however vivid, are faulty in many respects, as I discovered when I read the many letters which Esmond wrote in the ensuing days to Mother Rat and his father and sister and friends, as well as to his immediate boss Michael Hornby, and to several others in the firm. The building did not burn to the ground: in 2009, with the help of the writer Radwa Ashour, who herself lived nearby, I found the side street Sikket el-Fadl, and I recognised W.H. Smith's premises from the turban topknots at the four corners, which had clearly survived the blaze. In his letters Esmond indeed marvels how ferro-concrete resists fire better than other materials.

I only remember him coming home once and walking with his briefcase along that long wall of curtained light by the windows, and falling down, becoming a dark shape on the floor. But in his letters, he writes that he drove in and out of Cairo several times that day, taking stock of the mounting crisis, getting through the jam on the Qasr al-Nil bridge past the guardian lions, to check on the premises and on the situation in general. He knew, he writes, that fires were being set in the city early that day, and he went back and forth to check the spread of the attacks and watch for the riot spreading and reaching Sikket el-Fadl. As it was getting late, he was still hoping the shop would escape notice.

There had been rumbles of trouble throughout his time in Cairo: threats of further boycotts of various British goods, and riots – for example, the nasty incident when one of his staff, (was it Nasrallah?), had been roughed up by anti-British protestors demanding to know why he was working for the enemy.

I knew none of this at the time: I was only aware of us as a family living in style and having a wonderful time.

~~~

This is what Ilia remembered and told me when I asked her, not long before she died, to tell me about that day.

When Ilia saw the smoke rising from downtown Cairo and realised the city was burning, her first thoughts, she told me, were to 'bundle up you two, my little girls, and grab my jewellery – the half-moon diamond rings Mother Rat gave me, which Max brought on Esmond's instructions to our flat in Bari during the war, and some other lovely things I'd been given. I thought when my father fell down that he was dead and I was very scared, for you two and for me, and for him. The mob would be coming for us too, and I was thinking how we'd get away from them. I wanted to sew my jewellery into my dress, along with the compact which Dimitrino presented to me as a tribute, so he said, though he wasn't really one for the ladies, as I discovered – but there wouldn't be time. I thought the crowd would rush the bridge, and we were very close to it, so I would run down the fire escape at the back of the building, holding on to you with one hand, and with Laura on my hip in the other arm and we'd take cover and hide in the scraggy bushes along the road. The Club wouldn't be safe, it would be the first place they'd come looking for us because those people hated us for drinking – though I never drank much – and for swimming in our bathing costumes, and what with women playing golf and everyone going to the races.'

When I first heard her plan to gather up her valuables and run and hide, it seemed, I'm ashamed to say, naive and melo-dramatic. Now I know better: every refugee tries to secrete something they can sell in exchange for survival – for food, water, shelter – and a passage out, and the more compact and concealable the items are, the more efficient. The writer Rachel Lichtenstein, in her book about her forebears, *Diamond Street*, reflects on the miniature scale of the tools of the trade, as she gathers up those her grandfather and his fellow jewellers in Hatton Garden used to mend watches or adjust engagement rings: 'all these tools', she writes, 'could have easily fitted into the pocket of an overcoat . . . like the diamonds that some merchants managed to escape with from war-torn Europe, sewn into the hems of their clothes'.

In Italy in 1944, when Iris Origo on her estate, La Foce in the Val d'Orcia, learned the front was coming ever closer, she had the same instinct of self-preservation. She and her family stood at a high end of the social scale, but she set about bricking up their moveable goods in the walls.

Ilia knew she was lucky to have anything to secrete about her person; she had known that ever since Mother Rat's gift of the two diamond rings arrived in Bari. 'I resolved,' my mother went on, 'that if we were spared that day, I would never again . . .' She did not tell me what she was never again going to do, but the words rose in the air between us . . . She would be good, she would take the world as it came, in the person of the husband she had not known when she married him but now feared . . . She wouldn't shrink from him any more.

Many among the dead and wounded were Egyptians, and several of the businesses attacked were Egyptian, too: the Opera House was a monument to an ambitious and glorious era, but Ismail's extravagance had placed his country in hock to foreign money . . . so that grand building was associated with the long history of dependency. Other targets – Cicurel's – were landmarks, owned by the super-rich cotton magnates and landowners, who were Egyptian but also European. The many places of entertainment were popular with Cairenes, and not only with French-speaking groups or cosmopolitans, as several cinemas screened films in Arabic, which explored stories of struggle that reflected ordinary Egyptians' problems. Esmond had begun stocking Arabic books and papers, too.

Some interests had supplied the petrol for the fires, but even after all this time, it is still not known exactly how the uprising was organised or how it was supported and given the means to do its work. The riots broke out 'spontaneously', it is repeated, and no single group or groups claimed responsibility, then or now. The nationalist, fascist-sympathising Socialist Party, which had grown out of the banned movement Young Egypt (Misr al-Fattah), entertained ideas and aims that showed their members were in sympathy with the riots, and their leader Ahmed Husayn was charged and imprisoned; the Muslim Brotherhood, also nationalist but, then as now, more ardently and severely pious than other parties, had long denounced urban pleasures, drinking and dancing, sex not only with women but also with men (seen as Western debauchery, though Arabic culture with its glorious bisexual love poetry and enthusiastic drinking songs, has its own hedonistic history). The precise early targeting by the arsonists of Shepheard's Hotel as well as 200 cinemas and theatres corresponded to the Brotherhood's ideals. Cairo's police stood by – were they involved, too, were they in sympathy or merely helpless? Or were the politicians in charge of their orders hedging their bets to see who came out the winners from the violence? Esmond thought so: he railed against the political class for doing nothing to quell the riots until much too late in the day, and blamed the ruling parliamentary party, the anti-British Wafd, for actively encouraging the destruction. The revolutionaries were drawn mostly from the effendis, and the combined modernity and national traditionalism of their views was marked by their dress: a fez on their head, and a long tunic over loose trousers (this complex history runs through Naguib Mahfouz's *Cairo Trilogy*). Esmond also suspected Russian interests behind the scenes.

Some historians now suggest, contradictory as it may seem, that British intelligence was behind the uprising, acting as agents provocateurs to scare the king into greater compliance with British plans for the country. (In Esmond's letter to the board on 14 January, he wishes 'the British [would move to] re-occupy Egypt – which is only likely in the case of large riots here producing a breakdown in law and order . . .') It seems difficult to credit, but it was a time of feints and plots.

Donald Maclean had been working in the Embassy as head of Chancery; he'd disappeared the year before and, in January 1952, his whereabouts were not yet publicly known.

Individual Egyptian army elements were clearly involved, but the army did not take the credit or the blame in so many words, even though the Cairo Fire was swiftly followed by the coup which brought the Free Officers to power: it has never been ascertained how directly the Officers were involved in the turmoil and the destruction, but eventually, the king was deposed. On 26 July, six months after the Fire, Faruq acquiesced in his fall without a squeak, sailing out of the country that had placed such belief in the tall teenage prince; the new regime saw him off on his private yacht, the *Mahroussa* ('the Protected' – an epithet for both Egypt itself and Cairo), to the sound of a twenty-one-gun salute (the agreement with the new regime required that he disembark at Naples and the vessel be returned to Egypt). No guillotine or tribunal or prison cell for the king who was still only 32 years old: he lived out the rest of his days in beautiful places – in Capri, in Switzerland.

Like Erisychthon, Faruq was cursed with ravening hunger – he could not stop eating, he could not stop acquiring. Jewels, watches, linen, suits, shirts, pictures, furnishings, the toys and gadgets he especially liked, cars and more cars, diamonds, diamonds, diamonds – it was as if the entire stock of one of the luxury department stores in post-war Egypt had been bought up by him. At his death in 1965 at the age of 45, he is said to have weighed around thirty stone (200 kilos).

When some of his possessions were auctioned, two friends of mine who live in Zurich – the art historians and curators Bice Curiger and Jacqueline Burckhardt – were curious about the sale. They bid for – and won – a pair of pyjamas. Bice said, 'They were made of the finest silk, of course, with a big F on the pocket, crowned, and they were so vast that we could have dressed an elephant in them.' She gestured, spreading her arms. 'Both of us could fit inside them.' Everything Faruq owned was monogrammed: the F was the propitious letter of the family, revealed by a fortune teller to his father Fuad; Faruq's sisters were called Fawzia, Fazia, Fathia and Faika, his first wife Farida and his children all had names – given at birth or adopted on marriage – which began with that letter. It had not proved strong enough magic.

A few days after the Fire, the editor of the paper *Al Assai*, which was Saadist in allegiance (i.e. an offshoot of the Wafd), nevertheless generously offered the English bookseller 'shelter' in their building, and Esmond moved there, on a temporary basis. He needed to take stock of the losses, the outstanding bills, and to answer the messages of sympathy that were coming in, many from compatriots in the same predicament – diplomats, clergy, businessmen, doctors, charity workers – but also from friends. Some, like Dimitrino, strike a genuinely distressed note: 'one of the saddest things about the Jan 26th incidents is the thought of all those beautiful books and engravings . . .'

Esmond's photograph of the display tables in the bookshop, after the fire.

Several Egyptians wrote, and Englishmen who had married Egyptians. From John Plant, who had designed the golf course at the Club where Esmond had enjoyed many a round, came a handwritten note: 'You did something of great value for Egypt, Esmond. I dare not ask you, myself, to start again, but I shall pray most sincerely that you will.'

Plant was married to the painter Dora Khayatt (Esmond has noted on the letter: 'of that important Egyptian family'). They would leave in 1956, after the Suez crisis, and settle in Philadelphia, where the professor of Arabic and translator Roger Allen made friends with them. 'He used to tell wonderful stories,' Roger told me, 'about driving a car around Cairo with royal licence plates! Apparently, he once stopped in the middle of Sulaiman Pasha/Talat Harb Square and asked a policeman where he could park. "With that licence, sir," he was told, "you can leave it where it is or wherever you like!"'

Sir Robert Greg, who was gravely ill (he would die the following year), wanted Esmond to come and visit: 'How shall I return to you the second Vol. on Italian printing houses? Or will you retrieve it the next time you come and see me? . . . I shall miss the Club more than I can say when you and your wife leave us. It has made all the difference to my life here.'

The king's librarian at the Abdin Palace wrote in regret, saying how much their collections had been enriched by new and second-hand books, though the young king had abandoned the hopes his bookplate had promised.

The secretary of the Muhammad Ali Club offered Esmond an automatic membership should he ever come back to the city.

Nasrallah, from the shop – one of the staff who was to lose his job – wrote on a half-page of an exercise book:

Dear Mr Warner,

I came to wish you goodbye. I am sorry you were not at home.

Please try to forget all unpleasant souvenirs from Egypt & remember only that despite all fugitive misunderstanding you are leaving here – and especially with me – the living souvenir of one of the most human persons I have ever met.

Yours, really sincerely,

Nasrallah

Another, the driver Ahdam Mohamed Alim, also expressed genuine affection:

As I felt serving you, I have a few words which I could not say to you while I was working for you.

During the two and a half years I worked for you I found in you so many great manners which are rarely found in managers except hate and disgrace to their staff that which was never of your manners.

You have been to us more than a friend or a father and I would not forget how helpful you were when you hear of anything that might has happened to anyone of the staff – good or bad . . .

Georges Dimitrino wrote to both Esmond and Ilia, separately, with varying degrees of affection. He did not want them to leave.

The letter-writers represent a certain milieu – over the next decade or so, most of them would be joining the steady exodus. Esmond wrote to his parents: 'the European & rich Egyptian communities have quietly got the wind up and are slipping out to Europe, etc, at a great pace. Cairo will be very empty of the *gratin*, especially the wives, this summer.'

A fortnight later, Esmond reported to his parents:

To Sir Pelham and Lady Warner
3 Malvern Court
London SW7
15.2.52

My dear Daddy,

It has really pretty well knocked me out to see all that had patiently been built up over the last 4 years & now was a good going concern wiped out.

I feel like a <u>defeated</u> General must feel!!

And what security does the future here hold? If we do make a new treaty and withdraw from the Canal Zone and there are no British troops near, another Communist/Fanatic may go so much further than even 'Black Saturday'.

There was a complete censorship on the story here till a few days ago, when it was completely lifted, & the papers are now full of photographs & gruesome stories.

However, Esmond attended the reception held for the death of King George VI, and was greatly cheered when he was moved up to sit among the senior diplomats:

only 4 rows behind old Prince Muhammad Ali, who sat alone in the front row on left, representing the king. There was an interesting ecclesiastical procession of all sorts of costumes, orthodox, etc., patriarchs, old bearded men with curious and varied head-dresses & large pectoral crosses.

We sang 'God save the Queen' at the end. I never thought I'd live to do this! What a great name is Elizabeth for a Queen. I just read Ponsonby's 'Recollections of Three Reigns' most interesting what a <u>bully</u> Q. Victoria was! And what a human character KE VII was! He threw a <u>Garter</u> through the porthole of his yacht because the design was wrong!

What a magnificent memorial the king's funeral must have been. I expect you saw a lot on the television. We, the English, are masters of ceremonial . . .

Orders made before the riots were arriving as if nothing had happened, and he was busy: 'We had a very large book mail in just after the fire so are "in business" & our Zamalek little shop (Isis) was not touched.'

But when Michael Hornby arrived in Cairo in March to assess the situation, he found that 'Living in Cairo at the moment is like living on the lower slopes of a volcano. The main eruption has taken place, but there is an uncomfortable sensation that it may be followed by another, and the question is whether the stream of lava will this time engulf your village, or whether it will slide harmlessly by.' He stayed with them in the flat (since Shepheard's was gutted), and decided the volcano was still rumbling and 'the business is to be closed finally not later than June 28 1952'.

His presentiment was right: the Cairo Fire called time on a world and an era. Soon after, Gamal Abdel Nasser emerged as the leader of the coup; he became president in 1956, the first to be elected – in a referendum – to the post. In the face of British and French fury, he took the historic step of taking control of the Canal. Nasser was loved, trusted, and re-elected, again by referendum, twice more, in 1958 and 1965. In 1967, he became president until his death three years later.

～～～

The letters Esmond wrote home to London made me realise that when I heard those first words of his I remember, 'It's burning', he meant the premises of his work, not the whole city, as he already knew, and so did my mother, that parts of downtown were already on fire, and that when he fell to the ground howling – that terrible memory of a father felled – he had realised that the fires had reached the shop. You can hear the former army officer speaking in these accounts he gave, and the anger that would lead him to demand war, revenge, the might of British imperialism to bear down on Egypt in the aftermath that ended in 1956 with the Suez crisis – when the 'tripartite aggression', as Egyptians call it, ended in defeat for France and Britain and Israel.

He howled, his glasses fallen to one side, for the loss of his work in Cairo and for the hard-won status he'd achieved. He was 44 years old, and this was his first endeavour almost on his own, his first significant job; he hoped he'd found a way of keeping up that intensity of life he longed for.

'I shall never be the same man again,' he wrote to Michael Hornby, and though his words are melodramatic, it is the case that a man who had chosen to marry a Catholic, a southern Italian, who dreamed up a scheme to work in Cairo, who relished the mix and motley of Cairene society, drew in on himself into a thoroughly British outlook of a certain stripe. Until fairly recently I used to see his kind in the street, usually around St James's, going into their gentlemen's clubs, in their pre-war Savile Row suits now battered and faded, punctured by a hatching moth here and there, as they went in to make up a hand at bridge or thump the headlines in the *Daily Telegraph*. 'We'll beat the pants off the Egyptians,' I remember my father exulting in the kitchen over breakfast one morning in the autumn of 1956, during the Suez crisis.

~~~

'Ilia does not want to move. She is obdurate,' Esmond told his parents. Nevertheless, in June 1952, we were on our way back to England a few months ahead of my father. Our leaving was not a flight, and the insurance paid for the damages. But my mother's spontaneous reactions reveal something age-old in the stories of flight, and if I were to find myself unhomed, I too would take her jewellery: her diamonds and her amethyst flower ring, much less valuable than the diamonds on monetary exchange terms, but more profoundly saturated with her personal flair, her striking flamboyance. She always wore these rings on her manicured hands, which were nevertheless knobbly from laundry and other work, something she minded. I'd put them in a zip bag from airport security, dig them into a pot inside a saucepan (essential equipment), and in the same soil plant a cutting from the passion fruit vine growing in my garden. It came from hers, where it spread in rampant wild profusion on a southern wall. A passion vine will take even in climates far from its native habitat – as Ilia did, after she was transplanted (though she always breathed an air of the south).

My mother flew with us, her two daughters, first to Rome and then on to London. Laura was not quite two. In Rome I was given a beautiful new Italian doll, made of porcelain, painted, standing up in a box with a cellophane window through which I could see her, very much not a baby doll in appearance, but a poised child, wearing a broad-brimmed straw hat, with a bow for a topknot, and trimmed with pink chiffon to match her party dress, with its puffed sleeves and a rose on a ribbon at her waist. If it weren't for her short white socks and the sound box in her tummy which called out 'Mamma' in a piteous voice when you bent her over, she could be a proper grown-up lady showing herself at her best in the *passeggiata* of a summer *festa*.

Her head is fixed to tilt to one side, as if she is considering what lies ahead, and her long-lashed lids still close over her blue glass eyes; she holds her arms out, hands lifted as if about to greet you or speak. She was a treasure. When I unwrapped her from her box, she wiped all other memories of that return to London, except for the spectacle of magenta-mauve cherry blossom on the trees lining the old road into town from the airport.

I called her Margaret after the young princess whose picture in the English papers Doris showed me soon after I arrived in the flat in South Ken.

~~~

Maybe Abdel in his babouches, Mohammed with his rattan carpet beater, Ahmed the doorman at Soliman House, maybe Nanny One whom I so thoughtlessly rejected and maybe Nanny Three, Adriana Barakat, with their bags of sugar-dusted pistachio-stuffed lokum, and the suffragis, bawabs, nadils, receptionists and barmen, valets and drivers, shop assistants, barbers, hairdressers, beauticians, delivery men, attendants and receptionists who worked in the hotels and the clubs, the restaurants, department stores, garages and other services, especially in the places where the English and the French enjoyed themselves, along with the businessmen, agents, journalists, diplomats, maybe these Egyptians took part in the rebellion. Or their friends and associates did. Maybe even some of the staff at the shop felt a certain solidarity with the attackers? It does not seem that the fellahin came in from the fields and the villages to join in the rioting. No, those who worked with the elite and for them – who knew them – composed the groups who threw themselves into the uprising and raised the fires. Some of them I might have known personally and loved as a child loves those who care for her, Nanny One whose name I have lost and Nanny Three, who was called Barakat, 'blessing'. And the van drivers, Ahdam Mohamed Alim and Nasrallah. Although I can't enter their minds and besides, even if I could, shouldn't ascribe to them thoughts or deeds, I can imagine that while the destruction and its consequences made them anxious for their livelihoods, they hoped for a new time that would bring change for the better and restore their pride.

The burning of books – the scene repeats over time, in reality and in fantasy: books and fire set up a fundamental antinomy, emblematic of a catastrophic destiny, a final apocalyptic omen of a civilisation ending. Books and flames are haunted by history, especially in Egypt where the Library at Alexandria, where the Bible was translated into Greek, was founded by Alexander the Great, but was destroyed many times – in the third century CE, Christians set about deliberately burning works of pagan philosophy. History is spotted with zealots consigning books to the flames.

In the Acts of the Apostles, after some of the Jews in Ephesus have witnessed miracles St Paul has wrought by invoking the name of Jesus, and then found that mere hankies that Paul has touched have also worked wonders of healing and calmed down sufferers from illness and distress, they follow suit, and call on Jesus too. The seven sons of a high priest are giving this a try on a case of possession but the spirit inside their disturbed patient scoffs at them, and goes on to attack them horribly, stripping them and belabouring them and chasing them out of his house naked and bleeding. The author of Acts then tells us, 'A number who had practised sorcery brought their scrolls together and burned them publicly' (Acts 19). The writer points out that this was a painful sacrifice, for 'they counted the price of them, and found it fifty thousand pieces of silver' (Acts 19:19). The scene was painted for Notre Dame in Paris, in one of the huge 'Mays', pictures of biblical subjects commissioned by the city's goldsmiths and other guilds and offered every year from 1630–1707 during the month of May, Mary's Month, to her cathedral. Eustache Le Sueur's picture of the book-burning scene hangs in the Louvre and escaped destruction in the fire of 15–16 April 2019. Le Sueur paints a heap of books on a bonfire in the foreground; they're mostly contemporary volumes, printed and leather-bound, but some writing tablets and scrolls poke out of the flames here and there, and one bearded old man is approaching with an armful of scrolls and manuscript boxes. The artist isn't disapproving, or pushing the act of burning books safely back into a barbaric past, but reminding the viewer that the righteous indeed consign false knowledge to purifying fire. He was living in times of furious contention between different branches of Christianity and continuing denunciation by Catholic scholars of other religions, including above all Islam. 'In this way,' writes the author of Acts, 'the word of the Lord spread widely and grew in power' (Acts 19:20).

'A number who had practised sorcery brought their scrolls together and burned them publicly' (Acts 19). Eustache le Sueur, *The Preaching of St Paul at Ephesus*, 1649.

The emperor Qin Shi Huang (259–210 BCE), founder of the Qin dynasty, the all-powerful reforming ruler who expanded the territory of 'China' to the south and the west, consolidated the Great Wall, and was eventually buried with a multitude of terracotta guards and companions to keep him safe and entertained in the afterlife, was intent on controlling knowledge, and notorious for banning wholesale quantities of books and destroying them – then in irreplaceable manuscript form, of course. Or so the legends about him claim, legends intended to exalt his reign as inaugural of a new time. Mao Zedong took him as his guiding light, and during the Cultural Revolution also encouraged the purification of knowledge.

That is the point: burning books marks the end of a world view and the beginning of a new one.

It is also a kind of genocide, Susan Orlean argues in her *The Library Book*, where she adopts the word 'libricide'. It is 'a way to wipe out the history of a people'. The Nazis, the Inquisition, the targets of anti-clerical attacks by Voltaire, have singled out books because they are living mouthpieces, forming a collectivity over time. When the Los Angeles Central Library was burned down, in what was widely suspected to be a deliberate arson attack in 1986, it wasn't only local Angelenos or even Americans who lost their memories, but the larger community comprising all the future readers who would have used the library; they suffered this 'libricide' (over 900,000 loans yearly – in the 1920s, 1,000 books were being checked out every hour). 'It was the loss of a sanctuary,' Orlean writes. There were suspects, but the perpetrators were not found. Aldous Huxley, imagining London in the future *Brave New World*, strips his scientific utopia of books: only his 'Savage' has a mouse-gnawed copy of Shakespeare which has been preserved from earlier wholesale destruction. In Margaret Atwood's nightmare nation of Gilead, frenzies of book burning are encouraged by the authorities.

Eerily, arson is a crime that effaces its own trail: the murder weapon is consumed with its victims.

In 1995 the writer Edmund White collected essays he had written over the previous twenty-five years and called it *The Burning Library*: it was the first time I'd heard the saying, 'Whenever an elder dies, a library burns down.' Vaguely labelled 'African' (as far as I can discover), the proverb mourns above all the knowledge and wisdom lost with the deaths of an old man or old woman, the emphasis falling on minds and memories, not books per se. It's therefore significant that this piece of common wisdom specifies burning. For books are lost to rats and mice, weevils and worms, termites and ants, or simply to rain coming through the roof. Yet in imagination and in symbolism, fire has elemental power, and fantasies of overturning oppressors crave for cleansing conflagrations, not dust mites and mildew.

The men whom the young boy led to the bookshop were carrying jerrycans of petrol; reports mention others in the uprising were equipped with hessian which they soaked in paraffin and when they entered a building, like the Turf Club, they broke up the furniture to build a fire. You need to pour fuel on books to set them on fire, especially if they are set tightly side by side on shelves or piled up on a table. As Ray Bradbury has made known, they will ignite at Fahrenheit 451 – that is 238 degrees Celsius – a raging heat that in his novel, requires special flame-throwers. In an ordinary hearth, parchment will buckle and shrink, and printed books singe along the edges; if you want to reduce them to ashes, like the heap of grey dust which I remember with the lavatory bowl sitting in it, you have to dowse them thoroughly first. A burning book is a paschal lamb in a riotous rite of sacrifice.

Opening a bookshop in Cairo after the war seemed a civilised idea, and I have always felt that it was an uncanny presage of my future – and my way of life, reading, writing, piling the books high in my house – that my first memory should be the sight of its charred contents. But now, in the epoch of soft power, I see how such an enterprise might have looked to an Egyptian filled with hopes and ambitions for the autonomy of his people, and wounded by the humiliations still inflicted on them over the decades following the independence from European powers supposedly achieved in 1922.

Two years after the Cairo Fire, in 1954, we moved to Belgium, where Esmond was to manage the Brussels branch of W.H. Smith's. It had a splendid art deco swirl of a staircase and an English tearoom on the first floor and I spent my early bookworm years there, listening out for my father's booming voice and eruptions of jokes with customers. He enjoyed front of house just as he had in Cairo and was still making friends with enthusiasm. But after Egypt, Belgium in the 1950s was dowdy in Ilia's eyes, and a social backwater in spite of the arrival of Captain Peter Townsend, in exile, and the excitements of the 1958 World's Fair and the silver spheres of the Atomium. Laura and I went to Les Dames de Marie, a convent of extreme traditional tendency where Pope Pius XII was venerated as a living saint. At the age of nine, I was sent to boarding school in England, St Mary's, Ascot, as my father worried I was never going to become a proper Englishwoman.

We all came back to England in 1959; with his bonhomie and his indefatigable appetite for social contacts, Esmond enjoyed talking to customers in the bookshop in Cambridge; Bowes & Bowes's handsome and historic site opposite Senate House drew much passing trade from dons and students; he opened two smaller branches down Trinity Street, one specialising in foreign languages and the other in sciences (neither were profitable, and besides, shoplifting was a problem). By dint of much pleading (the lessons were expensive), Ilia learned to drive and freed herself from isolation in the bleak and cut-off village of Lolworth on the Huntingdon Road. At the wheel of a Triumph Herald coupé, she cut a startling figure in what was then a staid provincial town, with her big sunglasses and a Hermès headscarf tied under the chin as worn by the Queen, a 1960s variation on a hijab. Esmond planted a garden and grew marvellous roses. After he retired – early (the new branches he'd opened on the university campuses of that decade lost money, too), he tidied up the library of Brooks's Club in St James's, in order to make room for the sequence of occasionally risqué dilettanti portraits which came when the St James's Club closed down, in exchange for their members' admission to Brooks's. He often stayed at the club, at a cut rate, for his room was on the top floor with no lift. Ilia, in those days, was teaching Italian at a crammer's to young people often in trouble; smoking was allowed in class, astonishing as that now sounds, and her cough became chronic. She was very gifted at winning her students' confidence and getting them the grades they needed. She would stay as 'a PG' (a paying guest) with Sadika in Kensington. My parents would go out together to social engagements, of which there were still very many.

Esmond died of a heart attack after coming back home from a hearty Sunday lunch with friends; it was 1983. Ilia soon moved to London and embarked on her *vita nuova*, at last.

∼∼∼

The Cairo Fire had a brutal effect on my father's state of mind; he was right when he told Michael Hornby he would never be the same man again. It embittered him: during the Suez crisis, he roared with fury every morning over the news in support of maximum 'punishment' – the voice of that younger man, the officer who'd felt sympathy with the prisoners of war he saw sitting under the desert sun, grew rough and vengeful. During the early 1960s, I rose in equally vehement revolt against him and all he stood for. Nasser seemed to me a shining liberator and a unifier, justified in his defiance of the British and his seizure of the Canal.

In 2014, when I was invited to give the Edward Said Memorial Lecture at the American University in Cairo, my host was a tall young woman professor in the English literature department, called Tahia Abdel Nasser – unlike some of her coevals, her hair was loose and uncovered. I noticed her last name but thought it might be common in Egypt. The downtown campus of the university is near Tahrir Square, and murals to the Martyrs of the Arab Spring in the streets nearby were painted over by the authorities every day, only to reappear again overnight. After my talk, Hoda and Nadia Gindi, sisters who used to teach at Cairo University, invited Tahia and me to dinner. Both straight-backed, elegant and silver-haired, still active in political resistance, they told me they remembered the smaller bookshop on the island, the Isis. Their apartment, so similar in style to ours in nearby Soliman House (art deco wrought iron on the lift, the stairs and the doors) now seemed, with the passing of time and my grown-up size, much less lofty and vast.

At the end of the meal, Hoda asked Tahia if she would allow their cook to come out to greet her. She said, 'Of course.' An old man appeared, in his apron, and bent over Tahia's hands and kissed them, murmuring heartfelt words, with tears in his eyes. After he had withdrawn back into the kitchen, my host explained: 'He was thanking Tahia for her grandfather, for setting the country free.'

This is how I thought of Nasser too. But either age has dimmed my own ardent longing for liberation, and moved me closer to my father's views, or the last half-century and more of rising ethnic nationalism and bigoted demagogues – by no means only in Egypt – has modified my ideas. Even since I began trying to remember what it was like growing up in Cairo, the turmoil of the Middle East has intensified, and strife – Homer's terrible demonic Eris – has whirled across the map, visiting fury and hatred and bigotry and all their consequences – war, famine, drought, sickness – on millions of people. The circadian rhythms of history have brought me face to face with resemblances between that mixed-up, morselled, polyglot society of Egypt, before Nasser's secular dictatorship, and the hopes of a new era of openness and tolerance called for by the revolutions of 2011 in North Africa and Egypt. There are profound differences between them, since no river can be turned back in its course, let alone the Nile, but I have found myself increasingly wishing that the diasporic mosaic of the Mediterranean was still in existence, in spite of all I know about its corruption, jaw-dropping carelessness and inequalities. Thousands of displaced people – Syrians, and refugees from North, East and West Africa – are composing a new commons, however many walls rise and bales of razor wire are rolled out to keep them out or pen them in. But the form that commons takes needs a political will to tolerance and equality that, at the time of writing, is not developing. The rhythmic pulse of history nevertheless keeps returning to these ideals again and again and they need attending to and struggling for. The broken aims of Art et Liberté, the intellectual movement growing out of the horrors of the First World War, were reprised in the ideals of the Arab Spring.

The first protests in Egypt in 2011 were called on 25 January, annual 'Police Day' in memory of the deaths in Ismailia that triggered Black Saturday. The events of that day – the violence, the riots, the looting and destruction – had come to seem for Egyptians a promise of liberation. Oppressive and corrupt authorities who colluded in their malfeasance with foreign interests had met their ignominious end. The Cairo Fire was a presage of the recovery of the Canal four years later, and the true rejection by Egypt of colonial rule.

It did not take long for this hope to be crushed. As I write, the presidency of General Abdel Fattah el-Sisi, who took power in 2014, has been extended, in the interests of stability and security, with the full agreement of parliament to the necessary amendments to the constitution, to continue until 2030. That day of the Cairo Fire turns out to mark the start of long decades of military regimes, which do not look as if they will be ending soon.

20

Shabti

Shabtis were buried with Egyptian pharaohs, queens, princesses, viziers, and their clerks and lesser officials. They are the labourers of the other world, who work on behalf of the deceased to meet their needs and provide for their comforts during eternity. Standing stiffly with arms tightly folded, figurines in wood, clay, stone and glazed turquoise faience, they're surrogates – copies, dummies – of the dead man or woman, who was often a pharaoh or a queen, a dignitary, a scribe who was in the position of making ambitious arrangements for eternity. When demon overseers in the world on the other side of life put each soul to the hard labour of the corvée and other penalties, the *shabti* would magically assume the task, and with flails, hooks, seed baskets and other tools, carry out the necessary duties – and the substitution was satisfactory. The more powerful of the dead set up thirty-six overseers and 365 *shabtis* in their tombs, to ensure there was one at work on

their behalf every day of the year. In earlier periods, miniature assemblies – showing fishponds and slaughterhouses,
granaries and cattle pens, bakers' ovens and butchers' sham-
bles – would provide the departed with complete scenarios
of the work on their estates.

Ilia first saw an array of them in the National Museum in
Cairo, which she liked to visit, often with a friend after
Esmond, worried about unrest in the city, stopped her going
out on her own. The magic spell, inscribed on their bodies,
summons them to action: they must come to the call and say,
'Here I am,' and carry out all the tasks demanded of them.
'Shabti' is a play on the verb 'to answer', so shabtis answer
and obey; they play-act someone else, and live their lives,
speak their lines and fulfil orders to work well enough that
the gods are pacified.

These answerers figure in the rituals of the dead, serving
the several parts of their master or mistress: the *ka*-spirit is
that part of a person that remains on earth and continues to
need all the appurtenances of an easy life: bread and shelter,
wine and music; the material body remains in the tomb with
the *ka*, and has been mummified in oils, spices and perfumes
so that it will withstand mortal corruption and thrill schoolchildren who in thousands of years will still be flocking to
see them in London and Paris and Berlin. Besides these other
parts of a person in the ancient Egyptian psychology are their
names and their shadow, and, probably the most familiar
aspect of all, the *ba*, or soul-bird, which flies away to the
other world.

~~~

Serried ranks of these figurines were on view in a poky alcove
in the Ashmolean in Oxford in the mid-1960s when I used
to visit the museum, which is next to the Modern Languages

building, the Taylorian, where I went to lectures; the *shabtis* have now been moved and are displayed more luminously, alongside model soul-houses and ships and other necessities, and they flank the pantheon of hybrid animal gods and goddesses – cobras, vultures, jackals, lions, hippos, cats, lionesses. *Shabtis* were run off assembly lines en masse in moulds, sometimes glazed, at other times painted, the artisan streaking in the stiff wigs with the same paint as the dark kilt, and rendering the feet with a splash of colour – reddish ochre for a male figure, paler sienna for the female; they do not have to be carefully made; they are dummies, but not dumb. They live in relation to the dead, trying to keep faith with them. Their time is a continuous now, as their *raison d'être* is to keep going and give respite to the subjects whom they substitute in the afterlife.

~~~

I'm fumbling towards an analogy with writing, or at least with the kind that Margaret Atwood describes as 'Negotiating with the Dead'. In the case of a writer, a ghost is a kind of *shabti* (in French, the term for ghostwriter used to be *nègre*), who takes on their subject's identity and labours in the public arena of this world on behalf of the other person. The ghostwriter steals with permission, taking up occupation of the story of someone who wants their story told but doesn't know how to do it. In many ways, translators also write the book again, in another language, with permission to take over the words: Helen Lowe-Porter, who was Thomas Mann's first translator into English, commented warmly that she acted as the 'Would-be writer . . . Who refuses to let go of her translations until she feels she has *written the books herself*'.

As the last provides the cobbler with a template for a client's foot, so tailors' dummies model the measurements of a woman's body – the dummy used to drape a dress or fit a jacket. They're sometimes moulded to the customer's shape – if the dummy is being used by a *sarta*, a professional dress-maker, the dummy might have an adaptable wire frame, to match different clients. Since Ilia had first set up the state-of-the-art Singer sewing machine she'd been given, she'd often muse that she'd like to have a tailor's dummy to work on, but one didn't come cheap.

Dummies also featured in the desert war Esmond lived through: artists helped create mock aerodromes to dupe German pilots, and built models of tanks so light that soldiers carried them above their heads like a papyrus canoe; camou-flage experts like Joseph Gray also designed cut-out silhouettes of troops to be mustered in the sand as decoys. At the landings in the south of France in 1944, elaborate false plans, with decoys and mock soldiers, were mounted – and successfully distracted the enemy from the real site of the action.

A publisher's dummy, on the other hand, is a mock-up of a book before publication, the same shape and size and quality of paper and boards, with the cover design and title and author of the book, but everything entirely blank inside. This kind of dummy used to be made – and are still by publishers who hold with book-making tradition, like the Folio Society. These blanks make perfect notebooks. Booksellers used to be presented with samples to encourage them to order the real book (a reverse of the *shabti*'s role, who acts to forestall any further demands on the dead man or woman whom he impersonates). As a bookseller, Esmond was always being presented with them, and my mother filled them with notes – recipes, guest lists, journals, lists of sayings and quotations and proverbs – after my father passed them on to her.

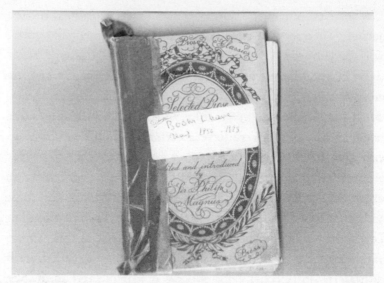

In a publisher's dummy of a selection from Edmund Burke, Ilia has kept notes of her reading, 1950–98.

One of the earliest notebooks is a slim octavo volume, the title printed on the boards in a rococo cartouche and written in secretary-hand flourishes, with exuberant interlaced exhibitions of penmanship: Selected Prose of Edmund Burke, *edited and introduced by Sir Philip Magnus (Falcon Press, no date). On this ornate front Ilia later stuck a label 'Books I have read 1950–1998'. In front of the word 'Books', she has later inserted, with a kind of conscious sense of her achievement, the word, '<u>Some</u>'. The inside pages are thick creamy laid paper and are filled with Ilia's distinctive, rather Gothic home-schooled handwriting – in pencil, mostly; to begin with she adds red biro, for outlining certain words and underlining others, and awarding three stars to her favourites.*

In the very first entry she made in May 1950, in Cairo, at the age of 27, when she had been married almost six years, she copies this sentence from Oscar Wilde's *De Profundis*: 'But while I see that there is nothing wrong in what one does, I see that there is something wrong in what one becomes.'

There are a few Italian books: *Neapolitan Gold* is a 1947 account of the city by a Milanese journalist, Giuseppe Marotta, who had moved to Naples and made its ways his speciality (he's the Italian precursor of Norman Lewis); there was enough curiosity in post-war Britain for the Hogarth Press to bring out a translation two years later, which Esmond had brought her from the shop. She also reads Iris Origo on Leopardi, and excerpts, in red biro, 'Indifference and gaiety are the proper emotions, not only for a sage, but for anyone who has had any experience of human life, and the wit to profit by it.'

Indifference and gaiety: she is finding instructions in Leopardi's thoughts.

I remember how she could rekindle a room filled with deathly dull 'old sticks' by putting on all her liveliness. She performed gaiety so it seemed real; she was masking the terrible, appalling anguish I found in her diaries.

Mostly, however, she was reading in English, and they are all recent books, which Esmond was bringing back from the shop for her as they arrived; they show his taste, but the responses are hers.

In January 1952, the month of the uprising and the burning of Cairo, she makes three entries, including Walter Baxter, *Look Down in Mercy* (a forgotten novel today, it's a pioneering exploration of desire, with a gay encounter at its heart – Jamie and she discussed it, I feel sure). She awards it three stars.

In February 1952, when the bookshop has just been burned down and the troubles are continuing, she awards only one star to HRH the Duke of Windsor, *A King's Story*. Over the summer that year, when the women, as my father put it, had been sent ahead to England, Ilia goes on reading – including Violet Trefusis' recent memoirs, *Don't Look Round*. She keeps making notes on passages that strike her: in Albert Camus, *The Outsider*, she finds these words: 'Those who arouse love, even if it is disappointed, are princes who make the world worthwhile.' And again, later, 'Lying is not only saying what is not true . . . It is also . . . saying more than is true, in the case of the human heart, saying more than one feels.'

She loved Camus; she cried the night that his death was announced on the telly. I remember her sitting on the sofa, her face screwed up for someone she knew only through his writing.

She copies out these words from Charles Frazier, *Cold Mountain* (also awarded three stars): 'she said, "Marrying a woman for her beauty makes no more sense than eating a bird for his singing."'

Later, she gives three stars to Fausta Cialente's *Cortile a Cleopatra* and adds, 'a book which took me back . . . to the days of my innocence' (Cialente returned to Italy after Nasser's rise to power and translated Lawrence Durrell's *Alexandria Quartet* into Italian). Natalia Ginzburg is a constant favourite.

On the flyleaf of the back cover, Ilia (true to a lifetime of thrift, using every scrap), adds a declaration, in Italian, 'This is a very inadequate notebook. Many books which I've read I haven't registered here, such as for example, Marina's books which I read when they had hardly been published.'

She is addressing me; she knows that after she has died, I will go through her things – alongside Laura, I'll be her executor – and she wants me to know that she was reading, thinking, facing the world and the experiences it threw at her with discriminating thought based on wide reading. And she doesn't want me to think that she left me out (I know she read me, and liked some of my books, though *The Lost Father*, the other one that's mostly about her, gave her mixed feelings – as this one, the one I am now writing, would, too, if she could read it). 'I don't want to be exposed,' she said, or rather cried out. 'I don't want people reading about me.' I was crushed,

I had wanted to please her. (A few years later, reading that book again in Italian, she told me she liked it better.)

Often personal writings like these share that impulse the dying Keats expresses so pungently in his last poem:

This living hand, now warm and capable
Of earnest grasping, would, if it were cold
And in the icy silence of the tomb,
So haunt thy days and chill thy dreaming nights
That thou would wish thine own heart dry of blood
So in my veins red life might stream again,
And thou be conscience-calm'd – see here it is –
I hold it towards you.

Ilia's reading notes and her closing declaration aren't filled with eerie menace, unlike Keats's fierce challenge issued to those who come after him Her script, which shows signs of the troubles that were afflicting her sight in her last years, holds out to me her living hand, elegant, fine-fingered, though by the 1990s gnarled with arthritis, but scented with the lemon she always kept by the kitchen sink, alongside the soap, to get rid of onion and garlicky and washing-up-glove rubbery smells; even in her closing days, her fingers were still crowned with long smooth carefully tended nails – filbert nails. They used to be varnished deep red (painted while watching the telly – never waste a moment, that was her way), adorned with the half-moon diamonds, the amethyst flower ring.

I am trying to be her *shabti* and answer to her ever-present ghost. Or so I think, as I sift through her notes and hear her vanished voice. Maybe I can whisper her lines on this side of life, to continue her being and register her experience by responding to the traces of her acts? If I take the hand she

holds out from her self-archiving and note-taking can I inter-
pret her and relate the story?

Unlike most friends of writers, she would eagerly read the
books they wrote, but she gives Jamie Chantry's first venture
– *Stash*, a thriller – only one star. Thrillers weren't to her taste
anyway but she was disappointed again and again in friends'
efforts, even when, after my father died in 1983 and she moved
to London, they had become part of her close circle of beaux
and *soupirants* or even lovers.

Coming across her diaries of this period, all in Italian, the
writing agitated and sometimes desperate, filled me with rage
on her behalf against him. The scenes aren't to be repeated
here: her ghost would shudder at the memory of those times
of deep unhappiness. Yet she didn't destroy these notebooks,
several volumes of them, brimming with more hopes of love.

The sense that she had found herself too late after the
marriage to Esmond grew and grew. One year, she sent me a
birthday card, with the message, 'How lucky you are to be
young!'

~~~

It has taken me over a decade since my mother died to look
through her clothes again. After my sister and I emptied her
wardrobes and her chests of drawers, I kept all the outfits she
made herself, from the 1940s in Cairo to the 1960s and 1970s
in Cambridge. Because I no longer sew, words that were
familiar in her vocabulary are no longer in use in mine or have
acquired a different meaning.

For example, *basting*; the loose stitches used for the initial
stages of making of a dress, hardly in use any more, for the
word usually now describes moistening a roast with its own
juices to stop it drying out in the oven. *Selvedge*: the sealed
end of a roll of material which will not unravel and cannot

be pulled out of shape or draped to fall in another way besides the straight, unlike fabric cut on the *bias* which can then, my mother showed me, be fashioned to fall in loose folds, or stretched to fit a longer length of material to make a frill or a ruffle.

How such terms lend themselves to metaphor: basting for the shallow safety of the unexamined love, for the flight from scrutiny and close attention; selvedge for the limit, which is a kind of safety, a holding place, a fixed address; and bias – to think that the concept of bias comes from this material property of fabric, that it will lend itself to a shape by clinging, by slanting, by accommodation.

～

She holds out her hand to me through the notebooks she did not destroy, the reading notes I found on her bedside table after she had been taken to the hospital for the last time, and she calls to me to answer, to witness the arc of her life.

And yet, when a *shabti* toils in the underworld, he or she is also acting to divert demons from the proper subject of their purposes; writings may also become part of a strategy to disguise the truth – not intentionally, but as a consequence of wishfulness. A memoir like this one, which needs must be unreliable, since it is not possible to know your parents or their lives and yours before the age of six, substitutes for what really happened and who they really were; its work on their behalf inevitably misremembers or misrepresents, or, at best, embellishes, failing to set out what really took place.

Epilogue

26 January 2008, London

Wrapped in gleaming high-end florist's cellophane, Dr Karg's Classic 3-Seed biscuits come in packets of six. Made in the 'Family bakery since 1950' in Schwalbach, Germany, with a heraldic crest showing two lions rampant, the 'organic wholegrain crispbread' is knobbly all over and satisfyingly stiff, the three seeds – sunflower, sesame and linseed – studding the surface like cabochons on a medieval missal's silver cover. The biscuits turned up in Mehmet's, my local corner shop, around 1995, and they became a family favourite, living up to the promise of the packet to give 'a cracking good bite'; unlike a loaf of bread, if you kept them wrapped up, they didn't get stale.

~~~

Ilia was lying in the bed in the nursing home. Her long limbs, wasted to the bone, barely raised the coverlet; her face was disappearing into an arrangement of its planes and angles and hollows, the veins beneath showing through her transparent skin; her eyes terribly dimmed, when she opened them, which was not very often. She was already an effigy that over time brass-rubbings and footsteps have worn away. More footsteps were coming closer and taking her, except that she was still drawing breath, very shallow and intermittent so that as we sat beside her, Laura and I and others from the family who came as often as they could to visit, we waited for each breath as it seemed the next intake might not come, the interval always seeming longer, the pulse more delayed.

She developed a tiny frown between her brows, which contracted now and then with her passing thoughts, which testified that inside, she was feeling things: a stab, a pang, provoked her to give a sudden tiny cry. Her hands then hovered, searching for the wire to the bell to call the nurse and fluttering over her face to make sure the oxygen tube was still in place. She didn't want to hear me read to her any more.

Now and then she cried out, 'It's terribly cold.'

Or, often, '*Acqua! Acqua . . .*' Sometimes, '*Bicchiere, bicchiere.*' ('A glass, a glass.')

Propping her up, I could feel her bones, light as leaves.

She grimaced as she tried to swallow.

'Put me in a barrow, darling. I'm dead.' She seemed a nestling, fallen from the tree.

No, rather the frail husk, the cracked eggshell which lies on the ground.

And then, with a sudden strength, she'd order, 'Bury me. Bury me.'

~~~

'Pray for us, now and at the hour of our death': the closing words of the Hail Mary were taking on a brilliancy for me, like cut diamonds in my head. As my mother lay there, that imploration to the Virgin to pray for us *at the hour of our death* blazed with knowledge of the end and its cruel difficulty. I would have liked to be able to pray, but I can't. Not any more.

She had never abandoned the Catholic faith of her childhood, however badly priests behaved. I remembered that there had been in Cambridge a monk she liked, Father Sylvester Browne, OP, from Blackfriars. She found his sermons full of insights and he used to hear her confession and he was simpatico and sensitive to her doubts and anxieties. They became friends outside the ambit of the confessional and the Mass. An anthropologist by training, he confided in her, too, and she liked him when he told her that he suffered from doubts now and then and didn't always stay steadfast in his trust that God was good.

It occurred to my sister and me that Mummy might like to see him, that if he could perform the sacrament of extreme unction, it might bring her some comfort. It wasn't clear she wanted it, but she didn't reject the thought altogether, as far as we could tell.

We tracked down Father Sylvester to the retirement home for old Dominicans in his home town, Glasgow, and invited him to London. He arrived, in his old black suit and polo-neck jumper, carrying a small scuffed overnight bag. His once strong tall frame, that I remembered from twenty years before, was now hollowed by age, his thick lenses scratched and smeary, in sturdy frames that dated to the time Ilia had known him well. The sight of his dignified shabbiness took me back to my teenage years when everyone in England was so much less spruce, and what they wore was darned and patched and shiny, when dry-cleaning was expensive and not often resorted to.

We were having breakfast, about to set out for the nursing home, when I asked him if he had everything he needed to perform the last rites. His bag, which looked sufficiently medical for him to officiate, was still upstairs in the bedroom.

He expressed surprise.

'But you know, your . . . don't you need to bring, what's it called . . . your instruments? And the hosts?'

He hadn't thought of them, he told me. He hadn't realised that we were wanting him to do that.

I couldn't believe that he had come all the way from Glasgow, without the materials necessary. I had imagined that battered bag would contain a portable altar, with little compartments for the Eucharist, the oils and the salt, whatever. Like in a vitrine at the V&A: a chrismatory, a pyxis, a lidded container. Nothing fancy, not up to the standard set by the Magdalene, but something exactly purposed for the last rites. That he would give Ilia Communion and bless her and anoint her.

'What about olive oil? And ordinary bread?' I said, help-lessly, waving at the bread board where a loaf from the Co-op stood.

'No,' he said, 'that won't do. The bread must be unleavened.'

I looked about the kitchen. 'I do have these,' I said, holding up a packet of Dr Karg's 3-Seed biscuits.

The old monk's face brightened. 'Yes, that will do fine.'

I took the packet, which had been opened. There were three biscuits left.

When we entered Ilia's room, she didn't express happiness or surprise at Robert's appearing at her side, yet I sensed that the unexpected sight of him after so long seemed to stir some sparks of the life force in the muddy depths of her agony.

He took one of the Dr Karg biscuits and, in an undertone, with his right hand making the sign of the cross, consecrated it and then broke it into little pieces and offered her a crumb of a corner. She could barely manage even that morsel, for her lips were dry, her throat parched, and it was very hard for her to swallow.

Then he made small crosses over her eyes, her ears, her nose, her mouth, her hands, and gestured towards her legs. I couldn't hear the words, as he was hardly even whispering, but the ritual is short, direct, asking for forgiveness for any wrong done by the senses and even by the power of motion: *Per istam sanctam unctionem et suam plissimam misericordiam, indulgeat tibi Dominus quidquid per visum . . . per odoratum . . . per gustum et locutionem . . . per tactum . . . per gressum . . . deliquisti.*

Most of the biscuit was left, the triple seeds strewn here and there on the bed, and the fragments, fallen on the bedclothes, risked disappearing into it. I was making a move to begin to gather them up when Father Sylvester shot out his hand to prevent me. He pushed me from the bedside with far more energy, authority, indeed priestly power than he had shown before that moment, and commanded me, 'Don't touch! They're consecrated!'

I moved away and he carefully brushed the morsels together and spilled them into his handkerchief to keep them safe.

~~~

I am not sure how much difference the sacrament or his visit made. It is impossible to tell how my mother would have faced her death if she had not seen her friend, who happened to be a priest who'd understood her worries and her sins, if she had not been shriven and blessed according to the custom of the church she was born into and remained loyal to always. But not quite always, for towards the very end, which came a few days later, she became angry with the god in which she had believed all her life, when the cruelty of her sufferings as she lay dying seemed to her so unjust after all that she had done not to be a sinner.

'Why do I have to suffer like this?' she whispered in her tiny hoarse voice. 'When I have tried so hard to be good. It is not just . . . *non mi sembra giusto.*'

Beyond that softly uttered cry, I could see the long years stretch, years of her unhappiness, her self-denial on our, her children's, account, her consent to how things had to be, during all that time when she had done all she could to keep everything together.

I remembered how, when I must have been about 12 or 13, I suppose, I was standing by the sink while she was doing the washing-up; I was drying the cutlery and the crockery as she put them on the draining board and she was crying and she couldn't wipe away her tears because she was wearing clumsy rubber gloves. 'One day,' she was saying, 'I will leave your father, but I can't, not now, not yet.'

Chronology

1798–9	Napoleon's expedition to Egypt; scientific explorations
1801	British defeat French
1805–48	Muhammad Ali governor of Egypt
1822	Printing press set up in Bulaq, Cairo
1859	Work begins on Suez Canal
1867–79	Khedive Ismail
1869	Opening of Suez Canal
1871	*Aida* performed in Khedivial Opera House in Cairo (24 December)
1882	Riots in Alexandria; Khedive Tawfiq restored by British; British take control of the Suez Canal
c.1883	Gezira Sporting Club founded; 150 acres on island of Zamalek, exclusive to British Army and authorities; tennis, polo, racing, a swimming lido, eight croquet lawns, etc.
1883–1907	Sir Evelyn Baring (Lord Cromer) becomes Consul General, effectively ruler of Egypt
1899	Setting up of Anglo-Egyptian condominium
1906	The Dinshawai incident, executions of pigeon farmers
1914–18	First World War
1915	Egypt placed under British 'Protection' – till 1922

1917	The Balfour Declaration
1919	Independence leader Saad Zaghloul sent into exile. Widespread uprising ('the 1919 revolution'); elite Egyptians allowed in Gezira Sporting Club
1922	King Fuad I comes to power; Egyptian independence
1924	Saad Zaghloul becomes prime minister, dies three years later
1933–6	Sir Miles Lampson (Lord Killearn) High Commissioner
1936	Anglo-Egyptian Treaty; Faruq (aged 16) succeeds King Fuad
1939–45	Second World War
	26 May–11 June 1942: Battle of Bir Hakeim: French forces defend position near Tobruk against Rommel's Panzerarmee Afrika
	1–27 July 1942: First Battle of El Alamein: British forces stop Rommel's second advance into Egypt
	23 October–11 November 1942: Second Battle of El Alamein: Allied victory over the Axis powers, defeat of Germans in Africa
15 May 1948– 10 March 1949	Arab–Israeli War
1951(late)	Gezira Sporting Club taken into Egyptian control
26 January 1952	'Black Saturday'. The Burning of Cairo ('the 1952 revolution')
22–23 July 1952	Free Officers take charge; Faruq abdicates
1953–4	Egypt becomes a republic; Muhammad Naguib president
1954–70	Gamal Abdel Nasser president
26 July 1956	Nasser takes over the Suez Canal; British and French go to war with Egypt, and lose

1967	Six Day War with Israel; Canal closes
1970	Death of Nasser; Sadat succeeds him
1973	Yom Kippur War with Israel
26 March 1979	Egypt–Israel Peace Treaty signed by Egyptian president Anwar Sadat
1981	Sadat assassinated
1981–2011	Hosni Mubarak president
1988	Naguib Mahfouz wins Nobel Prize
2011	Arab Spring
30 June 2012	Mohamed Morsi president
3 July 2019	General Abdel Fattah el-Sisi takes power, removing Morsi in a *coup d'état*
2020	Death of Mubarak

Notes

All translations, when not attributed, are by the author.

vii   *Shabti* spell: adapted from the wall label to the *shabtis* in the Egyptian collection, Ashmolean Museum, Oxford, the British Museum, London, and the catalogue of the *shabtis* in the collection of the Queen's College, Oxford. The Egyptologist Richard Parkinson comments, 'The word *shabti* is apparently derived from the word for "persea-wood", which is apparently what the original *shabtis* were carved from. However, the Egyptians themselves re-interpreted the word as being derived from *usheb* "to answer", so the word is sometimes written as "*ushabti*". (But this is a later etymology).' Personal communication, 1 April 2020.

7   I wish!: https://www.thelocal.it/20181005/italian-word-of-the-day-magari. (accessed 10 April 2020).

8   'I'll wait for him': ibid.

8   'We were alone': ibid.

12   'not of this earth': Roger Caillois, *'Recette'*, in *L'Ecriture des pierres* (Paris: Gallimard, 1966), p. 133; *idem, The Language of Stones*, trans. Barbara Bray (I've slightly amended) (Charlottesville: University of Virginia, 1985).

15   'a little Italian cavalry schooling': Dan Vittorio Segre, 'The Man on the White Horse: Amedeo Guillet, 1909–2010', http://www.amedeoguillet.com/ww2-in-africa/#comments (accessed 15 January 2019).

17 '. . . not universally considered beneficial': Jean Chevalier and Alain Gheerbrandt, *Dictionnaire des symboles* (Paris: Robert Laffont/Jupiter, 1982), pp. 26, 353–4.

24 anthology of English and American literature: *Antologia della Letteratura Inglese e Americana*, eds. Aurelio Zanco and Silvio Molena (Florence: Nuova Italia, 1942).

27 a good chum: http://www.cottesmore-hunt.co.uk/chhistory. html (accessed 15 January 2019).

45 'London is not beautiful': Carmelo Colamonico, *Paesi et Popoli della Terra: Antologia Geografica per la Scuola Media: L'Europa* (Milan: Francesco Villardi, 1941), p. 133.

63 textbook about Europe: Colamonico, op. cit.

64 Italian royal family: Guido Masieri, *Le Glorie di Casa Savoia dal Conte Biancamano a Vittoria Emanuele III* (Florence: Rino Bertazzi, 1936).

64 fables: [Carlo Alberto Salustio] Trilussa, *Le Favole* (Milan: Mondadori, 1922).

64 a large, linen-bound volume: Giuseppe Novello, *Che cosa dirà la gente?* (Milan: Mondadori, 1937).

65 'an elderly woman': George Seferis, *A Levant Journal*, trans. Roderick Beaton (Jerusalem: Ibis, 2007), p. 29.

66 '. . .what an awful thing. . .': Ibid., p. 29.

66 'his own piece of flotsam': Ibid., p. 62.

68 '. . . the new warmer climate all right': Esmond Warner, Letter, 29 November 1945.

70 'Old customs and old practices' etc.: Colamonico, op. cit., p. 137.

72 '*la prima speranza*': Trilussa, Er Professore de filosofia', op. cit., p. 137.

72 '*La squartai come un pollo*': ibid., pp. 96–7.

73 'Her intimate friends': Novello, op. cit., p. 56.

73 'After the rape of the Sabines': ibid., p. 101.

85 Robert Burns, from 'Address to the Deil [*sic*]', *The Complete Poetical Works*, ed. James Currie (Edinburgh: D. Appleby, 1845), p. 72.

85 'a kind of artless shoes': Samuel Johnson, James Boswell et al., *A Journey to the Western Islands of Scotland; and, the journal of a tour to the Hebrides* (London: The Folio Society, 1990); https://www.electricscotland.com/history/journey/jour18.htm (accessed 15 August 2020).

86 . . . 'feathered Mercuries': Marjorie Plant, *The Domestic Life of Scotland in the Eighteenth Century* Highland (Edinburgh: Edinburgh University Press, 1952), p. 195. https://archive.org/stream/domesticlifeofsc006837mbp/domesticlifeofsc006837mbp_djvu.txt (accessed 15 August 2020).

87 'Oh! would I were': John Betjeman, 'The Olympic Girl', https://allpoetry.com/The-Olympic-Girl.

92 'Or perhaps it is from Old Irish *barrog*': http://www.etymonline.com/index.php?term=brogue (accessed 10 April 2020).

92 'She spoke in a declamatory, emphatic way': Roy Foster, personal communication, 2 April 2020.

104 'blonde' . . . meat jelly': F.E. Le Mesurier, *Sauces French and English* (London: Faber & Faber, 1947). My parents' copy is annotated with Arabic translations of, for example, nutmeg, paprika and capers.

103 'she spilled her spikenard': Anne Carson, *Nox* (New York: New Directions, 2010), no page numbers.

123 King Faruq's Bookplate: The historian Hussain Omar has identified the sheikh as Rifa'a Rafi' al-Tahtawi, an Imam, linguist and translator and 'the pre-eminent intellectual of the period', whom Muhammad Ali sent to Paris with around thirty young men 'to study in Paris and bring back the modern sciences in Egypt'. The Rifa'l mosque was built later, at the turn of the century 'as a ceremonial space and burial grounds of the dynasty . . . The argument seems to be: Egypt's modernity is a gift of the dynasty and therefore inextricable from it.' Personal communication, 19 June 2020.

130 The cosmopolitanism . . . 'morseling': Reynolds (2012), pp. 4–5, 39–40.

138 'a . . . rather devilish old rake': E.C. Hodgkin (ed.),

Thomas Hodgkin. Letters from Palestine 1932–36 (London; New York: Quartet Books, 1986).

145 'this coast of Provence': 'Passant souviens-toi / des volontaires du groupe de Commandos d'Afrique / débarqués les premiers / sur le sol de la patrie / le 14 août 1944 à minuit / et dont les corps jalonnent sur cette côte de Provence / le chemin de la libération du territoire.'

180 'list of lesbian musicians': https://en.wikipedia.org/wiki/ includes the warning: 'This category may inappropriately label persons'.

187 the *madrab* Abdel wielded: my thanks to Omar Berrada for helping me identify this word.

202 enraptured by the spectacle: David Cannadine, *Ornamentalism: How the British Saw Their Empire* (Oxford: Oxford University Press, 2001).

203 'he looked as if he wasn't quite a gentleman': see Alison Smith et al., *Artist and Empire: New Dynamics*, Exhibition Catalogue, Tate Britain, London, 25 November 2015–10 April 2016.

204 skilful studies: Wilkie's drawings are in the Ashmolean Museum, Oxford.

210 'charming' looks: My thanks to the staff in the Prints & Drawings Room for showing me his work. Sir Herbert Maxwell, *The Honourable Sir Charles Murray, KCB: A Memoir* (Edinburgh and London: William Blackwood & Sons, 1898), pp. 58–60; and H.E. Maxwell, 'Murray, Sir Charles Augustus (1806–1895)', rev. H.C.G. Matthew, *Oxford Dictionary of National Biography* (Oxford: Oxford University Press, 2004), online edn, January 2008, http:// ezproxy.ouls.ox.ac.uk:2204/view/article/19596 (accessed 1 July 2014); Sir Charles Augustus Murray (1806–95): doi:10.1093/ref:odnb/19596.

212 polychromatic marble carvings: see Laure de Margerie and Edouard Papet, *Charles Cordier: Les Nubiens 1848–1851* (Le Havre: MuMa, 2011).

213 Named 'Obaysch': Wilfrid Blunt, *Country Life*, 13
November 1975; *The Ark in the Park* (1976); see also
John Simons, *Obaysch: A Hippopotamus in Victorian
London* (Sydney: Sydney University Press, 2019),
pp. 33–115.

214 'What connection is there': Virginia Woolf, 'Three
Guineas', in *A Room of One's Own and Three Guineas*, ed.
Morag Shiach (Oxford: Oxford University Press, 2000),
p.180, photograph appears facing p. 200.

215 'Am I a Snob?': Virginia Woolf, *Moments of Being:
Autobiographical Writings*, ed. Jeanne Schulkind (London:
Pimlico, 2002), pp. 62–77.

216 '. . . sameness throughout the jelly': Virginia Woolf, 'The
War from the Street', in *The Essays of Virginia Woolf 1919–
1924*, ed. Andrew McNeillie, Vol. 3 (London: Hogarth
Press, 1988), p. 4.

217 'My first recollections . . .': Pelham Warner, *My Cricketing
Life* (London: Hodder & Stoughton, 1921), p. 1.

224 'our language and our culture': Jean Cocteau, *Maalesh:
Journal d'une tournée de théâtre* (Paris: Gallimard, 1949), p. 61.

224 'secret reports': ibid., p. 97.

225 'The life of the leisured classes': ibid., p. 97.

228 Sarah Bernhardt and Rachel: Rachel's surname was Félix,
but like Colette, she is known by her first name only:
Sophie Basch, *Rastaquarium: Marcel Proust et le "modern
style"*: *Arts décoratifs et politique dans À la recherche du temps
perdu* (Turnhout: Brepols, 2014), pp. 170–1, quoting Jules
Guérin and Paul Ginisty, *Les Rastaquouères. Etude parisienne*
(1883), p. ix.

228 'flashy foreigner': http://www.oxforddictionaries.com/
translate/french-english/rastaquouère. '. . .betrays the
Nation': Basch, op.cit., p.153.

228 Dada rant: Sarah Hayden, '*Jésus-Christ Rastaquouère*: Francis
Picabia's Anti-Art Anti-Christ', *Irish Journal of French
Studies*, 13 (2013), 41–67; Frances Richard, 'I am a

beautiful monster', http://www.bookforum.com/inprint/014_03/878 (accessed 10 April 2020).

229 'good-for-nothings': Silviano Santiago, 'The Cosmopolitanism of the Poor', trans. M. Edwards and Paulo Lemos Horta, in *Cosmopolitanisms*, eds. Bruce Robbins and Paulo Lemos Horta, with an afterword by Kwame Anthony Appiah (New York: New York University Press, July 2017). He quotes from Gilberto Amado, *Mocidade no Rio e Primeira viagem a Europa* (Youth in Rio and First Voyage to Europe) (1956), in which the contrast lies between the outsider's lack of polish and French *goût*: 'I began, naturally, to be delighted by the masterworks of French cuisine. I raised my already reasonable aptitude for opining knowingly, and not approximately, like a *rastaqüero* or *meteco*, on these matters of sauces and condiments.'

230 'despite these careful rejiggings': Tom McCarthy, *Tintin and the Secret of Literature* (London: Granta, 2006), p. 45.

232 James Bond were cast in Ivar's mould: see Ivar Bryce, *You Only Live Once: Memories of Ian Fleming* (London: Weidenfeld & Nicolson, 1975).

233 Jean Painlevé: films include *La Pieuvre* (1928), *Bernard-L'hermite* (1930), *L'Hippocampe* (1934).

233 Colette's husband, Willy: Basch, op. cit., p. 171, from *Les histoires les plus spirituelles de Willy* (Paris: n.d.), p. 60; she dates it, on the grounds of typography, to *c*.1915.

233 a journalist who became a Dreyfusard: Georges Maurevert, *L'Art, le boulevard et la vie* (Nice–Paris: N. Chini–H. Floury, 1911), p. 331. Maurevert had worked on Drumont's *La libre parole* but changed his views. Basch, op. cit., p. 171.

234 'the condemnation of "modern style"': Basch, op. cit., p. 153.

243 H. would write to her: This first letter to Sadika was written on 16 September 1961 and the last in 1964, the year of his death.

245 'lines of Persian Poetry': letter 90 to Sadika Tancred, 18 May 1964.

247 Tara: The house has the same name as the villa in Gezira which became notorious as the wartime playground of high-living English officers during the war, among them Paddy Leigh-Fermor, but I don't think it can be the same house because a letter of my father's mentions how lovely the Delta was looking as they drove there. See Cooper, *Cairo in the War*, pp. 283–8, plate 33, f.p. 179, fig. f.p. 354.

249 'For love is like health': Naguib Mahfouz, *Palace Walk* (November 1998 in Ilia's notebook), three stars.

260 'where the holy family rested in the shade': Nicholas Warner, *The True Description of Cairo: A Sixteenth-Century Venetian View* (Oxford and London: the Arcadian Library with Oxford University Press, 2006), 3 vols., 2:57–65, 121, 136–9.

261 Benoît de Maillet: M. L'Abbé de Mascrier [M. de Maillet], *Description de l'Egypte, contenant plusieurs remarques curieuses . . . composée sur les Mémoires de M. de Maillet* (Paris: Louis Genneau and Jacques Rollin, 1735), pp. 110–12.

263 'We were loath to leave the garden': Florence Nightingale, *Letters from Egypt: A Journey on the Nile 1849–1850*, selected and intro. Anthony Sattin (London: Parkway Publishing, 1988), p. 185.

267 'the land of spices': George Herbert, 'Prayer (I)'. https://www.poetryfoundation.org/poems/44371/prayer-i (accessed 16 August 2020).

267 'I also participated yesterday': Anthony Barnett on Agnes Heller, https://www.opendemocracy.net/en/can-europe-make-it/next-hundred-years/ (accessed 10 April 2020).

267-8 'Jessye Norman and Kathleen Battle': https://www.youtube.com/watch?v=UqlDbqKaFks Accessed 14 July 2020 pp. 269-70

267 'If I can believe': Nightingale, op. cit., pp. 175–6.

270 translations of scripture vary: English did not always render the Hebrew *tsori* as 'balm'. John Wycliffe has

'sweet gumme', John Purvey 'rosyn'; it was Myles
Coverdale who in 1535 chose 'balm' in one passage,
following closely the Vulgate 'balsamum', but in
connection with Gilead he called it 'triacle'. The Geneva
Bible coined the phrase 'balm in Gilead'.

271 a kind of clerical joke: Lewis Carroll, *Alice's Adventures in
Wonderland*, ed. Hugh Haughton (London: Penguin, 2003),
p. 66.

271 the phrase stuck: the name of Gilead has reappeared in
settings that hint at a longing for paradise and a profound
betrayal of that longing: alongside Margaret Atwood's
Republic of Gilead, in *The Handmaid's Tale* (1986) and *The
Testaments* (2019), Marilynne Robinson's *Gilead* (2004)
evokes a small town in the American Midwest with a
hidden history of involvement in the Indian slaughter and
the racial persecutions of the Civil War.

271 Kew Gardens' Plant List: See http://powo.science.kew.org/
taxon/urn:lsid:ipni.org:names:127676-1 (accessed 16
August 2020).

271 It seems that the land of spices must be a queendom:
Josephus, *Antiquities* 8:2; Laurence Totelin, 'Botanizing
Rulers and their Herbal Subjects: Plants and Political
Power in Greek and Roman Literature', *Phoenix*, Vol. 66,
No. 1/2 (Spring–Summer 2012), 122–44, https://www.
jstor.org/stable/10.7834/phoenix.66.1–2.0122 (accessed 9
August 2018). However in Rome male rulers also coveted
balsam trees. Some were brought to Rome and paraded as
trophies in the triumphs celebrating the conquest of
Jerusalem. Pliny the Elder writes that 'of all scents, that
which is ranked highest is balsam. Of all the countries, it
has been vouchsafed only to Judaea, where formerly it was
found only in two gardens, both belonging to the king
. . . The emperors Vespasian and Titus exhibited this
variety of tree to Rome.' He then goes on to
anthropomorphise the trophy, as if it were a human: 'This

tree is now a slave; it pays tribute together with its race'
(*Historia Naturalis* 12:111–13).

272 trials on a cure: https://www.bloomberg.com/news/
articles/2020-02-03/gilead-drug-to-undergo-human-trials-
in-china-to-cure-coronavirus.

273 'all goodly fragrant woods': Richard Pankhurst, *The Ethiopian
Borderlands: Essays in Regional History from Ancient Times to the
End of the 18th Century* (Lawrenceville, NJ: The Red Sea
Press, 1997), p. 9; D.M. Dixon, 'The Transplantation of
Punt Incense Trees in Egypt', *Journal of Egyptian Archaeology*,
Vol. 55 (August 1969), 55–65, https://www.jstor.org/
stable/3856000?seq=1 (accessed 10 April 2020).

274 largest Refugee Complex: see Ben Rawlence, *City of
Thorns: Nine Lives in the World's Largest Refugee Camp* (New
York: Picador, 2016).

286 'thanks to the sacrifice of his beloved': Giorgio Vasari, *Le
Opere*, eds. D. Passigli et al (1838), p. 633.

290 'You know the book has marks': G.E. Shelley et al., *Handbook
to the Birds of Egypt* (London: John van Voorst, 1872).

291 'Delta looked quite lovely': EPW letter, 27 November
1948 (I have moved the date).

296 'I used to work for the British Army': I am paraphrasing
from Fausta Cialente, *The Levantines*, trans. Isabel Quigly
(Boston: Houghton Mifflin, 1963), and Francesca Rubini,
'*Diario di guerra (1941–47) di Fausta Cialente. La memoria e
il racconto*', *Bollettino di italianistica* (January–June 2014),
1:61–84.

297 '*Levantinismo* . . . But the peasant *is* Egypt': Cialente, *Ballata
Levantina*, p. 141; trans. Quigly, slightly adapted, p. 141.

319 '. . . and it was the tyrant father': Virginia Woolf, 'Sketch
of the Past', in *Moments of Being*, op. cit. p. 123.

320 'in a corner of the cage': ibid.

332 'Mr Said's granite-like exterior': Nadia Gindi, 'On the
Margins of a Memoir: A Personal Reading of Said's *Out of
Place*', *Alif*, 20 (2000), 290.

341 'all these tools': Rachel Lichtenstein, *Diamond Street: The Hidden World of Hatton Garden* (London: Hamish Hamilton, 2012), p. 99.

345 'one of the saddest things': Raymond Flower, fellow bookseller, wrote, in French, 'I regret above all the considerable toll of old rare books which you kept in your office among which were so many rare finds, very difficult to obtain. My friends and I were in the habit of foraging among them and I cannot recall ever leaving without carrying off with joy a work indispensable to my research or a rare edition which would become an ornament to my library.'

349 'Living in Cairo at the moment': Michael Hornby, 'Report on Visit to Cairo, March 28–April 6 1952'.

349 'the business is to be closed': *idem*, Memo, 5 April 1952.

355 900,000 loans yearly: Susan Orlean, *The Library Book* (New York: Simon & Schuster, 2019), p. 38.

356 'Whenever an elder dies, a library burns down': https://www.goodreads.com/author/show/88231.Amadou_Hampâté_Bâ (accessed 10 April 2020).

363 '*Shabti*' is a play on the verb 'to answer': see note to p. vii above.

364 '*written the books herself*' (emphasis in original): Helen Lowe-Porter, letter to Thomas Mann, quoted in Kate Briggs, *This Little Art* (London: Fitzcarraldo, 2017), p. 91.

368 'This is a very inadequate notebook': '*Questo è un elenco molto insufficiente dei libri che ho letto non ho registrato qui, per esempio i libri di Marina che ho letto non appena pubblicati.*'

369 'This living hand': John Keats, https://www.poetryfoundation.org/poems/50375/this-living-hand-now-warm-and-capable (accessed 12 April 2020).

Bibliography

Aciman, André, *Out of Egypt* (New York: Riverhead Books, 1994)

Adès, Harry, *A Traveller's History of Egypt* (Adlestrop: Chastleton Travel, 2007)

Ahmed, Leila, *A Border Passage: From Cairo to America: A Woman's Journey* (New York: Farrar, Straus & Giroux, 1999)

Alhadeff, Gini, *The Sun at Midday: Tales of a Mediterranean Family* (New York: Pantheon Books, 1997)

Ashour, Radwa, *Blue Lorries*, trans. Barbara Romaine (Doha: Bloomsbury Qatar, 2014)

Art et Liberté. Rupture, War and Surrealism in Egypt (1938–1948), eds. Tim Fellrath and Sam Bardaouil, Exhibition Catalogue (Liverpool: Tate Liverpool; New York: Art Reoriented; Paris: Éditions Skira Paris, 2018)

Bardaouil, Sam, *Surrealism in Egypt: Modernism and the Art and Liberty Group* (London; New York: I.B. Tauris, 2017)

Bradbury, Ray, *Fahrenheit 451* (1953) (New York: Ballantine Books, 1966)

Bryce, Ivar, *You Only Live Once: Memories of Ian Fleming* (London: Weidenfeld & Nicolson, 1975)

Burdett, Charles, 'Italian Fascism, Messianic Eschatology and the Representation of Libya', *Politics, Religion and Ideology*, 11:1 (March 2010), 3–25

Cavannante, Alfredo and Matteo D'Acunto (eds.), *I profumi nelle società antiche: produzione, commercio, usi, valori simbolici* (Salerno: Pandemos, 2012)

Cave, Terence, *Thinking with Literature* (Oxford: Oxford University Press, 2016)

Cecil, Edward, *The Leisure of an Egyptian Official* (London: Hodder & Stoughton, 1921)

Chevalier, Jean and Alain Gheerbrandt, *Dictionnaire des Symboles* (Paris: Robert Laffont / Jupiter, 1982)

Cialente, Fausta, *Ballata Levantina* (Milan: Feltrinelli, 1961).

Cialente, Fausta, *Interno con Figure* (Rome: Editori Riuniti, 1976)

Colla, Elliott, *Conflicted Antiquities: Egyptology, Egyptomania, Egyptian Modernity* (Durham, NC and London: Duke University Press, 2007)

Cooper, Artemis, *Cairo in the War, 1939–1945* (London: Hamish Hamilton, 1989)

Fahmy, Ziad, *Ordinary Egyptians: Creating the Modern Nation through Popular Culture* (Stanford: Stanford University Press, 2011)

Gansel, Mireille, *Translation as Transhumance*, trans. Ros Schwartz (London: Les Fugitives, 2017)

Gauthier, Gilles, *L'Épopée du canal du Suez*, Exhibition Catalogue Musée du Monde Arabe (Paris: Gallimard, 2018)

Ghali, Waguih, *Beer in the Snooker Club* (London: Deutsch, 1964)

al-Ghitani, Gamal, *Zayni Barakat* (1971), trans. Farouk Abdel Wahab (Cairo: American University in Cairo Press, 2004)

Goldschmidt, Arthur, Amy J. Johnson and Barak A. Salmoni (eds), *Re-Envisioning Egypt 1919–1952* (Cairo and New York: American University in Cairo Press, 2005)

Golia, Maria, *Cairo: City of Sand* (London: Reaktion Books, 2004)

Golia, Maria, *Photography and Egypt* (London: Reaktion Books, 2010)

Goodden, Henrietta, *Camouflage and Art: Design for Deception in World War 2* (London: Unicorn Press, 2007)

Grafftey-Smith, Laurence, *Bright Levant* (London: John Murray, 1970)

Hoffman, Adina, and Peter Cole, *Sacred Trash: The Lost and Found World of the Cairo Geniza* (New York: Schocken Books, 2011)

Josipovici, Gabriel, *A Life* (London: London Magazine Editions, 2001)

Kerboeuf, Anne-Claire, 'The Cairo Fire of 1952 and the Interpretations of History', in Goldschmidt et al. (eds.), pp. 194–216

Lagnado, Lucette, *The Arrogant Years: One Girl's Search for Her Lost Youth, from Cairo to Brooklyn* (New York: HarperCollins, 2011)

Lively, Penelope, *Moon Tiger* (London: André Deutsch, 1987)

Lively, Penelope, *Oleander, Jacaranda: A Childhood Perceived* (London: Viking, 1994)

Luckhurst, Roger, *The Mummy's Curse: The True History of a Dark Fantasy* (Oxford: Oxford University Press, 2012)

Maalouf, Amin, *Adrift: How Our World Lost Its Way*, trans. Frank Wynne (London: World Editions, 2020)

Mahfouz, Naguib, *The Cairo Trilogy* (1956–7): *Palace Walk*, trans. William Maynard Hutchins and Olive Kenny; *Palace of Desire*, trans. William Maynard Hutchins, Olive Kenny and Lorne Kenny; *Sugar Street*, trans. William Maynard Hutchins and Angele Botros Samaan (London: Black Swan 1994)

Mahfouz, Naguib, *The Quarter*, trans. and ed. Roger Allen (London: Saqi Books, 2019)

Makdisi, Jean Said, *Teta, Mother and Me: An Arab Woman's Memoir* (London: Saqi Books, 2005)

Makdisi Cortas, Wadad, *A World I Loved* (New York: Nation Books, 2009)

Manning, Olivia, *Fortunes of War: The Levant Trilogy* (1987–91) (New York: New York Review Books Classics, 2014)

Mansfield, Peter, *The British in Egypt* (London: Weidenfeld & Nicolson, 1971)

Mikes, George, *How to Be an Alien. A Handbook for Beginners and More Advanced Pupils* (London: Allan Wingate, 1946)

Naggar, Jean, *Sipping from the Nile: My Exodus from Egypt: A Memoir* (Las Vegas: AmazonEncore, 2008)

Napier, Priscilla, *A Late Beginner* (London: Michael Joseph, 1966)

al-Nuwayri, Shihab al-din, *The Ultimate Ambition in the Arts of*

Erudition, ed. and trans. Elias Muhanna (London: Penguin, 2016)

Omar, Hussain, 'The State of the Archive: Manipulating Memory in Modern Egypt and the Writing of Egyptological Histories', in William Carruthers, ed., *Histories of Egyptology Interdisciplinary Measures* (New York: Routledge, 2014), pp.174–183.

Origo, Iris, *War in Val d'Orcia: A Diary* (London: Jonathan Cape, 1947)

Origo, Iris, *A Chill in the Air: An Italian War Diary 1939–40* (London: Pushkin Press, 2017)

Ovenden, Richard, *Burning the Books: A History of Knowledge under Attack* (Cambridge, Mass: Belknap Press, 2020)

Palieri, Maria Serena, *Radio Cairo. L'avventurosa vita di Fausta Cialente in Egitto* (Rome: Donzelli, 2018)

Pea, Enrico, *Vita in Egitto* (Milan: Mondadori, 1949)

Pea, Enrico, *Moscardino*, trans. Ezra Pound (1955) (New York: Archipelago Books, 2005)

Philipps, Roland, *A Spy Named Orphan. The Enigma of Donald Maclean* (London: The Bodley Head, 2018)

Rafaat, Samir, with Suzan Welson, *A Brief History of Zamalek* (Zamalek: The Palm Press, 2001)

Reynolds, Nancy Young, 'Commodity Communities: Interweavings of Market Cultures and Consumption Practices, and Social Power in Egypt, 1907–1961' (PhD thesis, Stanford University, 2003)

Reynolds, Nancy Young, *A City Consumed: Urban Commerce, The Cairo Fire and The Politics of Decolonisation in Egypt* (Stanford: Stanford University Press, 2012)

Robb, Brian, *My Middle East Campaign* (London: Collins, 1944)

Rodenbeck, Max, *Cairo: The City Victorious* (London: Picador, 1999)

Ross, Alan, *Colours of War: War Art 1939–45* (London: Jonathan Cape, 1983)

Rossant, Colette, *Apricots on the Nile: A Memoir with Recipes* (London: Bloomsbury, 2001)

Roy, Xavier, and Gamal al-Ghitani, *Reviewing Egypt. Image and Echo* (Cairo and New York: American University in Cairo Press, 2010)

Said, Edward, *Out of Place: A Memoir* (London: Granta, 1999)

Say Shibboleth! On Visible and Invisible Borders, eds. Boaz Levin, Hanno Loewy and Anika Reichwald, Exhibition Catalogue, Judisches Museum Hohenems, 2018

Skelton, Barbara, *Tears before Bedtime* and *Weep No More* (1987, 1989) (London: Faber & Faber, 1993)

Soueif, Ahdaf, *Mezzaterra. Fragments from the Common Ground* (London: Bloomsbury, 2004)

Soueif, Ahdaf, *Cairo* (New York: Pantheon Books, 2012)

Soueif, Ahdaf, *The Map of Love* (London: Bloomsbury, 2014)

Stadiem, William, *Too Rich: The High Life and Tragic Death of King Farouk* (London: Robson Books, 1992)

Subin, Anna Della, *Not Dead But Sleeping* (New York: Triple Canopy, 2017)

Viscomi, Joseph John, 'Out of Time: History, Presence, and the Departure of the Italians of Egypt, 1933–present' (PhD thesis, University of Michigan, 2016)

Warner, Ilia Terzulli, *You Can't Get Blood Out of a Turnip* (London: Stacey International, 2005)

Wilfrid Blunt's Egyptian Garden/Fox Hunting in Cairo (1901) (London: HM Stationery Office Uncovered Editions, 1999)

Wilkie, David et al., *Paintings and Drawings by Sir David Wilkie*, Exhibition Catalogue, Royal Academy London 1958, with introduction by John Woodward (London: Royal Academy of Arts, 1958)

Ziock, Hermann, *Guide to Egypt*, trans. H. Bitter and D. Harris (Cairo: Lehnert & Landrock, 1956)

List of Illustrations

Endpapers Mohammed and Abdel with MW, left, and Laura in carrycot, Cairo, 1951–2. And other photos by EPW.

Vignettes and papercut ornaments: Sophie Herxheimer.

p. 14 Max Harari, Asmara, Ethiopia, 1941.

p. 21 Esmond 'Plum' Warner (EPW), 1942.

p. 30 Ilia, during her honeymoon in Ravello, visiting the Villa Cimbrone, taken by EPW, June 1944.

p. 44 Ilia with her father-in-law the cricketer Plum (Sir Pelham Warner), going to the Royal Garden Party, July 1949.

p. 49 EPW, aged five or six, with his father, Plum Warner, Maidstone Cricket Week, 1911 or 1912, taken at Eyot House on the Thames. Photo from Dorothy D'Oyly Carte's family album by kind permission of Simon Frazer.

p. 205 David Wilkie, *Sotiri, Dragoman to Mr Colquhoun*, Constantinople 1840. By permission of the Ashmolean Museum, Oxford.

p. 206 David Wilkie, *Admiral Sir Baldwin Wake Walker*, 1840. Lithograph. (© Trustees of the British Museum)

p. 211 After Willes Maddox, *Charles Augustus Murray*, Cairo, 1852. Mezzotint reproduced with kind permission of the Warden and Fellows, All Souls College, Oxford.

p. 213 *Obaysch*, aged one and a bit, London Zoo, 1852. Photo: Juan, Count de Montizon.

p. 223 Staff outing of W.H. Smith's, Cairo (visit of board member Arthur Acland (in straw hat, and his wife on his right), 1950. By kind permission of the University of Reading, Special Collections (W.H. Smith Archive).

p. 240 Sadika Tancred, *c.*1945 by kind permission.

p. 246 Ilia with Seddiqi Pasha and friend (unidentified).

p. 260 'In this place the true balsam is gathered . . . This obelisk is made of a single block of hewn stone', from Matteo Pagano, *Veduta*, in Nicholas Warner, *The True Description of Cairo: A Sixteenth-Century Venetian View* (2006). By kind permission of the Arcadian Library, London, vol 2: 56–7, 136–7.

p. 264 The pyramids and the Sphinx from Matteo Pagano, *Veduta*, ibid. By kind permission of the Arcadian Library, London, vol 2: 62–3.

p. 270 Loading of cargo on to Queen Hatshepsut's boats, bas relief from Deir al-Bahari, Luxor, after drawings by Johannes Duemichen (1869), Auguste Mariette (1877) and Eduard Naville (1898).

p. 273 Jan van Scorel, *Mary Magdalene*, *c.*1530, Rijksmuseum, Amsterdam.

p. 276 Christmas party, Auberge des Pyramides? Or Shepheard's Hotel? (EPW waving, Ilia far right).

p. 286 Cola dell'Amatrice (Nicola Filotesio), triptych of *The Assumption of the Virgin*, 1515, Pinacoteca Vaticana, Rome. By kind permission of the Photograph Collection at the Warburg Institute.

p. 287 Cola dell'Amatrice (Nicola Filotesio), *St Mary Magdalene and St Gertrude/ Scholastica* [?] left-hand wing of triptych of the Assumption, 1515. Pinacoteca Vaticana, Rome. By kind permission of the Photograph Collection at the Warburg Institute.

p. 292 Christmas card from Cairo House, W.H. Smith, Cairo. 1949. By kind permission of the University of Reading, Special Collections (W.H. Smith Archive).

p. 299 'This is the fig tree of Pharaoh, which is very very ancient, where, we are told, the Madonna often sat in its shade', from Matteo Pagano, *Veduta*, ibid. By kind permission of the Arcadian Library, London, vol 2: 62–3.

p. 306 Nanny (1) at Gezira Sporting Club (MW 2nd child from right), 1949?

p. 333 The ruins of Shepheard's Hotel after the events of 26 January 1952.

p. 339 View from the flat in Soliman House of downtown Cairo burning, 26 January 1952. Photograph: EPW.

p. 345 Interior of the bookshop, after the fire. Photo: EPW.

p. 354 Eustache le Sueur, *The Preaching of St Paul at Ephesus*, 'May', annual votive painting offered to Notre Dame de Paris, 1649, Louvre, Paris.

p. 366 Ilia's notebook, with her reading notes, 1950–98. Photo MW.

Acknowledgements

In Egypt, on my first return visits since childhood, the British Council and the American University in Cairo were my hosts. I owe them a huge debt: in 2009, I was introduced to the late Radwa Ashour, novelist and academic, who helped me retrace my childhood haunts. In 2014, I was invited to give the Edward Said Memorial Lecture and hosted by Ahdaf Soueif, to whose generosity and inspiration I owe more than I can say. My mother's closest friend, Sadika Tancred, now in her nineties, has spoken with me many times about her years in Egypt, and I've exchanged reminiscences and thoughts with others connected to Cairo: the late Edward Said and Mariam Said, Claudia Roden, Gabriel Josipovici and Donald Sassoon; also with the sadly missed Michael Sheringham and Eric Hobsbawm. The expert knowledge of Nicholas Warner, Salima Ikram at AUC, Alastair Hamilton, Elizabeth McGrath and Paul Taylor of the Warburg Institute, Joe Murray of the Arcadian Library, and many others whose books are entered in the bibliography have inspired and informed me. At the beginning of the research, I visited the

W.H. Smith's archive, then kept in house; they have since moved to Reading University, and I am very grateful to Guy Baxter for his help; letters, reports and transcripts from the W.H. Smith archive are reproduced by kind permission of the University of Reading and WHSmith PLC. Many of my inspiring colleagues at Birkbeck, London, and All Souls, Oxford, have been a source of precious insights, references and information. Wen-chin Ouyang, at the School of Oriental and African Studies, has introduced me to writers from the Arabic world who have been rich sources of information. Staying with the late Rick Mather and David Scrase, who has also now died, led me to the sites of Allied landings and hand-to-hand fighting in Rayol and Le Canadel. The staff of the London Library, who have been valiantly sending out books by post during the Covid-19 lockdowns, have been an invaluable support. Helen Simpson's incisive but gentle interest has been a mainstay throughout: it was her inspiration to include vignettes. I am infinitely grateful to Sophie Herxheimer, artist and poet, for accepting the task with her tonic high spirits and showing such sympathy with the subjects.

Among early readers, Maria Golia and Hussain Omar generously spared me many historical and local errors; those that remain are my own responsibility. Rachel Kneebone gave me the staunchest and most generous encouragement, a point of sharp apprehensiveness, as did Darian Leader. I am most grateful to them both, and also wish to express warm thanks to Maggie Staats Simmons, Roy Foster, Kate Daudy and George Prochnik for their perceptive responses. Colleagues invited me to read and talk about the book as it slowly progressed and I appreciate the stimulus this gave me, their responses and their students': the late Tony Judt invited me to the Remarque Institute, New York University, where I began to think and read for this book; I read from early drafts at Hermione Lee's life-writing seminar in Oxford, and as part of the Weidenfeld

Lectures at St Anne's, Oxford, which I was invited to give by Sally Shuttleworth and Matthew Reynolds. Mariët Westermann, Philip Kennedy and Paulo Horta at New York University, Abu Dhabi, and Dominique Jullien and Sowon Park and their students at the University of California, Santa Barbara, spurred on my explorations; Charles Burdett included me in the conference, *Transnationalities*, at the British School in Rome; Julia Bell asked me to speak about the book to our Birkbeck creative writing students. Sylvia Whitman entertained me warmly when she invited me to read at Shakespeare & Co. in Paris. The *London Review of Books* has published two sections, now reworked here, and I thank the editor, Mary-Kay Wilmers, very much indeed for showing such interest, and for her team's scrupulous care. Jackson Lears and Stephanie Volmer, at the US journal *Raritan*, have also been a source of huge encouragement.

I also wish to thank David Godwin for introducing me to Arabella Pike, the editor of this book, who took it on with such faith; I am very grateful to her and to her team at William Collins, especially Iain Hunt, for making the book happen during this long and unsettling period of the pandemic. Antonia Karaisl has helped most splendidly with research and logistics – many thanks to her, too.

Above all, my thanks go to my sister Laura Gascoigne, my son Conrad Shawcross, and both their families, and Graeme Segal for his steadying companionship, especially during the long penumbra cast by the coronavirus.

I've been writing the book or a long while and many more friends and chance acquaintances have greatly helped, but please forgive me as I shan't have remembered each of you.

Kentish Town, August 2020

Permissions

I would like to thank: Antonia Fraser, for her kind permission to quote her father's letter (p. 37), and Roderick Beaton, for kind permission to quote from his translation of George Seferis, *Levant Journal* (Jerusalem: Ibis Editions, 2007); I have made every effort to contact others for their permission but the pandemic has meant these messages have remained unanswered. Many other quotations fall within fair use. In one case, permission was unfortunately not given, so the passages in question have been anonymised and paraphrased. For picture permissions please see the List of Illustrations.

Cast of characters

Family

Agnes 'Mother Rat' Warner, Lady Warner, née Blyth (1886–
   1955), daughter of Henry Blyth, partner in Gilbey's & Son
Harold 'Father Badger' Henderson (1901–72), naval attaché,
   Cairo, RN captain
Mungo Henderson (1935–2018), their son, stockbroker
Doris Smith, Lady Warner's companion
Elizabeth ('Betts' or Betsy) Warner (1905–96), Mrs Harold
   Henderson, Esmond's sister, mother of Mungo
Emilia 'Ilia' Terzulli (1922–2008); Mrs Esmond Warner from
   1944, daughter of Luigi Terzulli (1895–1931) and Maria
   Filippa Pansini Terzulli (d. Chicago 1956); youngest sister of
   Annunziata, Purissima and Beatrice (all born Chicago,
   returned to Bari 1921, died USA).
Esmond Warner (EPW) (1907–82), lieutenant-colonel, Royal
   Fusiliers (London Branch), 8th Army; in Italy, in charge of
   Intelligence for No.3 Section; married Ilia Warner 1944;
   bookseller in Cairo, Brussels, Cambridge
Laura Warner (b.1950), Laura Gascoigne, art critic and writer,
   daughter of Esmond and Ilia, sister of Marina
Marina Warner (MW) (b.1946), writer and teacher, daughter of
   Esmond and Ilia, sister of Laura
Sir Pelham 'Plum' Warner (1873–1963), the 'Grand Old Man'
   of British cricket. Born Port of Spain, Trinidad, father
   Charles Pelham, Attorney General, mother Rosa Cadiz.
   Played in West Indies team (his brother Aucher captain),

then in the England team, which he captained for ten Test matches; in 1904, brought back the Ashes, same year married Agnes Blyth (qv); founded the *Cricketer* 1921 and edited it till 1963; manager of the England team 1932–3 during notorious Bodyline tour; president of the MCC 1950. The Warner Stand at Lord's is named after him. His ashes were scattered on the pitch.

Close to family

Adriana Barakat (Nanny 3)
Ahmed, the bawab, Soliman House, Sharia el Gezira
Sylvester Browne, OP, joined Dominican order in 1950; anthropologist, Ilia's confessor
Ivar 'Burglar' Bryce (1906–85), said to be a principal model for James Bond, restored family seat of Moyns Park, Essex
Eulalie Buckmaster (1901–?) (Marina's godmother), daughter of Olympian polo player and Master of Foxhounds Walter Buckmaster; sister of Beryl, a keen huntswoman; chatelaine of Moreton Manor, Warwickshire
Penelope Chetwode (1910–86), married John Betjeman in 1933; keen horsewoman and author of travel writings, sister of Roger Chetwode (1906–1940), who drove across Europe to Albania with Esmond, Long Vacation, 1927
Hildegarde (Loretta Sell) (1906–2005), cabaret artiste and singer
Basil Lubbock (1876–1944), boat designer, yachtsman and marine historian; married Dorothy Warner 1912 (Aunt Dot, d.1944)
Sadika Miligui (1922–), married Christopher Tancred in 1944
Frank Pakenham (1905–2001), later Lord Longford, politician and prisoner reformer; Marina's godfather
Elizabeth Pakenham, née Harman (1906–2002), later writes as Elizabeth Longford
F.E. Prestridge, Esmond's batman
Violet Trefusis, née Keppel (1894–1972) (Marina's godmother), writer in English and French; lover of Vita Sackville-West as

pictured in Nigel Nicolson's memoir of his parents, *Portrait of a Marriage*; lived and died in Bellosguardo, Florence

Lady Joan Villiers (1911–2010), Mrs David Colville, sister of 'Grandy', Earl of Jersey

Mohammed and Abdel, staff in the flat

Nanny 1

Nanny 2

C.M. Wells (1871–1963), Esmond's housemaster at Eton; cricketer, rugby player, classics scholar, and dabbler in the stock market

The Firm (W.H. Smith's)

Sir Michael Hornby (1899–1987), Esmond's friend and boss; vice-chairman; 1928 married Nicolette Ward (1907–88), their son Simon Hornby (1934–2010) succeeded him as chairman. Other board members: Billy Smith, 3rd Viscount Hambledon (1903–1948); his brother David Smith, Dick Troughton, Arthur Acland.

Ben Mendelssohn, Esmond's deputy in the bookshop, and Maisie, his wife

Among those working for W.H. Smith's Cairo House: Ahdam Mohamed Alim, Ziza Botton, Pauline George, G. Nahas, Nasrallah, and Labiba Zaki.

More dramatis personae (italics = imaginary personae)

H. Iranian diplomat and politician; innamorato Sadika Tancred (qv)

Muhammad Ali (1769–1849), Ottoman governor of Egypt 1805–48

Jamie Chantry, author of Stash, *a thriller*

Fausta Cialente (1898–1994), Italian novelist, left Trieste for Cairo, author of *Cortile a Cleopatra* (1936) and *Ballata Levantina* (1961) and short story writer; broadcaster on Radio Cairo during the war; died in Eastbourne, England

Georges Dimitrino, member of Art et Liberté movement; poet and belleletrist

Queen Farida (1921–88), married Faruq in 1938

King Faruq (1920–65), ruler of Egypt 1936–52

Princess Fawzia (1921–2013), Faruq's eldest sister, first wife of Mohammed Reza Pahlavi of Iran; Princess Fazia (1923–94), Faruq's second sister; Princess Faika (1926–83), Faruq's third sister; Princess Fathia (1930–50), Faruq's youngest sister

Nicola Filotesio (1480/9–1547/59), known as Cola dell'Amatrice; painter in Le Marche; Vasari deemed him provincial, but paid tribute to his wife's heroism

Sir Robin Furness (1883–1954), deputy director-general of Egyptian State Broadcasting and deputy chief censor in Egypt; later professor at Fuad I University, then Oriental Secretary to the High Commissioner; after the War director British Council in Egypt; married Joy; daughter Mary born in 1946

Sir Robert Greg (1876–1953), British commissioner for the Egyptian Debt 1930–40

Major Chetwode ('Chatty') Hilton-Green (1895–1963), fellow officer of Esmond, keen horseman

Khedive Ismail or Ismail Pasha (1830–95), ruler of Egypt 1863–79

Sir Miles Lampson, later Baron Killearn (1880–1964), High Commissioner to Egypt and the Sudan, 1934–36, then UK Ambassador till 1946

Mary Magdalene, Saint, died ?c. 70 CE in South of France

Sir Charles Augustus Murray (1806–95), diplomat; author of rightly forgotten works, *The Prairie-Bird* (1844), and *Hassan or The Child of the Pyramid. An Egyptian Tale* (1901)

Claudia Roden (1936–), born in Cairo, writer and specialist on Middle Eastern cuisine; author of *A New Book of Middle Eastern Food* (1968) and many other cookbooks

Sir Thomas Russell Pasha (1879–1954), chief of police, Cairo 1917–46

Edward Said (1935–2003), professor of comparative literature at Columbia University, author of *Out of Place* (1999) and many influential (and polemical) cultural studies

Anna Sosenko (1909–2000), American songwriter and manager of Hildegarde (qv)

Ahmed Seddiqi Pasha, owner of Tara, a pleasant retreat

Sir Baldwin Wake Walker (1802–76), surveyor of the Royal Navy 1848–61; captain of Ottoman fleet

Sir David Wilkie, RA (1785–1841), British genre painter and portraitist; travelled to Cairo, Syria et al. for his health; died in Malta

Beryl Wynne, horsewoman, married to headmaster of 'the Eton of Egypt'

Index